CAMARO
SPECIAL EDITIONS

Matt Avery

CarTech®

INCLUDES COPO, YENKO, ZL1, Z/28, GMMG, AND MANY MORE

CarTech®

CarTech®, Inc.
6118 Main Street
North Branch, MN 55056
Phone: 651-277-1200 or 800-551-4754
Fax: 651-277-1203
www.cartechbooks.com

Edit by Bob Wilson
Layout by Connie DeFlorin

ISBN 978-1-61325-491-2
Item No. CT658

Library of Congress Cataloging-in-Publication Data Available

Written, edited, and designed in the U.S.A.
Printed in China
10 9 8 7 6 5 4 3 2 1

All photos courtesy of Matt Avery unless otherwise noted.

DISTRIBUTION BY:

Europe
PGUK
63 Hatton Garden
London EC1N 8LE, England
Phone: 020 7061 1980 • Fax: 020 7242 3725
www.pguk.co.uk

Australia
Renniks Publications Ltd.
3/37-39 Green Street
Banksmeadow, NSW 2109, Australia
Phone: 2 9695 7055 • Fax: 2 9695 7355
www.renniks.com

Canada
Login Canada
300 Saulteaux Crescent
Winnipeg, MB, R3J 3T2 Canada
Phone: 800 665 1148 • Fax: 800 665 0103
www.lb.ca

TABLE OF CONTENTS

HOW TO USE QR CODES

QR codes are a convenient way to access additional information through your smartphone. **You will find them throughout this book.** To use them, simply open the camera on your phone and hold it over the QR code. Then, follow the prompt that appears on your screen.

If no prompt appears, you may need to download a free QR scanner from either the Apple App Store or Google Play.

Scan QR codes for **OVER 70 PAGES OF ADDITIONAL CONTENT** *in this book!*

ACKNOWLEDGMENTS

Thank you to my wife, Becca, for her love and support, and a huge thanks to Senior Advisor Vince Miller for his invaluable assistance with this project. Many more thanks to the following:

Chevrolet Senior Staff

- Scott Settlemire: brand manager, Camaro/Firebird, Chevrolet (1996–2002)
- Adam Barry: senior creative designer, Camaro, Chevrolet (2010–present)

Technical Advisors and Subject Matter Experts

- Jon Mello, Jim Pearse, Lance Hill, Brian Henderson, Joe Barr, Bill Kummer, Tom Benvie, Bill Bradley, Tony Habeeb, Dennis Dickman, Lee Douthitt, Jim Hairston, Mike Rhudy, Peter Parr, Mike Brienza, Mark Strembicke, Jim Smith, Aaron Thornton, Jim Simon, Vince and Sally Miller, Andrew McCall, Ryan Datko, and the GMMG Registry.

Performance Advisor

- Harold Sanford

Other Special Thanks

- Rob Kutzler and the Waukegan Harbor and Marina team
- Mark Pieloch and his staff at the American Muscle Car Museum, including Ed Dedick and Andrew Mackey
- Empire State Muscle Cars, 123 Auto Sales, Newton Motor Co., Naperville Autohaus, Collector Car Gallery
- All the vehicle owners and enthusiasts across the country who supported and aided in the completion of this undertaking

Many special-edition Camaros have been created over the years. For the scope and purposes of this book, I zeroed in those I deemed most notable and significant, working hard to bring you the most pertinent and accurate information about these cars.

FOREWORD BY ADAM BARRY

This book is the definitive source for all things regarding Camaro special models and editions. Special editions are just that—special. Here, the author worked diligently to compile the facts and data that set each and every one apart.

The Camaro is a car that transcends time, age, and social status. Since the very beginning, it's been about self-expression, being a companion to owners who love the feeling that only a sporty automobile provides. Put the pedal down and feel the torque and exhilarating sound of an engine roaring, and it's all packaged inside a beautifully shaped design.

I fell in love with the Camaro at age 14. My father owned a repair shop, and a local high school senior dropped off his 1968 Hugger Orange SS coupe for a tune-up. It rumbled into the garage, and after one look, I knew I wanted a car like this. Ten years later, I was hired as a designer at General Motors.

Not long after, I joined the Camaro team, making my boyhood dream come true. It's a passionate group that understands our customers want to stand out from the crowd, even when that crowd is fellow Camaro owners. The goal is to take the Camaro and find ways to further set it apart in both looks and performance. This leads us to craft a variety of unique versions that allow everyone to find his or her own special slice of the Camaro Nation.

I'd like to personally thank Camaro fans for so passionately loving and supporting the vehicle. That's the fuel that inspires and drives us.

Adam Barry
Chevrolet Senior Creative Designer,
Camaro (2010–present)

FOREWORD BY SCOTT SETTLEMIRE

I had the rare privilege of growing up in a Chevrolet dealership with my uncle and father. So, when I first got a glimpse of a new Camaro in September 1966, it was love at first sight. I remember it well. It was a Bolero Red Camaro convertible, and it was the most beautiful car I'd ever seen. It's been a love affair ever since, and I remember every year when the Camaro was revealed and the excitement that we all experienced. I can't help but reflect on the following words:

"The name 'Camaro' means 'pal, friend, or comrade,'" Eliot M. "Pete" Estes said. "Thus, it suggests the real mission of our new automobile: to be a close companion to its owner, tailored to reflect his or her individual tastes and at the same time provide exciting personal transportation . . . It suggests the comradeship of good friends, as a personal car should be to its owner."

Estes spoke those words in June 1966 when he revealed the name of the Camaro, and I often wonder if he had any inkling that the car would bring so many people together worldwide.

Karen Lewis once said the following at a Camaro gathering: "This is like one big family reunion—but I actually *like* all of the people here!"

I take my hat off to author Matt Avery for doing his due diligence over many years and doing so much research to capture so much information about Chevrolet Camaro special editions. In fact, I've learned quite a bit from reading his manuscript!

Now, sit back, grab your favorite beverage, and enjoy!

In Camaro comradeship I remain,

Scott Settlemire
a.k.a. the "Fbodfather"

INTRODUCTION

What do you look for in a pal, friend, or comrade? If you're into four-wheeled sports machines, you look to the Camaro. It is the car that Chevrolet designed to be best buds with motorists across the globe. With a name inspired by a French phrase that means "close acquaintance," the model quickly became a far-reaching icon that was synonymous with speed, personality, and performance.

At the launch in September 1966, Chevrolet General Manager Pete Estes cast the vision for the brand-new automobile. He proudly declared it to be a close companion of owners that was tailored to the owner's individual taste while being exciting transportation.

Both of those fuel-fed visions readily came to fruition. With pleasing looks and an ability to meet a variety of driving wants and needs, the Camaro became a friend to all. No one pulled the Hugger in closer than those with a heavy right foot. Enticed by the vehicle's long hood, short deck, and wide-open engine bay, the car was the perfect canvas, allowing everyone from hobbyists to full-blown race teams to custom craft a Camaro into the ultimate dream machine.

For more than 50 years, the Camaro has been the thumping heartbeat of America, developing a rock-solid rapport with an ever-growing group of worldwide fans and followers. Whether throttle down on drag strip blasts, tight corner carving, or around-town cruising, the Camaro has forged a bond with the hundreds of thousands of owners who have happily slipped behind the wheel. The car has been used to pace races, celebrate landmark milestones, and has been the foundation for numerous high-performance efforts.

Camaro Special Editions takes you on a decades-long journey to examine the pinnacles and high points of the model's lineage, focusing on the most noteworthy and significant special editions. These are the versions of substance and scale found in Chevrolet showrooms that have dazzled and delighted drivers and collectors on countless motoring excursions.

Whether modern, retro, or classic, these heavy-hitting Camaros are the hot ones that continue to rev emotions and get rumbling bowtie-loving hearts racing.

The Camaro has always been a friend to those who love the open road.

## CHAPTER 1

LIMITED FACTORY OFFERINGS

Right out of the gate, the Camaro was intended for performance driving. That fuel-fed legacy led to no shortage of special editions from Chevrolet that were ready for the starting line or grid. These pedal-down pursuits continued to be refined by the hot asphalt of competition and the intense passion to pursue first place and top finishes on road courses and drag strips the world over.

These factory-fast, special-edition Camaros were built ready for competition but were also streetable (with one exception) and readily found in showrooms. Each was designated from arbitrary regular production option codes that have since become legendary. Having proven their mettle, the likes of Z28, L89, ZL1, B4C, and COPO (Central Office Production Order) leapt right off the ordering-book pages and into the hearts and minds of enthusiasts, collectors, and fans who continue to champion their capabilities.

What started as a limited track-focused package quickly led to the Z/28 becoming one of the most desirable first-generation Camaros.

1967 Camaro Z/28

Prior to the Camaro's launch, Vince Piggins, Chevrolet's manager of product performance, recognized the growing popularity of sanctioned sedan road racing and wanted a factory-built Camaro that could be a serious competitor. Internal confidential correspondence from the summer of 1966 revealed the savvy gearhead knew the Sports Car Club of America (SCCA) was expanding this class of competition for 1967.

A suitable Camaro fit into guidelines set forth by category. Competing cars were intended to be near street legal, modified only slightly for safety, and—of utmost importance to automakers—identifiable as vehicles that could be purchased at a local dealership and driven home. To enforce this standard, the Fédération Internationale de l'Automobile (FIA) stipulated that 1,000 identical cars had to be manufactured and distributed to certify it was indeed a production car and not some one-off, purpose-built race car.

Engine size was another restriction. The SCCA capped the class's maximum displacement at 5 liters or 305.1 ci. After looking over its available engine lineup, Chevy engineers had to mix and match pieces to create something that worked within these guidelines.

There was the 250-ci 6-cylinder, but it certainly wasn't powerful enough. On the opposite side of the spectrum, the 327- and 350-ci V-8s were too big. If Chevy had offered the Camaro with the 283 engine, that's more than likely what it would have moved forward with, but Vince wanted to make the most of the opportunity. He proposed using the 327's block paired with the 283's crankshaft to make a 302-ci engine. It was readily approved and given the green light by Chevrolet General Manager Pete Estes. Other changes included giving the engine items such as the "30-30" camshaft from the Corvettes, 11:1 pistons, a high-volume oil pump, pan baffles, mechanical lifters, and a newly designed intake manifold.

The track-ready Camaro was arbitrarily named the Z/28, after the internal regular production option (RPO) code with which its equipment was grouped under. The moniker wasn't a hit out of the gate and took time to catch on with internal staff and enthusiasts.

A total of 602 Z/28s were produced in 1967 with the goal of having them compete in SCCA racing. In this inaugural year for the Z/28, no specific badging was used to call out the package.

The 302-ci V-8 was potent, featuring mechanical lifters and a 4-barrel Holley carburetor. This example is unrestored and features the cowl plenum air intake and the smog emissions equipment. The smog equipment was usually one of the first items to be removed when the cars were new.

Performance Upgrades

The Z/28 foundation was limited to sport coupes, and the Rally Sport Package RPO Z-22 provided the basic appearance equipment that was improved with additional options.

Under the hood, inspiration was taken from earlier high-performance Corvette engines, including the L79. The 302 was fitted with mechanical lifters that wouldn't float at high RPMs, the crankshaft was nitride coated, and an 8-inch harmonic balancer was installed. There was also a new fan clutch assembly that was capable of operating at a higher RPM and featured a five-blade fan.

The car's Holley 800-cfm 4-barrel carburetor was fed by bigger fuel lines that were enlarged from the 327's 5/16 inch to 3/8 inch. The engine was dressed up with various chrome pieces, such as rocker covers (found on that year's L79 Chevelles and Corvettes), oil-filler tube and cap, and air-cleaner cover.

The whole setup breathed through a dual exhaust system (RPO N61) that consisted of dual pipes and low-tone mufflers without resonators. The transmission was the close-ratio M21 Muncie 4-speed manual that used the L79's 10.5-inch clutch, which was also used on L88 powertrains. The L88 used a 10.5-inch clutch, but it was a different part number and had much heavier pedal pressure. It featured an inherently stronger closer-spaced 2.20 first gear that was exclusive to Z/28, L78, and Corvettes. A rear-axle gear ratio of 3.73 was the base option but could be exchanged for other ratios too. Positraction was not standard (except with 4.10, 4.56, and 4.88 ratios) and had to be ordered separately.

All told, the Z/28 was officially rated at 290 hp. However, even period reviews stated that with modifications allowed by the rules of the racing series, the total output was closer to 400 hp, surpassing that of the Cougar 289 (380 hp), Mustang 289 (370 hp), and the Barracuda and Dart's 273 (360 hp).

Brake Upgrades

Knowing the rigors of aggressive laps around a racetrack, Chevy engineers pulled out all the stops in putting together several robust brake packages.

RPO J50 (adding power assist to the front brakes) and RPOJ52 (upgrading the front drums to 11-inch disc brakes) were deemed to be mandatory Z/28 options. Customers could

1967 Camaro Z/28: Performance Content and Equipment							
Engine 302-ci V-8 (RPO Z28)	Carburetor	800-cfm Holley 4-barrel and 3/8-inch fuel lines					
	• Mechanical lifters • Special accelerator linkage • Five-blade fan assembly						
	RPO L79 Items	• Fuel pump assembly • Air cleaner • Water pump • Fan and generator drive belt • Dual water pump and fan pulleys					
	Chrome	Rocker covers, oil filler cap, oil filler tube, air cleaner cover					
Exhaust	Dual with low-tone mufflers without resonators (RPO N61)						
Transmission	4-speed manual Muncie (with low 2.20:1 first gear ratio)* (RPO M21)						
Steering	20:1 lock-to-lock (lowered from standard 24:1)			Opt		Power (RPO N40)	
Suspension	Heavy-duty front and rear springs and shock absorbers (RPO F41)						
Rear Axle	*Available with Positraction differential						
	3.73 gearing	Optional					
		Economy (RPO H01)		3.07			
		Performance		3.55			
		Special service		3.31, 4.10, 4.56, 4.88			
Brakes	Front	RPO J50*	Power assist	$42.15	Rear	Drum brakes	
		RPO J52*	Disc brakes	$79.00			
Optional	RPO J56	Heavy-duty front discs and rear metallic drum linings (also required RPO J50 and J52)			Price	$26.35	
					Total	205 cars	
	RPO J65	4-wheel drums with 1/2-inch-wider shoes than RPO J56			Price	$36.90	
					Total	1,217 cars	
Wheels	15x6-inch steel with trim rings and hub caps						
Tires	7.35x15 inch "NF" nylon red stripe high performance						
*	Required options						

In addition to power assist for the front brakes, customers could upgrade their Z/28's front drums to 11-inch disc brakes (RPO J52).

RPO J56 added phenolic heat insulators to the caliper pistons, helping to keep the brake fluid from boiling during heavy use.

RPO J56 also exchanged the rear brake-drum shoes for those with segmented linings that helped with heat dissipation.

step up further by adding the Corvette-inspired RPO J56, which upgraded the front discs with phenolic heat insulators on each of the caliper's four pistons. The insulators helped keep the brake fluid from boiling while racing.

The package also included swapping out the rear shoes with a fade-resistant, metallic lining that was segmented into separate sections to further aid heat dissipation. The rear drums and springs were also upgraded for better performance. The J56 option was a Z/28 exclusive installed on 205 cars.

Suspension Upgrades

The Z/28 offered a quicker manual steering ratio over the standard Camaro. The Z/28's lock-to-lock ratio was lowered from the standard 24:1 to 20:1, which provided a quicker response while turning. Nothing was changed for buyers who selected the power steering option, except for a deep-groove pulley on the power steering pump.

Power steering wasn't very popular on the Z/28. It only appeared on about 9 percent of the cars built that year. The relatively new system was thought to be complicated, fussy, and simply another item to maintain. Racers wanted components that were simple and lightweight.

The Z/28's suspension was the heavy-duty RPO F41 option, which upgraded the springs and shock absorbers. The very early production Z/28s featured a round traction bar mounted on the passenger's side of the rear. By early March 1967, this was upgraded to a heavier-duty traction bar with a rectangular cross section. For unknown reasons, Chevrolet only opted to place a traction bar on the ride side rather than on both sides like Pontiac chose to do on its Firebird 400.

New 15x6 steel wheels wrapped in NF nylon 7.35x15 high-performance, red-stripe tires were also added.

Exterior Touches

The Z/28's exterior received a pair of painted racing stripes in black or white (depending on the body's paint color) over the hood and down the decklid. The stripes had a neat visual element on the passenger's side of the rear decklid, featuring a cutout around the Camaro badge. A smaller cutout on the stripe also appeared on the front upper valance panel as well. While not seen often, either a white or black vinyl top was available.

Pricing the Z/28

When ordering a Z/28, buyers paid $358.10 for the package plus the required two options: power front disc brakes ($121.15) and the 4-speed manual transmission ($184.35).

Inside the car's cabin, bucket seats were the norm, but a bench seat was also available. Air conditioning wasn't offered. In this inaugural year, 602 examples were sold to customers.

No air conditioning was offered inside the cabin, but other options could be added. This example was ordered from Williams Chevrolet in Lebanon, Pennsylvania, with a push-button radio.

1968 Camaro Z/28

With the popularity of the model, Chevrolet offered it again in 1968. Still only available on coupes, the option cost $400.25. The biggest addition was front fender badges.

Rear spoilers (RPO D80, $32.68) weren't included in the package but were offered as an RPO option as well as dealer add-ons. A total of 7,199 Z/28s were created in 1968.

1969 Camaro Z/28

Sensing the model's continual momentum and track-proven success, Chevy offered it again for 1969. The Z/28 option now cost $506.60 and had to come with either a tachometer or special instruments, a 4-speed transmission, and power front or four-wheel disc brakes. Positraction was recommended.

The package included the 302-ci V-8 with bright accents, dual exhaust, a heavy-duty radiator, and a temperature-controlled fan. Underneath was quick-ratio steering and special front and rear suspension components. At each corner, 15x7 E70X15 special white-lettered, black-wall tires were mounted, and the wheels had special center caps and trim rings.

Exterior body additions continued to include a pair of painted on rally racing stripes as well as rear bumper guards, an auxiliary valance panel, and a rear deck spoiler. New this year was the inclusion of the Z/28 badge not only on the front fenders but also on the rear panel and in the grille on the driver's side.

The formula was a total success with sales increases of nearly three times from the previous year, having 20,302 cars

In 1968, the Z/28 returned and was now sporting "Z/28" fender badges. This example was purchased new at Brigance Chevrolet in Oak Park, Illinois, by Joe Koski, who worked at the dealership. Joe still owns the car today.

One of the rarest Camaros is this Fathom Green 1968 Z/28 convertible—the only one in existence. It was commissioned by Chevrolet Product Performance Manager Vince Piggins for the brand's general manager, Pete Estes.

This Rally Yellow 1969 Camaro Z/28 was sold new at Green Chevrolet in Pontiac, Ilinois, and was equipped with the dealer-installed cross-ram manifold.

One of the rarest elements that can be seen on a Z/28 is the aluminum cross-ram intake manifold with dual 600-cfm Holley carburetors.

built. The combination possessed all the right ingredients for the model to go down as one of the most desirable Camaros on the planet.

1970–1974 Camaro Z28

In 1970, the Z28 performance-oriented trim returned on the second-generation Camaro. A big change was with the size of the engine. It was no longer was restricted to 302 ci but now utilized a 350-ci V-8. The powerplant debuted with 360 hp, which was reduced gradually in subsequent model years due to tightening emissions regulations. By 1974, it had been reduced to 245 hp and 280 ft-lbs of torque.

The Z28 trim returned on the Camaro's second generation, now equipped with a 350-ci V-8.

The pair of painted rally stripes returned, and new exterior additions included painted five-spoke wheels and a black-finish grille. In 1973, air conditioning was offered for the first time but only when the automatic transmission was selected. The Z28 trim appeared in 1974 but was discontinued for the 1975 and 1976 model years. The package price steadily increased year to year, costing $572.95 in 1970 and rising to $640.05 in 1974.

1977–1981 Camaro Z28

After a two-year hiatus, the Z28 trim returned in 1977. Horsepower dropped again for the 350-ci V-8, this time featuring 170 hp. In subsequent model years, it climbed to a high watermark for this series of 190 hp in 1980. Cars sold in the stringent California market received even lower ratings. In the last two years of the run, they received a smaller 305-ci V-8 engine that was only paired to an automatic transmission.

Suspension upgrades were still the norm for the package as were exterior additions, such as body-colored wheels. A new feature was multicolor accent stripes that highlighted the wheel wells and lower rocker panels and outlined the rear panel. They also formed a design on the hood. Various elements were painted black, including the lower rocker panels, grille, and headlight bezels. The bumpers, door handle inserts, and sport mirrors all came painted body color.

In 1978, a simulated hood scoop with a black-painted throat was added along with louvers on the front fenders. In 1979, a new three-piece front lower air dam and front wheel opening flares were added to the package. The side striping was revised to now include a thick lower two-tone stripe that wrapped from that front air dam to the bottom portion of

During this era of Z28, horsepower was down, but colorful exterior accents were available.

the doors and culminated in a large Z28 identification on the doors. The lower rocker panels were no longer painted black but body color, and the Z28 identification in the front grille moved above the grille.

In 1980, the lower striping became tri-tone (available in seven combinations), while the fender louvers became one integrated vent. The front Z28 identification graphics moved from above the grille (which was now body color) to inside of it. A 15x7 aluminum five-spoke wheel became optional too. The simulated hood scoop was exchanged for an added hood cowl that was now functional. It included a blackout graphic on top, "Air Induction" graphics on the cowl, and highlights of tri-tone striping. At the rear, the Z28 identification graphics moved from above the rear deck panel to a badge located on the fuel-filler door positioned between the taillights.

In 1981, the sills returned to being painted black.

1982–1992 Camaro Z28 and IROC-Z

1982–1992: Camaro Z28 and IROC-Z: Trim Availability				
Years	1982–1984	1985–1987	1988–1990	1991–1992
Trim(s)	Z28	Z28 and IROC-Z	IROC-Z	Z28

In 1982, the third generation of the Camaro featured a Z28 trim. Power came from a 5.0L V-8 equipped with a 4-barrel carburetor. It could be fitted with an optional cross-fire injection (CFI) that when selected could only be paired to an automatic transmission. The CFI option was not available in California. The suspension was upgraded with items such as a rear sway bar and special spring rates.

For its appearance, the front and rear facias were painted body colored with color-keyed contrasting wraparound lower

panels. The upper body panels and wheels were given black accents, such as black dual hood scoops (functional with the CFI option), a black grille, and black door handles and locks. The driver's seat could be equipped with an optional L/S Conteur bucket seat that featured an adjustable head restraint, thigh and lumbar supports, and lateral support for the cushion and backrest.

As part of the model's debut, a silver and blue version was featured as the pace car to the 1982 Indy 500 with a run of commemorative editions available for sale.

In 1983, the output of both engines (LG4 and LU5) increased, and a 5-speed manual was standard. In 1984 a high-output (HO) version of the 5.0L V-8 was offered under RPO L69 that had 190 hp and 240 ft-lbs. of torque. It was offered through the 1986 model year.

In 1985, a new engine was offered: a 5.0L V-8 with throttle port injection (TPI) as (RPO LB9). In addition, the lineup was joined with a standalone IROC-Z model (ordered under RPO B4Z) that received much of the Z28 content but was equipped with exclusive touches, such as a special ride and handling suspension and additional cosmetic items. Other updates included the five-spoke wheels that were now available in a charcoal finish, revised striping and nameplates, and larger rocker panels and fascia.

In 1987, the 5.0L V-8 H.O. engine (RPO L69) was discontinued, but a 5.7L V-8 TPI was made available. This was also the last year the LG4 engine was offered.

In 1988, the Z28 moniker was no longer offered, with RPO Z28 being used for the IROC-Z. It received a new lower stripe, and the IROC-Z decals were moved to the rear of the doors. The stripes and decals could be deleted with RPO DX3. Painted 15-inch aluminum wheels were standard, and an optional 16-inch wheel was available. A 5.0L V-8 with

In 1988, the Z28 moniker was dropped in place of the sporty package called the IROC-Z.

For the final two years of the third-generation Z28, the model received a domed hood (sans black vents) with coupes getting a rear wing, as is shown on this 1992 example.

EFI (RPO L03) was now offered. In 1989, the IROC-Z base 15-inch aluminum wheel now resembled the optional 16-inch wheel. That 16-inch wheel was only included with specific optional powertrains. A performance exhaust was included with the optional V-8 engines (including RPO LB9 and B2L).

In 1990, the 5.0L V-8 TPI became the standard engine. A limited-slip differential was standard and exclusive to the IROC-Z. A performance axle ratio (RPO G92) could be added, which brought 4-wheel disc brakes, performance exhaust, and output to 230 hp and 300 ft-lbs of torque. The RPO G92 option was first seen in 1985 and used to facilitate the content for the Canadian Player's Series race-oriented Camaros. The IROC-Z convertible came standard with 16-inch wheels.

In 1991, the IROC-Z model was dropped, and the Z28 model returned but with no stripes or graphics. New body additions included a domed hood (no longer featuring black vents) and a large rear wing (coupes only). A 5.7L V-8 TPI was optional on the Z28 coupe. The 16-inch wheels were now color-keyed to the paint finish coming in silver, red, or white.

In 1992, the Z28 (along with RS) could be equipped with an optional Heritage Appearance Package (RPO Z03) that celebrated the Camaro's 25th anniversary.

1993–2002 Z28

In 1993, the Z28 trim was included on the fourth-generation Camaro, which was now available only as a coupe or with T-tops. It was readily called out with a painted black B-pillar roof hoop and standard five-spoke aluminum wheels. Under the hood was a 5.7L V-8 with multi-port fuel injection rated at 275 hp. It was paired to an all-new 6-speed manual. As in 1967 and 1982, this initial year of the model's redesign was featured as the pace car at the Indianapolis 500, and dealer replicas were available for sale. While being Z28s, they received exclusive black and white exterior paint schemes and unique interiors.

In 1994, the Z28 trim was available on the newly launched convertible bodystyle. In 1995, the Z28 coupe could now be optioned with a body-color roof along with a new traction-control system called acceleration slip regulation (ASR) as (RPO NW9). The LT1 was now equipped with sequential fuel injection. In 1996, the mirror caps could now come painted body color, and the 150-mph speedometer was standard. Output was bumped to 285 hp. An SS trim joined the

The pinwheel-style wheels were standard on the fourth-generation Z28 from 1993–1996.

By 2002, like this example, Z28 output rose to 310 hp.

lineup, and when it was selected, Z28s received additional components. This first year was unique in that three markings (the engine air-filter frame, a center console cloisonné, and embroidered floor mats) showed "Z28 SS." This is the only time in Camaro history that these two performance trims appeared together on one Camaro. Subsequent years just showed "SS."

In 1997, a new 5-spoke wheel design was introduced. An optional 30th Anniversary Package (RPO Z4C) was available on Z28s (both coupes and convertibles), bringing elements such as monochromatic Arctic White paint, Hugger Orange stripes, and white wheels.

In 1998, the Z28 coupe could be optioned with a body-color roof and mirror caps. A big change was the engine, which was updated with the Corvette-sourced LS1. Components it featured included a deep-skirt aluminum block, powdered metal rods, and lightweight pistons. Another big change was the 4-speed automatic becoming the standard transmission, while the 6-speed manual was optional.

In 1999, a Zexel Torsen differential was used in the limited-slip rear axle. The Monsoon premium audio system that had only been standard on Z28 coupe was now standard on Z28 convertible.

In 2000, body-color mirror caps became standard along with a new 16-inch aluminum wheel design (available with an optional polished surface). In 2001, the LS1's output increased to 310 hp and 340 ft-lbs of torque. In 2002, the P245/50ZR16 Goodyear Eagle RSA tires became standard equipment along with a power steering cooler.

2014–2015 Camaro Z/28

When the fifth-generation Camaro was launched in 2010, it took another four years for the iconic Z/28 moniker to resurface. Unlike previous versions, this 2014 edition returned to the Z's original roots and launched as a hardcore track machine.

After a 12-year hiatus, in 2014 the Z/28 trim returned on Camaro. Harkening to its roots, this time it was a hardcore track machine. It was selected to pace the Indy 500, with this being of 1 of 3 pace cars created for those duties.

It was only available as coupe, came in five exterior paint colors, and cost $75,000. A single option was available, adding air conditioning and upgrading the single Z/28's lone audio speaker to the six that were standard on the Camaro SS. Speakers would have been left out entirely, but one was required by law for the safety belt chime.

In 2014, 515 cars were made.

Aero and Exterior Upgrades

On the exterior, every additional body component was installed to improve the car's aerodynamics. A front splitter was mounted along with a unique front fascia that featured a grille that was optimized to allow maximum airflow. Even the Chevy bowtie utilized an open design to help with engine cooling. Borrowing from the ZL1, the Z/28 used the same carbon-fiber hood extractor. Other additions included rocker and wheel flare moldings, front wheelhouse liners, and a belly pan.

At the rear, a spoiler was mounted with a "wickerbill," which is a small vertical tab at the edge of the piece that further improved drag. Final touches included Z/28 badging in the grille and on the front fenders and rear panel.

Engine Upgrades

The Z/28 was powered by a hand-built 7.0L LS7 engine that was sourced from the C6 Z06 Corvette. It delivered 505 hp and 481 ft-lbs of torque. Calling out the displacement, the engine cover featured a pair of red 427 badges. The only transmission option was a 6-speed manual transmission that was paired to a Torsen helical limited-slip differential.

A 7.0L LS7 V-8 engine sourced from the Corvette Z06 was installed under the hood. Output was rated at 505 hp and 481 ft-lbs of torque.

Suspension Upgrades

The suspension was heavily upgraded with Multimatic shocks with spool valve dampers, stiffer springs, and adjusted bushing rates. Brembo carbon ceramic brakes with monoblock calipers (six-piston in the front and four-piston in the rear) were installed. Both front and rear calipers were emblazoned with the "Z/28" script.

Special 19-inch forged aluminum wheels were painted gloss black, etched with "Z/28" on the outer edge, and were wrapped with 305/30ZR19 Pirelli PZero Trofeo R tires.

Interior Changes

Inside the cabin, the Z/28 included trim in a matte-metallic finish called Octane and special sill plates. Also included was a flat-bottom steering wheel with a Z/28 logo at the bottom, manually adjusted Recaro seats with an embroidered Z/28 logo, and a back seat that featured weight-savings measures such as an eliminated seat-back pass through.

More weight was removed through measures such as eliminating the tire-inflator kit (except for a few states where it was required by law), the removal of interior sound deadening and the trunk carpet, the installation of a smaller battery, and the use of thinner rear glass. Weight was also kept down by eliminating the high-intensity discharge (HID) headlamps and fog lamps and the option to omit the air conditioning.

The Z/28 package was carried over to the 2015 model year, and 1,292 were produced.

2014–2015 Camaro Z28: Performance Content				
427-ci V-8 (11.0:1) LS7 505 hp 481 ft-lbs	Aluminum	• Engine block • Ported cylinder heads • Flat-top pistons		
	Titanium	Connecting rods and intake valves		
	• Dry sump oiling system • Sodium-filled exhaust valves			
Exhaust	Tri-Y manifolds			
	Dual mode system with 3-inch-diameter pipes			
Transmission	Tremec TR6060 6-speed manual transmission			
Suspension	Multimatic monotube shocks with F1-style spool valves			
Rear Axle	3.91 (available with Posi differential)			
Brakes	F	Monobloc 6-piston calipers		
	R	4-piston calipers		
Rotors	Carbon-ceramic composite 2-piece			
Wheels	19-inch forged aluminum		F	19x11
			R	19x11.5
Tires	PZero Trofeo R 305/30-ZE19			
Vehicle Price	$75,000			

1967–1971 Camaro SS 396

After the Camaro's launch, it soon became clear that the model needed more power to stay in front of the competition. The 300-hp, SS 350 (RPO L34) wasn't going to cut it against the 1967 Mustang that had the new 390-ci V-8 with 320 hp.

Spurred on by Ford's actions, in January 1967, Chevy released the SS 396 trim. This hotter package, which was rolled out on the Chevelle in 1965, came with a Turbo Jet big-block

The SS 396 was the hottest RPO package available on the first-generation Camaro. It was fitting that this 1968 coupe in LeMans Blue was sold new at performance-oriented Brigance Chevrolet, in Oak Park, Illinois.

Interior additions included a flat-bottom steering wheel and manually adjusted Recaro seats.

	2014			2015		
Paint	Total	ACSP*	Total	Total	ACSP*	Total
Black	233	Yes	214	554	A/C	520
		No	16		No A/C	34
Summit White	122	Yes	110	332	A/C	317
		No	12		No A/C	15
Red Hot	96	Yes	85	224	A/C	214
		No	9		No A/C	10
Ashen Gray Metallic	34	Yes	29	132	A/C	128
		No	5		No A/C	4
Silver Ice Metallic	30	Yes	20	50	A/C	48
		No	9		No A/C	2
*	Air conditioning and speaker package costing $1,150					

While several iterations of the 396-ci V-8 were offered, the highest output was the 375-hp L78. In 1968, the option cost $500.30.

Chevrolet employed all types of tactics to offer Camaro customers hotter versions. One trick was borrowing from the Corvette, which was the case with the RPO L89 option.

396-ci V-8. It was equipped with dual exhaust and paired to either the M13 3-speed or M20 4-speed manual transmission.

Initially, two outputs were offered on the Camaro with 325- and 375-hp variants. The lower version (RPO L35) came with 10.25:1 compression, hydraulic valve lifters, and a 4-barrel carburetor. The top trim L78 received solid lifters, a special camshaft, four-bolt mains and 11:1 compression. From the exterior, these big-block Camaros were readily identified with painted black rear taillight panels.

In 1968, a 350-hp version (RPO L34) was introduced, adding a high-lift camshaft. In 1970, only the L34 was offered. In 1971 and 1972, the only 396 option was an LS3, which was rated at 300 hp and then 240 hp.

1967–1969 Camaro SS 396: Production			
	1967	1968	1969
L35 (325 hp)	4,003	10,773	6,752
L34 (350 hp)	N/A	2,579	2,018
L78 (375 hp)	1,138	4,575	3,823

1968–1969 Camaro L89

Still limited to 400-ci engines or less in the first-generation Camaro, Chevrolet turned to internal tricks to keep its pony car competitive. One strategy was borrowing from the Corvette's top tech. As such, RPO L89 was offered on the Camaro.

This option first rolled out in the Camaro in 1968. It was available in Super Sport coupes and convertibles (RPO Z27) equipped with the 375-hp L78 V-8. From there, the L89 option could be tacked on. This swapped out the heavy cast-iron cylinder heads for aluminum ones. Air conditioning was not available.

The L89 package added aluminum cylinder heads to the L78 396-ci V-8 engine, saving about 75 pounds.

The goal wasn't a bump in outright output, as the setup didn't produce additional horsepower. Rather, the ploy was all about weight savings. With the aluminum heads, the 396 engine weighed about 75 pounds less in addition to the savings of the L78's aluminum intake manifold. It may have reduced weight, but it didn't lower the price. After paying for the car, the L78 with L89 heads was available for $710.95.

The new cylinder heads brought other advantages too. Aluminum is simpler to repair versus broken cast iron, which is difficult to weld. They also dissipated heat faster. These were both positives for lead-foot competitors.

Few of those enthusiasts caught wind of the special setup, and even fewer had the funds to select the pricey option. Only 272 customers purchased it in 1968 and another 311 in 1969. Some of the low turnout is attributed to marketing. News of the L89 was extremely limited because Chevrolet still was trying to present itself as being out of racing.

COPO Camaros

In 1969, after two long years, Chevrolet dealerships encountered a breakthrough. They were now able to order a new Camaro equipped with an L72 427-ci V-8. Until that point, the largest engine option that was available was the 396-ci V-8, despite how the car's engine bay readily accommodated the L72 427 V-8.

Customers wanted more and in years prior, many dealerships launched their own internal speed shops and performance centers to satiate that need for speed. Interested Camaro owners purchased their car (usually in SS 396 trim) and then paid the dealer to perform the motor swap to the L72. Along the way, other upgrades and modifications were usually added.

While profitable, there was room to streamline the process—mainly recruiting Chevrolet to do the heavy lifting of installing the big engine right on the factory floor. That kind of move saved dealerships the added time and labor of having their technicians do the exchange.

Pioneering that innovation was Canonsburg, Pennsylvania, dealer Don Yenko, who was well-versed with leveraging Chevrolet's central office for these types of backdoor, underground projects. He received the green light from the brand's top brass and was rewarded with COPO 9561, which allowed him to order 427-equipped Camaros. It was a game changer, and for a while he was the sole recipient of such tantalizing four-wheeled fruit.

Word got out in the early summer of 1969, and soon other dealerships were jumping in and ordering their own 427-Camaro COPO 9561 creations. Some dealers added a second COPO to their Camaros, known as 9737, the Sports

The interiors could be fitted with a variety of options, but many owners preferred to keep them stripped down, which not only saved weight but also lowered the cost.

Car Conversion. This was a package first seen on Yenko's 1968 Camaros and included in his 1969 line. Some even went further and added the factory RS Z22 package, further driving up the already-high vehicle cost.

1969 COPO L72 Camaro: Factory COPO Additions	
COPO 9561	High Performance Unit
RPO L72	427-ci V-8 (all built at Tonawanda, New York, plant and featured orange painted blocks, oil pans, and cylinder heads)
RPO ZL2	Ducted cowl induction hood
RPO V48	Heavy-duty 4-core Harrison radiator
RPO F41	High-performance suspension with special springs and shocks
COPO 9737	Sports Car Conversion
	15x7 Rally wheels with E70x15-inch-wide-tread tires
	140-mph speedometer
	13/16-inch front sway bar
Mandatory Options	
RPO J50	Power front brakes
RPO J52	Front disc brakes

Other than the ZL2 cowl-induction hood, no exterior touches or badges callout the special powertrain equipment on the 1969 COPO Camaro. Due to the surreptitious nature, these cars weren't advertised or marketed.

Under COPO 9561, the L72 427-ci V-8 was installed. A heavy-duty radiator was also installed.

1970

Usually Chevrolet's COPO program was used in conjunction with outside dealership partners, such as Don Yenko or Fred Gibb. However, on occasion, it was utilized by General Motors itself to handle specific vehicle requests or (in the case of the 1970 Camaro) make improvements.

Approaching that year, the brand had plans to carry over the 1969 bodystyle, rolling out an all-new bodystyle in 1971. However, that changed when General Motors caught wind of new government safety regulations rolling out in January 1970, as the 1969 Camaro would not meet them. Retrofitting was an option, but it was deemed to not be the most budget conscious. As such, the company moved forward with advancing the new design that was supposed to debut in September 1970. Instead. It was pushed to the start of the new year with production beginning at the end of February.

Part of the scramble involved cutting short the final engineering for the Trans-Am-oriented Z/28 package. As such, the elongated, European-influenced design was fitted with a low-back one-piece fiberglass spoiler across the rear edge of the trunk lid (RPO D80). It worked with the boxier first-generation design but proved ineffective on the second generation.

Chevrolet was still officially not openly supporting racing but worked closely (mostly behind closed doors) with Jim Hall's Chaparral team that was comprised of three newly acquired 1970 Camaro Z/28s. Rumors long circulated about the working arrangement of the two with suspicions arising that Hall's efforts served as a backdoor test bed for new products.

During some of the testing with the trio of cars, an immediate flaw arose with the spoiler: it was too low. At speed on

COPO 9796 added a high-back spoiler to the 1970 Camaro, helping to improve downforce during high-speed cornering.

a racetrack, the cars lost traction going around corners, lacking sufficient downforce. A taller unit was deemed essential. Thankfully, one was already available—in a roundabout way. Competing Pontiac Firebirds had a taller spoiler and proved to be just the ticket.

Utilizing it proved to be tricky. Per the Trans-Am series homologation rules, any car competing had to have production figures of 2,500 units or 1/250th of the previous year's production (whatever was larger). For a new part exchange, Chevrolet had to show it was available on the production lineup. Vince Piggins, Chevrolet's performance product manager, stepped in, connecting with Jim McDonald, Pontiac's general manager, for approval to use the center section from the Firebird's three-piece spoiler. The endcaps weren't interchangeable, and A.O. Smith, the fiberglass supplier rushed to fabricate the needed pieces so as not to get behind with the race season. A design was created under COPO 9796 Rear Deck Lid Extension to be production ready. Later, a lower front spoiler in flat-black plastic was added to the COPO production vehicles sometime in May, as well as the race cars.

The high back spoiler was manufactured from April to the beginning of May while the front spoiler was installed on cars from late May to early June 1970. As such, there's a four-week period of COPO cars that were created that only had the rear spoiler. The front spoiler was never installed at the factory but rather shipped in the cars' back seats for installation at dealerships. If installed, it wouldn't clear the ramps for loading onto the transport trucks and rail cars.

2012–2021

In 2012, Chevrolet marked the return of the legendary COPO Camaro, offering 69 purpose-built Camaros, harkening back to the amount and intentionality of the 69 1969 Camaro ZL1s. These new cars were not street legal, and with the limited quantity, customers expressed their interest via the COPO Camaro mailing list with the final owners being randomized by an independent third party.

This new iteration was designed to compete in the NHRA's Stock Eliminator and Super Stock classes. All were hand-built as body-in-white body structures at the General Motors Performance Build Center in Wixom, Michigan.

They utilized a solid axle and were given a full chrome-moly roll cage. To reduce weight, most of the power accessories and sound deadening were left out along with the rear seat. Bucket seats were installed up front, complete with a safety harness, a competition floor shifter, and Chevrolet Performance gauges. Customers could select from three different engines and could participate in the assembly. They also could select a collector's package that included all three engines with each serial number

For nearly 10 years, Chevrolet has offered purpose-built COPO Camaros that aren't street legal but are perfect for track use.

matched to the car. The only transmission option was a Powerglide automatic transmission.

The cars did not receive a vehicle identification number (VIN) but were marked with a sequenced build serial number matched to the engine. They were available in five painted colors: Black, Summit White, Victory Red, Silver Ice Metallic, and Ashen Gray Metallic. A graphics package was made available coming in four colors.

BONUS CONTENT

Scan to view the 2012 production breakdown.

www.cartechbooks.com/ct658-qr2

2013–2022

Over subsequent years, changes and alterations were made to the program. In 2013, two new engines were offered as well as a manual transmission option. Other new performance content included a transmission cooler integrated with the radiator, revised front springs, and a dedicated racing wiring harness. Other additions included a "heritage" grille, standard-production (non-HID) headlamps, new exterior graphics with engine size callouts, and a revised interior package with custom carpet and a new switch panel.

In 2014, the engine lineup expanded to five. Other new additions included new racing seats, updated graphics, and a new wheel option. In 2015, the available engine lineup expanded to six different crate engine options. In 2016, a new

engine was added along with a Turbo 400 3-speed automatic transmission. In 2018, a Hot Wheels edition was available, and in 2019, an exclusive COPO Camaro 50th Anniversary special-edition package was offered. The look emulated vintage Chevy performance engines, sporting an orange block, chrome valve covers, and a black high-rise intake manifold.

In 2020, an exclusive black-and-silver paint scheme was offered, inspired by the John Force Edition. In 2022, a 572-ci big-block V-8 engine was available with pricing for a COPO Camaro equipped with that monster powertrain starting at $105,500. LSX-based small-block V-8 engines were still available with a supercharged 580-hp 350-ci V-8, and a naturally aspirated 470-hp 427-ci V-8 was optional. All engines were paired to an ATI Racing Products TH400 3-speed automatic transmission. In a radical departure, production was not limited to the typical 69 vehicles.

Under the hood is a naturally aspirated 427-ci V-8.

The interiors are gutted and fitted with items such as race seats, a roll cage, and additional switchgear.

This 2020 example, #27, was sold new through the legendary Berger Chevrolet dealership in Grand Rapids, Michigan. As part of its build, it was fitted with the Racer's Package, which added the parachute.

Camaro ZL1

The zenith for leveraging GM's Central Office Production Order program to create something truly fantastic fully manifested with the 1969 ZL1. It was every bit the exotic Camaro that Chevrolet desperately needed to command attention, and it performed well on drag strips everywhere. From its inception, it was to be the crown jewel, the glimmering flagship of the brand's pony car performance.

It couldn't come any sooner. Chrysler and its factory-backed race teams, such as Dick Landy and Sox & Martin, were red hot and frequently seen in the winner's circle.

Vince Piggins knew that something must be done. In the summer of 1968, he set his sights on the NHRA's Super Stock race classes, cooking up a Camaro creation that would crush the competition. He green-lit skunkworks research, led by Dick Harrell, to build a vehicle that could do just that. Harrell had already led the foray into the 427 dealer-conversion craze and continued to be a force on drag strips as a professional racer.

The 1969 Camaro ZL1 was a stripped-down track terror, boasting an aluminum 427-ci V-8.

For the apex Camaro to be considered "stock" in the eyes of the NHRA officials, 50 examples had to be built and available for public consumption. Enter a man named Fred Gibb.

1969 Camaro ZL1: Equipment				
427-ci V-8 COPO 9560 (430 hp)	Carburetor	850-cfm Holley		
	• Aluminum engine block, cylinder heads and air intake • Heli coil steel wire inserts • Block bolt threads • 4-bolt main bearing caps • 1/16-inch steel cylinder sleeves • Dual exhaust (RPO N10)			
	RPO K66	Electronic transistor ignition		
	RPO V01	Harrison 4-core heavy-duty radiator		
Transmission	RPO M21	4-Speed C-ratio manual	Stamping	ML
	RPO M40	Turbo Hydra-Matic 400		MM
Steering	Power steering (Cars #54, 55) RPO N40			
	Special steering (quick-ratio) (Car #68) RPO N44			
Suspension	Special performance front and rear suspension (RPO F41)			
Rear Axle	4.10 Positraction	12-bolt		
		Heat-treated ring and pinion		
Brakes	Power front disc brakes (RPO J52)			
Wheels	Rally wheels (RPO ZJ7)			
Tires	F70x14 white lettering (RPO PL5)			
Exterior	• Cowl-induction hood (RPO ZL2) • Air spoiler equipment (rear spoiler) (RPO D80)			
Interior	Standard black vinyl - Code 711			
Special COPO 9737	• "Sports Car Conversion" (Cars #3, 65) • E70x15 white-letter tires • Rally wheels • 13/16-inch stabilizer bar • 140-mph speedometer			

The engine featured upgrades such as four-bolt main bearing caps and Heli-Coil steel wire inserts. All that and more made it ready for performance use.

Gibb Chevrolet

Fred Gibb owned Gibb Chevrolet, in La Harpe, Illinois, a tiny farming community in the southwestern part of the state. Vince and Fred already had a close working relationship, pairing up on a similar backdoor performance car deal in 1968. There, they created 50 purpose-built, race-ready COPO Novas that paved the way for GM to install automatic transmissions behind their solid-lifter big-block V-8 engines.

That project was a smashing success. Hoping to catch lightning in a bottle again, Vince brought Fred onboard. In August 1968, he placed an order for 50 ZL1 Camaros.

COPO 9560

Under COPO 9560, all the cars (all coupes) received a special all-aluminum 427-ci V-8. Despite being a big-block, the material (besides dissipating heat) reduced weight, as it was only slightly heavier than a cast-iron small-block equivalent. The ZL1's V-8 tipped the scales around 520 pounds, closely matching that of the 302-ci V-8 found in the Z28 Camaro.

Officially, this wild wonder was rated at 430 hp, but when equipped with open headers and given a proper tuning, upward of 575 hp and 515 ft-lbs of torque was attainable.

Crafting the ZL1

Being destined for straight-line runs, Gibb's 50 cars were minimally optioned. All started off as RPO L78, 396-ci V-8-equipped Super Sport cars. From there, under COPO 9560, parts and components were either deleted or added.

Either an M21 4-speed manual or a Turbo Hydra-Matic 400 automatic transmission was installed, along with such items as a heavy-duty, four-core radiator, an electronic transistor ignition system, power front disc brakes, and a heavy-duty

Either the M21 4-speed manual or Turbo Hydra-Matic 400 automatic transmission could be installed.

suspension with a special COPO-built Positraction differential. One unique component was the ducted hood, which marked the first instance that a Camaro received a factory cowl-induction hood. Inside, they all came with standard black vinyl interiors with radios left out for weight reduction.

Keeping things organized, the set came in 5 paint colors grouped in sets of 10: Hugger Orange, Cortez Silver, Fathom Green, Lemans Blue and Dusk Blue. Within each set, 6 vehicles received manual transmissions, while the other four received automatics.

They were plain cars that lacked any kind of style trim, adornments, and badging that called out the car's muscle modifications.

The Wintery Delivery

The first two ZL1s, both painted in Dusk Blue, were built in the last week of December and delivered to Gibb Chevrolet. They arrived well after hours one cold night but weren't there long, being hurriedly rushed onward to Harrell's speed shop in Kansas City, Missouri, for final race prep for their debut at the AHRA's fifth-annual Winter Nationals. Harrell drove one while the other was wheeled by an up-and-coming female co-star Shay Nichols.

The Next 48 and the Send Back

The remaining 48 vehicles were built from the fourth week of February through the end of March. They began arriving in the tiny La Harpe dealership shortly thereafter.

While the cars were hot, the reception was not. At some point that spring, General Motors adjusted how these special projects were funded. Instead of having its research and development cost (in the case of the ZL1, a massive amount) wrapped up in the overall corporate budget, now it'd be applied directly to the cost of the vehicle.

All told, Fred was on the hook for around $360,000 of inventory. The staggering cost was near impossible to absorb, and Fred jumped on the phone with GM headquarters to resolve the matter. In a move that had never been seen before, Chevrolet allowed the cars to be returned. A total of 37 were sent back while Fred kept the remaining 13 to sell. He ended up selling 8 and transferring the other 5 to other dealerships.

BONUS CONTENT

Scan to view the 1969 ZL1's sales distribution by state.

www.cartechbooks.com/ ct658-qr3

The package included F70x14 white-letter tires and dual exhaust.

Camaro ZL1 #3 was ordered by Berger Chevrolet and is unique in that it's the only ZL1 that is painted Daytona Yellow and it is 1 of 2 to be fitted with COPO 9737.

BONUS CONTENT

Scan to view the 1969 ZL1's paint breakdown.

www.cartechbooks.com/ct658-qr4

19 More ZL1s and Program Shutdown

Later in the spring of 1969, 19 more ZL1s were built. Word got out about the program, and other dealers placed orders for their own ZL1 Camaros. Cars #55 and #68 stand out, being the only two to receive the RS package.

Citing the extremely high price, the ZL1 program (including an in-the-works radical street version built under COPO 9567 with metallic gold trim and badges and a proposed retail tag of around $8,500) was shut down in June 1969.

2012–2015 and 2017–2020

In 2012, Chevrolet resurrected a legendary moniker, offering a new ZL1 Camaro. At the time, it was the most powerful production Camaro ever, featuring an all-aluminum supercharged 6.2L LSA V-8 that delivered 580 hp and 556 ft-lbs of torque. Despite the extreme amounts of power, like its predecessor, it also came with a factory warranty. The cars started as 2SS and then were given the ZL1 upgrades.

They were available with either a 6-speed manual transmission or optional automatic transmission. Due to the extreme performance nature of the track-focused vehicle, it included an engine-oil cooler, a rear-differential cooler, and a high-performance fuel system.

Other unique features included magnetic ride control with Tour, Sport, and Track modes and an exclusive performance traction management with five different modes.

The ZL1's drivetrain was unique and featured a stronger driveshaft, a 9.9-inch cast-iron differential housing, and stronger axles. Brembo disc brakes were added with 6-piston calipers up front and 4-piston calipers in the rear.

The exterior of the vehicle received ZL1 badging along with aero-focused items, including an aluminum hood with a carbon-fiber insert, a front splitter, front tire air deflectors, a front fascia with air channels for engine and brake cooling, two belly pans (under the engine cradle and at the rear of the engine assembly), rocker panels, and a rear spoiler. Black-painted forged aluminum 10-spoke wheels were standard, but bright 5-spoke wheels were optional.

Inside, the cabin only came with a black interior with red stitching, a leather-wrapped flat-bottom steering wheel (complete with a ZL1 badge), suede microfiber seat inserts (which could also be had on the steering wheel and shifter),

After decades of dormancy, Chevrolet brought back the ZL1 moniker in 2012. It's 6.2L V-8 delivered 580 hp, which was the most of any Camaro to that point.

and stainless-steel trim on the foot pedals. The front-seat headrests were embroidered with the ZL1 logo, and another logo was mounted on the passenger's side of the dashboard. A lower "four-pack" auxiliary cluster was included that featured a boost gauge.

The vehicle came in eight available paint colors and had a base price of $54,995 with six options.

2012-2022 Camaro ZL1 Production							
2012	1,971	Coupe	1,971	Auto	671		
		Convt	0	Man.	1,300		
2013	7,956	Coupe	6,039	Auto	4,678		
		Convt	1917	Man.	3,278		
2014	2,436	Coupe	1,895	Auto	1,097		
		Convt	541	Man.	1,339		
2015	1,850	Coupe	1,561	Auto	897		
		Convt	289	Man.	953		
2017	3,048	Coupe	2,744	Auto	1,814		
		Convt	304	Man.	220		
2018	6,164	Coupe	5,542	Auto	UK		
		Convt	622	Man.	UK		
2019	3,343	Coupe	3,065	Auto	2,082		
		Convt	278	Man.	MJK	569	
					MH3	783	
2020	1,730	Coupe	1,515	Auto	1,289		
		Convt	215	Man.	MJK	239	
					MH3	202	
2021	TBA	Coupe	TBA	Auto	TBA		
		Convt	TBA	Man.	MJK	TBA	
					MH3	TBA	
2022	TBA	Coupe	TBA	Auto	TBA		
		Convt	TBA	Man.	MJK	TBA	
					MH3	TBA	

BONUS CONTENT

Scan to view the 2012 ZL1 coupe production breakdown.

www.cartechbooks.com/ct658-qr5

2013–2015

BONUS CONTENT

Scan to view the 2013 and 2014 ZL1 production breakdown.

www.cartechbooks.com/ct658-qr6

For 2013, the ZL1 was continued with the addition of a convertible option, a color touch radio with Chevrolet MyLink, and a frameless inside rearview mirror. Blue Ray Metallic was added to the available exterior paint options.

Because of the powertrain's extreme performance, the convertible platform was strengthened and reinforced with a strut tower brace, a transmission support reinforcement brace, an underbody tunnel brace, and a front X brace and rear underbody V braces. The convertible top was available in either black or beige.

For 2014, the ZL1 received several updates, including Recaro front sport seats, color driver information center and heads-up display readouts, and three new exterior colors: Red Hot, Bright Yellow, and Red Rock Metallic.

In 2015, the sole addition to the ZL1 was a new exterior paint color: Blue Velvet Metallic.

BONUS CONTENT

Scan to view the 2012–2015 ZL1 performance data.

www.cartechbooks.com/ct658-qr7

2017

After a year hiatus in 2016, the ZL1 returned in full force on the Camaro's sixth-generation platform for 2017. It weighed 200 pounds less than its predecessor and gained more horsepower and torque.

Under the hood was still a supercharged 6.2L V-8 (now an LT4), but it delivered 640 hp and 640 ft-lbs of torque. A 6-speed manual was standard, and a paddle-shift 10-speed

The fifth- and sixth-generation ZL1 Camaro has continued to evolve with upgrades in performance and capability.

The sixth-generation ZL1 featured a supercharged 6.2L V-8 engine with 650 hp.

automatic transmission was optional. The powertrain now featured 11 heat exchangers.

Suspension upgrades included an updated magnetic ride suspension, electronic limited-slip differential, and custom launch control. Brembo brakes were still used but were larger in the front with six-piston monobloc calipers bearing the ZL1 logo and 15.35-inch two-piece front rotors. Four-piston calipers were still used in the rear. The package included unique forged aluminum 20-inch wheels wrapped with the same tires as the previous generation.

Exterior aero additions included a new front fascia, carbon-fiber composite hood extractor, air splitters, and a rear spoiler. The center Chevrolet grille emblem was a "flowtie," which is a hollow bowtie that increases airflow. A black metallic stripe was optional, which added a center stripe on the roof (coupes only) and rear decklid and spoiler.

Inside the cabin, Recaro front seats were standard with a suede flat-bottom steering wheel and shift knob. Chevrolet's performance data recorder was also available.

BONUS CONTENT

Scan to view the 2017 ZL1 production breakdown.

www.cartechbooks.com/ ct658-qr8

2018 Camaro ZL1 and 1LE Extreme Track

For 2018, the ZL1 was carried over unchanged except for the addition of the 1LE Extreme Track Package option, which further improved the ZL1's track performance. It was only available as a coupe with the manual transmission and cost $68,495.

The $7,500 package included a radical rear wing, air deflectors, and dive planes on the front fascia. Lighter and wider 19-inch aluminum wheels were added wrapped in Goodyear Eagle F1 Supercar 3R tires. The suspension was upgraded with Multimatic dynamic suspension spool valve (DSSV) front and rear dampers, which allowed for an adjustable front-end ride height and camber plates and three-way-adjustable rear stabilizer bar.

More vehicle weight (around 60 pounds) was reduced with thinner rear glass and a fixed-back rear seat. Inside, standard equipment included dual-zone automatic climate control, a Bose premium audio system, heated/ventilated front seats, and a heated steering wheel.

Regarding its appearance, the hood received a Satin Black wrap, dark tail lamps and low-gloss black outside rearview mirrors were included, and the red brake calipers were highlighted with the 1LE logo.

BONUS CONTENT

Scan to view the 2018 ZL1 production breakdown.

www.cartechbooks.com/ ct658-qr9

2019–2022

BONUS CONTENT

Scan to view the 2019–2020 ZL1 production breakdown.

www.cartechbooks.com/ ct658-qr10

For the 2019 Camaro ZL1, no performance upgrades were made. Instead, enhancements and refinements were made, such as a full-display rear camera mirror, forward collision alert (coupes only), improved wireless charging, revised ambient interior lighting with new blended color options, and improvements to the performance data recorder.

For 2020, no changes were made to the ZL1. In 2021, changes were limited to the addition of a new exterior paint option, Wild Cherry Tintcoat (available for $495), and the capability for wireless Apple CarPlay and Android Auto.

1986–1992 GM Motorsports/ Player's Challenge Series Camaro

During the 1980s, Camaro performance, like the rest of the market, had dropped significantly. In a bold move, GM Canada sought to change that image and partnered with Player's Ltd. Tobacco Company, Sunoco, and Goodyear to organize a race series that pitted equally matched showroom stock IROC-Z Camaros and Pontiac Trans Ams against each other.

The event was called the GM Player's Series, and it was composed of eight races of about 20 laps at tracks scattered initially throughout eastern Canada. After a bump in popularity, a West series was added in 1987. The courses ran the gamut from ovals to road courses, all of which were sanctioned by the Canadian Automobile Sport Club (CASC). The series ran from 1986 through 1992 with more than 70 race events and $4 million dollars in prize money awarded.

The effort marked the first factory instance of a domestic automaker getting involved in Canadian motorsports with Chevrolet's goal being the acquisition of real-world testing in the pursuit of building better performance vehicles. It was also a brilliant marketing tool that revived the proven adage of "Win on Sunday, sell on Monday."

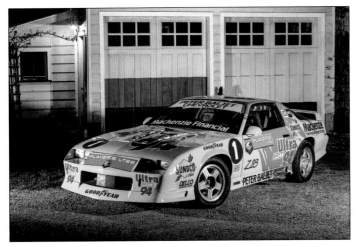

The third-generation Player's Series cars were part of a special effort by Chevrolet of Canada to boost the Camaro's performance and image.

1986–1992 GM Motorsports Player's Challenge Series: Paint Registry							
Paint	1986	1987	1988	1989	1990 (A)*	1991	1992
White	35	22	50	49	0	0	0
Black	8	7	9	10	1	5	0
Bright Red	5	17	10	12	10	5	6
Sedona Tan	7	4	0	0	0	0	0
Dark Blue	8	3	0	0	0	0	0
Taupe M.	0	0	1	0	0	0	0
Gunmetal M.	0	0	1	0	0	0	0
Black Sapphire	0	0	0	3	9	2	3
Arctic White	0	0	0	0	43	19	9
Dark Red	0	0	0	0	2	1	2
Quasar Blue	0	0	0	0	0	0	5
Dark Teal	0	0	0	0	0	0	2
Purple Haze	0	0	0	0	0	0	3
Total	63	53	71	74	65	32	30

1986–1992 GM Motorsports Player's Challenge Series: Interior Color Registry							
M. Gray	48	29	33	32	33	16	23
Black	15	18	28	35	23	14	6
Flame Red	0	0	0	0	9	2	1
Dark Carmine	0	4	8	7	0	0	0
M. Beechwood	0	0	0	0	0	0	0
Saddle	0	2	2	0	0	0	0
Total	63	53	71	74	65	32	30

*Built as 1991-model-year vehicles due to the 1990-model-year-Camaro production being cut short

1986–1992 GM Motorsports/Player's Challenge Series				
Engine	1986	RPO L69	1987–1992	RPO LB9
Exhaust	Walker exhausts		1986	Single side exit
			1987–1992	Dual side exit
	Chrome tips	1970 Chevelle SS		
	Caps	Removable, by Ozimek Industries, Inc.		
Transmission	5-speed manual (0.74:1 with OD)			
Brakes	Power 4-wheel discs	Rotors	12-inch	
		Calipers	1986–1987	Brembo
			1988–1992	PBR
Suspension	F	MacPherson strut/coil springs and sway bar		
	R	Delco performance tuned shocks, Salisbury axle with torque arm, lower control arms, track bar, and coil springs		
Tires	P245/50ZR16 Goodyear Gatorback			
	Spare	14 inch	1986–1987	
		15 inch	1988–1992	

Vehicle Ordering

To compete, interested drivers in possession of a CASC license purchased a new Camaro IROC-Z under RPO A4Q. Each could be financed, and typically, the dealer partnered with the driver for the marketing and exposure. Before being processed, all orders were evaluated and approved by the race director.

Breaking from the norm, the vehicles weren't stripped lightweight racers but rather came equipped with tinted glass, a window defroster, four-speaker AM/FM stereo cassette radio, tilt steering wheels, and power windows. Power windows were needed because a manual crank would interfere with a roll cage that needed to be installed.

All came ordered with the 5.0L high-output V-8 (RPO L69) paired with a 5-speed manual transmission. The engine option was not available to the public, although a claimed 75 were made. Sixty-three examples were sent to GM of Canada for the Player's Series.

For the first few years (until 1989), competitors were required to have their vehicles fully insured and registered for street use. To get them in the public spotlight, they were even encouraged to drive the Camaros to and from the track in addition to using them to attend promotional appearances. To help lower costs, this requirement was dropped in 1990.

Engine

Beginning from assembly, it was clear that this run of Camaros was special. It received bespoke performance upgrades in the same vein as the legendary COPO Camaros of the 1960s.

For power, the cars were ordered with the 5.0L high-output V-8 engine—one that was specially built by GM at its Flint, Michigan, facility. It was the same location where the Corvette Challenge engines were built.

All were fitted with blocks and cylinder heads taken from the same casting to ensure there was minimal variance between compression ratio and flow variations. Other uniform testing included checking camshaft lobes, flow-testing the fuel injectors, and giving close attention to piston clearance.

After a final inspection, each was put on a dyno to ensure that output within three percent of each other. They were then serialized and sealed with yellow epoxy paint to prevent tampering by drivers in pursuit of more power. These marks would be inspected prior to competition by technical inspectors.

When drivers ordered the cars in 1986, they had to place an order by March 15, 1986, specifying RPO A4Q. The vehicles (costing $8,7557.55) were shipped to Kerr Industries in Oshawa, Ontario, Canada, where the "as delivered" L69 engines were replaced with the "sealed" L69 engines. Kerr

The engines were specially built at GM's Flint, Michigan, facility, and all of them utilized blocks and heads taken from the same casting.

Safety equipment, such as a fire extinguisher and roll cage, was added to the cabin. Power windows were a must-have feature because the window cranks interfered with the cage.

Industries also installed the roll cages (designed by Bill Mitchell) and added the side exit exhaust and engine calibration prom. The company also installed the low-volume power-steering pump, track-specification struts, and a side-exit exhaust outlet on the passenger's side only. The base decal package was added, and the engine was calibrated with Players Series specifications.

Spare engines were produced using the same practices and were available each season in the event of engine failure. Each year, teams were required to race a new-production-year car, although cars from previous years were allowed with new-series engines. While the blocks did not receive a VIN matched to the vehicle, if found in a Player's Series Camaros, these would still be considered to be correct.

Other Upgrades

Other unique items to the Camaros included upgraded brakes; lower-ride-height coil springs, front struts, and shocks; and an improved fuel tank with internal baffling. The power-steering pump ran a lower pressure to help with cooling.

Race Team Additions

After the drivers had taken delivery of the vehicles, General Motors supplied additional equipment solely for race use. This included a specially calibrated engine computer program known as programmable read-only memory (PROM) that was set to optimize engine performance and provide driver aids, including a shift light and fuel cut-off. With a steering-wheel airbag added to the Camaro in 1990 and moving forward, race teams were provided with instructions on how to disable the airbag system. Also included by GM were instructions to adjust the vehicle's inner fenders to direct more air to the brakes.

Finally, series decals were provided for mounting on specific areas on the car. Teams could paint their vehicles or add additional sponsor graphics.

Race Requirements and Operations

Racers were required to add safety equipment, such as a roll cage and a fire extinguisher, and pay a refundable $5,000 bond. This ensured that racers wouldn't speed or stunt on public roads, that they wouldn't drink alcohol within 24 hours of a race, and that they would return the special performance parts, including the engine, to GM for evaluation.

The top teams were well-funded, multi-car outfits that were sponsored by companies such as Sony, Sunoco, Moto-Master, and Canadian Tire. At the other end of the spectrum were more grassroots individuals who financed their racing endeavors themselves.

On race day, drivers could remove the driver-side floor mat, spare tire, jack, exterior radio antenna, and air pump belt as well as adjust tire pressures and the alignment to suit their driving styles. Teams could also swap coil springs if they stayed above the minimum ride height. A race seat could be swapped in too. All the cars were required to use sponsor Sunoco or Mohawk (Sunoco's sister company) gas.

Before heading for the track, GM technicians inspected each car to make sure the rules were followed and competition was fair.

As part of the agreement, competitors were required to return many of the bespoke performance components, including the engine PROM.

Brakes

Out of the gate, it was apparent the stock brakes couldn't handle the heat of heavy use. To remedy the issue, each car was fitted with Brembo four-piston brake calipers. These were the same calipers found on the Ferrari F40, and they had special brackets to accommodate larger 12-inch rotors.

The setup was retained in 1987 with PBR heavy-duty Corvette calipers (modified to fit the F-Body spindle) being swapped in for the 1988 season and continuing until the end of the run in 1992. With the brakes becoming standard equipment in 1988 as part the 1LE Performance Package, they no longer needed to be returned.

Yearly Updates and Changes

In 1987, the cars were ordered under RPO A4U and were equipped with engine RPO LB9. When teams selected the options code packages, 24 teams opted for the base group option. Twenty-eight went with a medium options package including power windows and locks. One team elected for the deluxe options group. Power windows were desirable, as it was difficult to use crank windows with a roll bar.

In 1987, the series supplied a catalytic bypass exhaust system manufactured by Walker Exhausts (a division of Tenneco Canada Inc.). It provided dual dumps exiting on both sides of the vehicle, allowing spectators to feel the experience on both sides of the track. They were fitted with oval chrome tips from the GM parts bin, being stock items from a 1970 Chevelle SS. Removable aluminum caps were included for street driving and were made by Ozimek Industries Inc. in Ajax, Ontario, Canada.

In 1988, 19 teams selected the base options group, 49 went with the medium options package, and three opted for the top-tier deluxe package. The 12-inch performance brake package was now hand fit by PBR prior to the assembly line. Minor casting differences exist when compared to 1989 production. Due to the larger brakes, the spare tire was revised and supplied to teams midseason. The stock 14-inch spare wouldn't fit over the bigger brakes, so a 15-inch spare was included in the package. After 1989, the extra part was dropped because a 15-inch spare became standard equipment on the Camaro.

In 1989, the options code changed to R7U, which created an equal package for both the Camaro and Trans Am, resulting

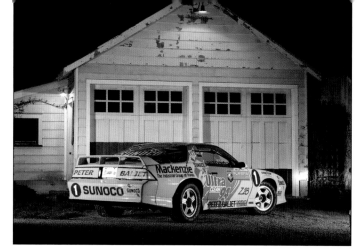

Despite the extreme modifications, the cars were street legal.

in nearly identical vehicle weight and price. R7U also included the newly created 1LE Performance Package group of options, which included 12-inch front brake rotors, front struts, rear shocks, stiffer control-arm bushings, and a higher-wall baffle fuel tank with a revised fuel pickup. The 1LE option also included the JG1 aluminum driveshaft and N64 aluminum spare for weight savings.

The package on Camaros also used the Trans Am's 36-mm front sway bar and 24-mm rear sway bar. Likewise, 1LE Trans Ams received the Camaros steering box brace, or "wonderbar." This year and moving forward, the only choice teams now had was the vehicle's paint color. The 1LE Performance Package option carried over into the fourth-generation Camaro through 1999 before returning with revised components in 2013 on the fifth-generation Camaro.

In 1990, the vehicles were built in two batches. The early cars were the 1990 model year in IROC trim, whereas the later cars were 1991 Z28s. All had the fuel tank modified by GM for port-injected cars, and all received the race-inspired high-wall baffled fuel tank and revised pickup. Other changes included the removal of the front rail re-enforcement (the wonderbar), which reduced the rear sway bar to 23 mm to reduce oversteer, and the addition of harder rear control-arm bushings to prevent wheel hop.

In 1991, the vehicles were still built as the 1991 model year with no changes in their creation, including the final year of production in 1992.

Winding Down

In 1989, a massive recession caused GM North America to pull out of sponsorship of any kind of race operations that were not related to direct sales. As such, it withdrew from the IROC competition.

In Canada, the Player's Series was helping with showroom sales and, as such, continued on. With the launch of the all-new fourth-generation Camaro in 1993, it finally was discontinued.

1989–1999, 2013–2015 1LE Performance Package

	1988	1989	1990	1991	1992
Total	4	111	62	469	685

The regular production option code of 1LE was introduced in 1988 and brought upgraded brakes, front struts, and rear shocks to be used on the track-destined Canadian Player's Series Camaros. Only four were equipped with them and were built in July and August 1988 for marketing purposes.

The 1LE option was drawn from the run of Player's Series Camaros and added mostly suspension upgrades.

1989-1992 1LE: Year-to-Year Changes

In 1989, the 1LE Performance Package required customers to order the top-level suspension. Camaros now received the Trans Am's larger 36-mm front sway bar and the 24-mm rear sway bar. As part of the larger front brakes, the rotor hub was slightly thicker and moved the front wheels outward. To compensate, outer bearings from the C10/B-body platform were used. Coil springs were added, which lowered the ride height.

Other additions included a new "high wall" fuel tank reservoir and the extended pickup that reached out to both sides of the tank as opposed to the stock style's one side. These measures provided more access to fuel during cornering. New

No changes were made to the interior, but the upgrades are definitely noticed when driving.

lower control arms (code LB) were added and were equipped with higher-density durometer bushings to prevent wheel hop.

When the 1LE Performance Package was ordered, it triggered lightweight items from the available regular production items. This included the aluminum driveshaft (RPO JL1) and aluminum space saver spare (RPO N64).

In 1990, the fuel tank became a regular production item for all port-injected Camaros, and the suspension bushings were improved. Other changes included reducing the rear sway bar by 1 mm to combat oversteer, and the chassis stiffener was removed.

1993–2000 Camaro Performance Package (RPO 1LE)

	1993	1994	1995	1996	1997	1998	1999
Total	19	158	134	64	46	101	74

With the all-new fourth-generation Camaro debuting in 1993, Chevrolet continued the 1LE Performance Package, making it available on Z28 coupes equipped with either the automatic or 6-speed manual transmission.

The 1LE option cost $310 and included an engine oil cooler and a special handling suspension system composed of larger stabilizer bars, stiffer shock absorbers, stiffer springs, and bushings. It did require the RPO QLC tires (P245/50ZR16 B/W). Cars equipped with the 4-speed automatic transmission (RPO MX0) required the optional performance axle (GU5). A power seat (RPO AC3 and later AG1) and the transparent roof panels (RPO CC1) were not available with the package.

In factory literature, the 1LE was described as being "engineered specially for professional racing and is intended for serious performance enthusiasts only."

In 1996, the package also included dual adjustable shock absorbers and bushings. In 1999, the package added a stiffer transmission mount for manual transmissions and stiffer Panhard bar bushings.

2013–2015 Camaro 1LE Performance Package

In 2013, Chevrolet brought the 1LE Performance Package back, making it available on 1SS and 2SS models through 2015. It came with an exclusive Tremec 6-speed manual transmission that featured close-ratio gearing that was optimized for road racing. As with the top-tier ZL1 Camaro, the 1LE's transmission used a standard air-to-liquid cooling system.

Many other ZL1 components were included in the 1LE package, such as a high-capacity fuel pump, short-throw shifter, and its front tires. Visually, it was set apart by a matte black hood graphic, front splitter, and rear spoiler.

2013 Camaro 1LE Production				
Total	1,826	1SS	413	
		2SS	1,413	
Paint	Total	Trim	Total	
Crystal Red	106	1SS	20	
		2SS	86	
Summit White	293	1SS	72	
		2SS	221	
Victory Red	316	1SS	76	
		2SS	240	
Ashen Gray Metallic	182	1SS	43	
		2SS	139	
Blue Ray Metallic	90	1SS	20	
		2SS	70	
Rally Yellow	92	1SS	28	
		2SS	64	
Black	529	1SS	78	
		2SS	451	
Inferno Orange	127	1SS	32	
		2SS	95	
Silver Ice Metallic	91	1SS	44	
		2SS	47	

2014 Camaro 1LE Figures				
Total	2,468	US	2,271	
		Canada	197	
1SS	676	2SS	1,792	
Paint	Total	Market	Total	
Crystal Red Tintcoat	97	US	92	
		Canada	5	
Summit White	577	US	533	
		Canada	44	
Red Hot	327	US	309	
		Canada	18	
Ashen Gray Metallic	241	US	220	
		Canada	21	
Blue Ray Metallic	120	US	104	
		Canada	16	
Bright Yellow	139	US	128	
		Canada	11	
Black	690	US	627	
		Canada	63	
Red Rock Metallic	148	US	136	
		Canada	12	
Silver Ice Metallic	129	US	122	
		Canada	7	

2015 Camaro 1LE	
Crystal Red	76
Summit White	741
Red Hot	351
Ashen Gray Met.	292
Blue Velvet Met.	85
Bright Yellow	166
Black	770
Red Rock Met.	109
Silver Ice Met.	147
Total	2,737

The B4C option, which was named the Police Package, essentially created an unbadged Z28 Camaro. It was intended to be used by law enforcement for high-speed pursuits. The only added performance component was trailing arms from the 1LE package.

BONUS CONTENT

Scan to view the 2013–2015 Camaro 1LE package content.

www.cartechbooks.com/ ct658-qr14

2017–2023 Camaro 1LE Performance Package

In 2017, Chevrolet offered the 1LE Performance Package on the sixth-generation Camaro in both SS and LT V-6 trim on coupes equipped with the 6-speed manual transmission. It continued the 1LE tradition of offering a potent package optimized for track use.

The V-6 package brought upgrades from the SS, such as components from the FE3 suspension, the fuel system, and the wheels. Both trims shared similar cosmetics in the form of a satin black hood wrap, mirror caps, and a blade spoiler.

BONUS CONTENT

Scan to view the 2017–2022 Camaro 1LE package content.

www.cartechbooks.com/ ct658-qr15

1991–2002 Camaro Police Package

In 1990, the Chevrolet Caprice sedan was the top-selling police car in America. While its large, roomy size made it ideal for general policing, it lacked agility (with a wide turning ratio) and speed for high-performance highway pursuits. Ford had the same problem with its LTD Crown Victoria but had solved the predicament by offering the Special Service Package 5.0L Mustang to departments ever since 1982.

1991–1992 Camaro Special Service Package: B4C

To fill the void, in the fall of 1990, Chevrolet debuted the 1991 Camaro RS equipped with its own Special Service Package. Ordered under Option B4C and costing $3,460, it brought a unique collection of options—most of which came from the Z28.

Buyers had their pick between the available pair of either the Z28's standard 5.0L V-8 or the optional 5.7L V-8, both coming with tuned port fuel injection. Other inclusions were the Z28's standard performance suspension, a 145-mph speedometer, and 16-inch aluminum wheels. They were wrapped with the Z28 coupe's optional 245/50ZR16 tires.

The interior was available in four colors: black, light brown, gray, or red. Standard cloth was the norm, but custom cloth was available as well, bringing a folding rear seat. Leather was not available.

The B4C option carried over to the 1992 model year unchanged.

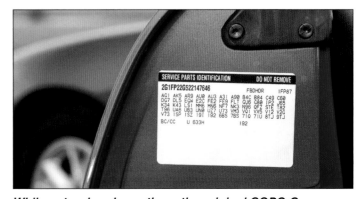

While not ordered exactly as the original COPO Camaros of the 1960s, RPO B4C follows in their spirit of undetected performance. In addition to B4C (RPO 1SP), the Preferred Equipment Group had to be ordered too.

1993–1997 Camaro Special Service Package: B4C

The Special Service Package B4C option carried over to the all-new fourth-generation 1993 Camaro. It was still only available on coupes and required base equipment group FCAB, plus the B4C option.

It still essentially brought Z28 upgrades with much of the content remaining. Notable changes included the LT1 5.7L V-8 now having more power (up to 280 hp). The standard transmission was the 6-speed manual, but the 4-speed automatic was optional.

Cloth or leather could be ordered for the interior. The majority of cars were equipped with the automatic transmission.

The packaging of the car was unique, differing from the Z28 in that it received a body-colored roof.

Inside, the cabins were equipped with cloth bucket seats with all three interior trim colors (Graphite, Medium Beige, and Medium Gray) available.

In 1994, the B4C option added a 140-amp alternator and the availability of the Flame Red interior color. Another change in 1994 was that the Caprice was now equipped with the same LT1 V-8, which improved its performance and made some departments rethink the Camaro strategy.

Changes to the 1995 B4C option were that it now required base equipment group 1SAX and the option to equip the interior with leather in Graphite or Medium Beige colors.

In 1996, the Special Service Package was ordered under base equipment group 1SA and now included a low-coolant indicator. The interior could now be had in Neutral (replacing Medium Beige), which was still available in cloth and leather.

In 1997, as seen across the Camaro line, Dark Gray replaced Graphite on the interior colors.

1998–2002 Camaro Special Service Package: B4C

In 1998, the Special Service Package was ordered under base equipment group 1SP in addition to the B4C. Changes included a 155-mph speedometer and RPO FE9 (federal emissions certification) being mandatory. Under the hood was the new LT1 V-8 with even more power at 305 hp.

In 2000, the only change to the Special Service Package was that it was now ordered under the Preferred Equipment Group 1SP as well as B4C.

In 2001 and 2002, no changes were made to the package. As the package was typically exclusive to law enforcement, this secretive allocation was in the same vein of the 1960s COPO Camaros that were built through similar backdoor channels. B4C Camaros were made available to the public, with limited examples being offered each year or dealerships selling former police examples. Owners who acquired them liked their Z28 performance paired with the lightweight, stripped-down nature. In 2002, 69 B4C Camaros were sourced as the basis of the run of GMMG-built ZL1 Supercars.

Throughout the run of B4C Camaros, police departments fitted the vehicle with exterior patrol gear, including a roof-mounted light bar, spotlight, and door insignias. It was also common for departments to keep them as unmarked units, which made them ideal for street racing enforcement.

BONUS CONTENT

Scan to view the 1991–2002 Camaro B4C equipment content.

www.cartechbooks.com/ ct658-qr16

When put into service by law enforcement, this is how you'd typically find Camaro B4Cs, equipped with patrol items, such as a light bar, spotlight, and reflective livery. This example was used for promotional duty with the Utah Highway Patrol.

1999 Camaro B4C: Production	Auto	6-Spd.
	184	12
Arctic White	50	3
Light Pewter Met.	25	0
Sebring Silver Met.	4	0
Navy Blue Met.	35	7
Bright Green Met.	1	0
Onyx Black	36	1
Mystic Teal Met.	1	0
Bright Rally Red	14	1

2000 Camaro B4C: Production	Auto	6-Spd.
Total	221	9
Arctic White	39	9
Light Pewter Met.	42	0
Sebring Silver Met.	70	0
Navy Blue Met.	18	0
Maroon	6	0
Onyx Black	42	0
Bright Rally Red	4	0

2001 Camaro B4C: Production	Auto	6-Spd.
Total	279	9
Arctic White	47	4
Light Pewter Met.	31	1
Navy Blue Met.	25	1
Maroon	7	0
Onyx Black	160	3
Mystic Teal	5	0
Bright Rally Red	4	0

2002 Camaro B4C: Production	Auto	6-Spd.
Totals	577	125
Arctic White	114	14
Light Pewter Met.	25	2
Sebring Silver Met.	33	12
Navy Blue Met.	42	8
Monterey Maroon Met.	29	2
Onyx Black	320	62
Police Two-Tone	13	0
Sunset Orange M.	1	7
Bright Rally Red	0	18

## CHAPTER 2

INDY 500 AND BRICKYARD EDITIONS

Being tardy to the pony car party, the Camaro desperately needed to make a splash in the marketplace. The perfect opportunity was pacing the 1967 Indianapolis 500, the largest auto race in the United States. It had been 12 years since Chevy last held the honor. If ever there was a place to show off the Camaro, this was it.

The idea surfaced during the holiday season of 1966 within Chevy's Indianapolis zone. Jack Bell, the region's manager caught wind of it and quickly presented it to his superiors. They liked it and so did the speedway's officials.

1967 Camaro Indy Pace Cars

Deeming the 1967 race as the perfect place to showcase an all-new engine in the Camaro, Chevrolet equipped the pair of pace cars (including a backup as was the norm) with the L78 375-hp 396-ci V-8.

Three such vehicles were sourced from Chevy's central office and delivered to General Motor's Milford Proving Grounds in late March of 1967.

For an even more vibrant look, the pair of pace cars (#92 is shown) received special white paint before being delivered to the track on April 24, 1967.

	Total
Test Mule	1
Pace cars	2
Festival committee	43
Speedway vehicles	10
Winner award	1
Brass hat cars #1	28
Brass hat cars #2	7–10
Display cars	3
Central office cars	8
Zone cars	20–30
Dealer replicas	320 (est.)

Special White Paint

As was customary for pace cars, they came as convertibles (with white tops) and came painted white, which was a color preferred by the track to help ensure that the vehicle remained visible during any kind of track condition. While Ermine White was available on Camaro, Chevrolet wanted them to be even brighter and sourced the brightest white paint available through the General Motors paint processing department.

More than likely, it was Truck White (Code 521), given that Chevrolet also loaned white pickups to the track for use and would want consistency across the range of supplied vehicles. It also could have been a white from Cadillac or perhaps extra time spent buffing. Whatever it was, something was different about the paint.

Besides being Super Sports, the Camaros received the RS package, but the factory D91 nose band was painted blue instead of black. A blue pinstripe was also applied, complementing the Bright Blue interior. Despite having a big-block engine, Chevrolet opted to leave the trio's rear cove as the body color (as opposed to the norm of painting it flat black). Subsequent big-block pace car replicas retained their black coves.

FSO Cowl Tag Data

Due to the special nature of the paint request, the Camaros received "FSO" stampings (called "COPO codes" by some Chevrolet staff) on the cowl tag, being part of a non-RPO Fleet and Special Order request.

These are identified with a paint code of "0." After the group of options trim code on the lowest line, a dash mark was followed by a collection of assorted processing numbers that included 050A, 050B, 061A, 062A, and 070A for Norwood, Ohio–built cars or L181A for those assembled in Van Nuys, California). Cars bearing a paint code of "C" (indicating RPO Ermine White paint) were still available as part of the pace car promotion if they included the second post-trim code dash and number combination.

Occasionally, solely the dash mark showed with the number combination left off. While seemingly random, this was part of the manufacturing sequence.

Final Prep

During evaluations, concerns of overheating and cabin noise arose along with an even greater threat: engine stalling. In 1967, the L78 was only paired to a 4-speed manual transmission. Given the heavy stop-and-go usage at the track and the additional promotional parades and appearances, the decision was made to dial the setup back for fear of stalling at a critical moment and the resulting brand optics of such an event.

Engineers then moved to converting the cars to L35 engines mated to M40 Turbo Hydra-Matic automatic transmissions. To ensure maximum durability, the engines were taken apart and given stronger internals. This included the camshaft and valve springs from the forthcoming L34 396 engine with 350 hp that debuted in the Camaro in 1968. The transmission and rear axle were also torn down and closely inspected to ensure perfect working order.

Bright blue interiors were used, pairing nicely with the white paint.

For visibility on track, flag mounts were added at the rear.

That attention to detail was carried over to the chassis and suspension, which were magnafluxed to ensure the metal's soundness. Heavy-duty metallic brakes were installed, and for good measure, extra brake shoes went with the vehicle in the event of overheating on race day. Extra wheels and tires were sent along as well to prepare for potential issues. Other heavy-duty components were installed, including steering knuckles, ball joints, and steering linkage. For a proper rumble, dual exhaust was added (from RPO N61) along with a heavy-duty battery, larger alternator, premium belts, and a larger radiator.

Of the trio, one vehicle served as the lead test mule, undergoing most of the evaluation resulting in it never leaving the proving grounds. More than likely, it was destroyed.

Festival Camaros

As was tradition, Chevrolet provided not only the official pace cars but also vehicles for the Indy 500 festival committee directors.

On April 1, following a breakfast at the downtown Indianapolis Athletic Club, the group headed across the street to the War Memorial Plaza where 33 Camaros were parked. Each had been ordered through Chevy's central office and mirrored the look of the pace car but was fitted in SS350 trim.

To identify the run, each vehicle was marked with blue number stickers affixed to the rearview mirror and ahead of the mirror on the driver's door. Track 1 and Track 2 (#90 and #92) were distinct in that their side numbers were affixed to the vent window.

BONUS CONTENT

Scan to view the full list of festival members, their roles, and city ties.

www.cartechbooks.com/ ct658-qr17

Speedway Camaros

As part of its commitment to the track, Chevrolet also provided another 10 Camaro pace car replicas for use by the directors and upper management of the speedway.

Three area dealerships were involved with the preparation of the commitment fleet. Johnson Chevrolet prepped the trucks while Bill Kuhn Chevrolet prepped 24 festival Camaros and the speedway's 10 Camaros. Nankivell Chevrolet prepped 19 festival Camaros.

Brass Hat Camaros

With Chevrolet playing full-court press from a marketing standpoint, a temporary office was set up at the Speedway Motor Hotel. Eight "brass hat" pace car replicas were assigned to remain outside the room in the hotel parking lot for easy access for central office personnel. An additional 20 or so Camaros were made available and assigned by the zone office.

Realizing that the allocation wasn't enough, a second batch of brass-hat Camaros were ordered to fill additional needs.

Numerous pace car replicas were created for festival use and to be part of Chevrolet's "Pacesetter" sales promotion.

Customers could equip their pace car replica with a big-block V-8, thus adding a painted black tail panel. This example was bought in April 1967 by an Air Force pilot in San Antonio, Texas. It is one of a few delivered with mag-style hubcaps.

Dealer Pace Car Replicas

As part of the massive promotional push surrounding the placement of the Camaro at the Indy 500, Chevrolet rolled out the "Camaro Pacesetter" sale. The promotion brought discounts to the model and included extra-charge options, such as a floor shifter for the 3-speed transmission, at no cost.

Most notably, it also allowed customers to purchase a replica of the pace car complete with the FSO Bright White paint, blue nose band and pinstripe, and blue interior. Door graphics were included but placed in the trunk and installed per the dealer and/or new customer's discretion.

Ordering was only open from the last week of February through the second week of March, and only cars ordered in the first week received the FSO Bright White paint. The remainder were painted Ermine White.

A variety of engines can be found on pace car replicas, including this 396-ci V-8.

The pace car replicas included the blue nose band, blue pinstripe, and door decals.

The dealer replicas matched the pace cars, receiving bright blue interiors.

Race Day

On May 30, the Camaro pace car was in full glory with Mauri Rose, a Chevrolet engineer and former racer, driving it around the track at the start of the race and for the victory lap. Pace cars wouldn't return to the track for caution conditions until 1979.

Upon the race's conclusion (on May 31 because it was delayed due to rain), A.J. Foyt was declared the winner, and later that evening, he was awarded the winner's Camaro pace car that Chevrolet had on display at the victory banquet. He caused quite a commotion, initially refusing to accept the vehicle until air conditioning and an automatic top were installed.

As part of the promotional push, in addition to the pace car placement, Chevrolet leveraged all kinds of additional exposure for the vehicle, including having it in the official program, on matchbook covers, in phone directories, and on paper pads.

1969 Camaro Indy Pace Car: The Hugger Returns

	Total
Pace cars	2
Winner award	1
Festival committee	33
Festival queen	1
Festival associates	8
Speedway vehicles	7
USAC officials	5
VIP and media replicas	75
Z11 convertibles	3,675
Z10 coupes	500

The pace cars were equipped with vibrant orange houndstooth cloth seat inserts

The pace cars were readily distinguished by their brand of tires. One wore Goodyear tires, and the other used Firestone. Here, both are shown together—an ultra-rare sight.

In 1969, ready for another media blitz, Chevrolet again secured the coveted spot of being able to provide the pace car for the 53rd annual Indianapolis 500. Having done so two years prior, this second time round, Chevrolet was able to kick it into high gear and really market the car.

Creating the Z11

The pair of Camaros that became the pace cars were built in the last week of March and delivered to the General Motors proving grounds to be made ready for track use. Greater efforts were taken than in 1967 to present both cars with as much factory performance equipment as possible.

Both were equipped as an SS/RS convertible fitted with a manual convertible top and cowl-induction hood (RPO ZL2). The cars came equipped with SS 396 L78 V-8 engines paired with the rare aluminum cylinder head option.

They were painted Dover White, and (despite being equipped with a big-block 396) had the rear panel and lower rocker panels left white instead of being painted black. The RPO D90 sport striping was left off, and the fenders received Hugger Orange fender striping (RPO D96 and part of the RS package, RPO Z22) instead. That matched the Hugger Orange Z/28-stylted stripes that were applied. Rally wheels with hubcap and trim rings were applied to the wheels.

Inside, a custom orange interior with orange houndstooth was installed. Other options on the car included a Turbo Hydra-Matic automatic transmission, Postiraction rear axle, power steering, console, special instrumentation, AM radio, front and rear spoilers, and a sport-styled steering wheel.

At the proving grounds, the engineers set to work further modifying the cars for heavy use. They disassembled and examined the engines, and fearing that the L89's aluminum cylinder heads might prove finicky during track use, they reinstalled the cast-iron heads from the original L78 setup. The transmissions were also torn down and closely inspected while the suspension components went through an added inspection process (being magnafluxed) to ensure durability.

To counter overheating, heavy-duty radiators were installed as well as temperature-controlled fan clutches. Other heavy-duty components included batteries, alternators, and a special six-bolt-specific torque converter (the same one installed on COPO L72 427 and ZL1 Camaros). The rare RPO JL8 four-wheel disc brake option was installed on both cars as well.

The pair received 15-inch wheels and F70x15 tires. To respect both tire manufacturers who sponsored the race, pace car #1 received Firestone Super Sport 200 tires while #2 had Goodyear Wide Tread GTs.

Other alterations included adding items such as two-way radios (complete with driver's side front fender antennas), chrome hood locks, a locking gas cap, and straps and clips to secure the convertible top.

The stock dual exhaust, which for 1969 exited straight out the rear, was swapped for the 1968 style, which dumped behind the rear valance. This allowed clearance for the pair of flag mounts that were installed. Handles on the windshield frame and a rear seat panel and similar door graphics to what were on the 1967 pace car rounded out the package.

BONUS CONTENT

Scan to view the 1969 Pace Car Equipment content and specifications.

www.cartechbooks.com/ct658-qr18

As was customary, the pace cars were equipped with flag mounts.

This pace car (#2) saw track use for the race.

Z11 Replicas

As now customary, Chevrolet provided a slew of additional vehicles, including a total of 131 pace car–replica Camaros. Forty-three served as festival cars, one was assigned to the race, seven were for the speedway, five for the United States Auto Club (USAC), and an additional 75 were for various duties. These replicas came equipped with additional options, such as a power convertible top, Soft-Ray tinted glass, custom deluxe seats, and front seat belts.

Dealerships also sold pace car convertible replicas designed with RPO Z11 (costing $36.90), which contained an assortment of equipment that closely matched that found on the pair of pace cars. The engine choice wasn't limited, and as such, the cars could be equipped with either the SS 350 or the SS 396. Options weren't restricted, and some of these replicas sported large price tags.

1969 Camaro Indy Sport Convertible: RPO Z11 Package Contents	
Package price	$36.90
RPO	Exterior
Z27	Camaro SS
Z22	Rally sport equipment
Code 911	Dover White Paint White body sill (instead of black) White rear panel (instead of black)
Z28	Hugger Orange stripes
Z22	Hugger Orange fender striping
ZL2	Air induction hood
ZJ7	Rally wheel, hub cap, and trim ring
RPO	Interior
Z87	Custom interior Orange Houndstooth cloth trim Code 720
RPO	Additional required options
M40	Turbo Hydra-Matic
G80	Positraction rear axle
N40	Power steering
C06*	Power convertible top
D55	Console
U17	Special instrumentation
U63	AM radio
D8G	Air spoiler (front and rear)
N34	Sport-styled steering wheel
YA1*	Custom deluxe seat and front shoulder belts (A39 and A85)
A01*	Soft-Ray Tinted Glass
Other	Indy 500 door graphics (included in the trunk)
*	Content not found on the official pair of pace cars

Z10 Coupes

To further broaden the appeal of the look, RS/SS coupes were also offered, receiving similar treatment but marked with RPO Z10. The package contained only the exterior equipment

The Z10 option brought the exterior looks of the pace car but with a coupe bodystyle. These were mostly sold in regions of the country where customers preferred the hardtop.

and paint and stripe treatment of the Z11 package. The door graphics were not included, and few, if any, received the orange houndstooth interior.

No Z10s were sent to the track because they were regional promotional vehicles that were sent to high-heat areas of the country where customers favored the hardtop versus the convertible.

BONUS CONTENT

Scan to view the allotment of additional vehicles supplied for track use.

www.cartechbooks.com/ct658-qr19

Race Day

To satisfy sponsorship contractual demands, one pace car was equipped with Goodyear tires while the other received Firestone tires. Both were used in the days leading up to the race to garner equal exposure for the two tire manufactures. To tell them apart, large white numbers (1 and 2) were mounted in the center of the windshield.

The pace car that saw track use was based on whatever brand of tires was on the race's pole position competitor. With A.J. Foyt holding that title and a deal with Goodyear, the Goodyear-equipped pace car (#2) was used with the Firestone counterpart serving as backup. With that settled, the numbers were removed, and a two-way radio and antenna was installed in Car #1, which was driven by Jim Rathmann. Rathmann won

the 1960 Indy 500 and was the operator of a Chevrolet dealership in Melbourne, Florida.

At the end of the race, winner Mario Andretti accepted a separate award pace car replica.

BONUS CONTENT

Scan to view the full list of festival members, their roles, and city ties.

www.cartechbooks.com/ct658-qr20

1978 Indianapolis 500 Festival Camaro Z/28

For the 1978 Indianapolis 500, Chevrolet, celebrating the Corvette's 25th anniversary, provided four black and silver 1978 limited-edition Corvettes for use as the pace car. Joining

White T-top Z28 Camaros were provided to the 1978 Indy 500 for use as festival cars. They came with gold-painted aluminum wheels and red and orange striping.

The cabins were equipped with a white vinyl and carmine interior, and the cars had an automatic transmission.

it was a fleet of additional vehicles, including 51 1978 Camaro Z/28s that served as the official festival car.

All came as T-tops painted white (Code 11/11), and they were accented with red and orange striping and gold-painted aluminum wheels. They also received a one-piece door decal. Inside, they received a custom white vinyl and Carmine interior (code XWR2), and they each had an automatic transmission.

Dealer Replicas

As part of the race festivities, Chevrolet reintroduced a "Pacesetter Sale" during the month of May. Promotions included offering dealerships the same door decals as found on the official festival cars to create dealer replicas.

Made by Kux Manufacturing in Detroit (and costing $22 a set), dealers were encouraged to mount the graphics to white Z/28s (and the sister Official Courtesy Car Monte Carlo) to emulate the look of the vehicles seen at Indy.

1982 Indianapolis 500 Commentative Edition Z28 Camaro

Total	Role	Total	Engine	RPO	Output
6,362	Pace Car	1	350 V-8 (CFI)	N/A	250 hp
	Backup	1			
	Festival	80	305 V-8 (4-bbl) or 305 V-8 (CFI)	LG4	140 hp
	Commentative	6,280		LU5	165 hp

After receiving a full redesign, the third-generation 1982 Camaro Z28 was selected as the pace car for the 1982 Indianapolis 500.

A backup was created, and both vehicles featured an exclusive silver and blue metallic exterior, Indy 500 graphics, sport mirrors, and stock Z28 15x7 aluminum wheels that were painted silver and accented with red highlights. They were wrapped with Goodyear Eagle GT black-wall tires.

Under the hood, they utilized a specially prepared fuel-injected 5.7L V-8 with an aluminum engine block, aluminum cylinder heads, and Cyclone headers. Compression was raised to 11:1, and output was rated at 250 hp and 310 ft-lbs of torque. This Cross-Fire injection (RPO LU5) was like the one used on the Corvette and featured vacuum-operated cold-air flaps in the scoops. The modifications and boost in power were necessary, as the paltry stock output was not sufficient for pacing duties.

The cars came with a power hatch and had no cruise control, air conditioning, or rear wiper. The ashtray was replaced with a panel that contained three switches for safety lights and the onboard fire extinguisher.

These pace cars were the first to be equipped with yellow safety lights (mounted on the roof), but they still retained the rear-mounted flags. In subsequent years, only the lights remained.

BONUS CONTENT

Scan to view the equipment and specifications of the 1982 pace cars and commemorative editions.

www.cartechbooks.com/ct658-qr21

1982 Commemorative Editions

The pair was part of a roughly 160-vehicle fleet that Chevrolet provided for track use, including Celebritys and S-10 pickups. The lot included 80 commemorative edition Camaros that mirrored the appearance of the pace cars and were used

Besides for the rear flags, the pace car is identified by its headlamp covers and Z28 embroidery on both front seat headrests.

The commemorative editions differed from the pace cars in that they had white-letter tires instead of black-wall tires.

The commemorative editions could be equipped, like this one, with the 5.0L V-8 with Cross-Fire Injection.

Festival and dealer replicas carried over the pace car appearance, being painted Silver Metallic with blue accents.

In addition to the blue and silver interior, the package added a special dash badge.

1982 Indianapolis 500 Camaro: Track and Festival Vehicles Registry

#	VIN **	Role	#	VIN **	Role	#	VIN **	Role
1	2CL100887 *	Pace car	27	27969	Track use	55	28112	Track use
2	7CL114283 *	Backup pace car	28	27180	Track use	56	27769	Track use
1	22261	Track use	29	28778	Track use	57	27105	F. parade
2	28646	Track use	30	27252	Track use	58	27346	F. parade
3	27244	Track use	31	27459	Track use	59	28546	F. parade
4	27693	Track use	32	27922	Track use	60	28631	F. parade
5	28151	Track use	33	28431	Track use	61	27010	F. parade
6	26977	Track use	34	27885	Track use	61	27071	F. parade
7	27029	Track use	35	28600	Track use	62	27279	F. parade
8	28734	Track use	36	28795	Track use	63	28315	F. parade
9	27600	Track use	37	28186	Track use	65	29117	F. parade
10	8582	Track use	38	28615	Track use	66	28566	F. parade
11	28041	Track use	39	27492	Track use	67	28845	F. parade
12	27558	Track use	40	22066	Track use	68	29660	F. parade
13	28811	Track use	41	22029	F. queen	69	29666	F. parade
14	28881	Track use	42	28766	Track use	70	23672	F. parade
15	28357	Track use	43	27433	Track use	71	29676	F. parade
16	28714	Track use	44	27803	Track use	72	29685	F. parade
17	27211	Track use	45	28394	Track use	73	29691	F. parade
18	127666	Track use	46	28469	Track use	74	29697	F. parade
19	28827	Track use	47	28276	Track use	75	29715	F. parade
20	26660	Track use	48	27636	Track use	76	29721	F. parade
21	27839	Track use	49	28695	Track use	77	29928	F. parade
22	28506	Track use	50	28677	Track use	78	29930	F. parade
23	27137	Track use	51	28076	Track use	79	32923	Courtesy car
24	28750	Track use	52	27728	Track use	--	26906	Winner's car
25	28007	Track use	53	28220	Track use	*	Following 1G1AP877	
26	28863	Track use	54	22295	Track use	**	Following 1G1AP87HCL1	

for festival and parade duties. These replicas were included in a run of 6,000 vehicles that were all built at the Van Nuys, California, assembly plant and sold at Chevrolet dealers. The package price was $900 and was ordered under RPO Z50.

The cars were painted Silver Metallic (RPO 16L). They were equipped with either the stock carbureted or fuel-injected 5.0L V-8 engine and either the 3-speed automatic or 4-speed manual transmission. All vehicles were equipped with special instrumentation, an AM/FM stereo, a leather-wrapped steering wheel, deluxe luggage compartment trim, and a blue and silver vinyl interior. The interior was identified with the special trim code of 26G, which was noted on the trim tag on the radiator support. A special Indy 500 badge was mounted on the passenger's side of the dashboard.

These replicas included the pace car decals but were not installed at the factory. Rather, a box containing the front and rear window "Camaro" banner script along with the door decals and Indy winged wheel decals for the sail panels were shipped enclosed in the trunk.

In addition to the lack of the light-bar and clear headlight covers, they differed from the pair of pace cars in several ways. They received white-lettered tires, and instead of a 140-mph speedometer, they utilized an 85-mph unit. They also included an adjustable driver's seat and could be equipped with options such as removable glass T-tops, air conditioning, four-wheel disc brakes, and tinted glass. A final differentiation is seen on the headrests. The pair of pace cars had "Z28" embroidered on both sides. The replicas had it only on the driver's side headrest.

1991 Indianapolis 500 Festival Camaro Z/28

In 1990, Chevrolet provided a specially prepared 1991 Beretta convertible that was painted yellow for use as that year's Indianapolis 500 pace car.

The brand also provided additional support and fleet vehicles. The allotment included 55 1991 Camaro Z/28 convertibles that were assigned to the festival committee and were available for track use.

They came painted Arctic White with a black top and were paired with a gray Custom Cloth interior and an automatic transmission. Decals were applied to the exterior. Most notably, a pink "chalked" Indy door logo was used.

The 1991 Indy 500 festival Camaros were painted Arctic White, highlighted with pink door decals.

1993 Indianapolis 500 Festival Camaro

Pace car	1		
Backup pace cars	2		
PR prototypes	5		
Festival cars	125		
Dealer replicas	520	US	500
		CAN	20
Factory replica	1*		
Total	647		

*Made for Chevrolet General Manager Jim Perkins and sole vehicle equipped with a 6-speed manual.

After debuting in 1993, the all-new fourth-generation Camaro (in Z28 trim) was selected to pace the 77th Indianapolis 500 on May 30, 1993. This marked the first time any model had been selected four times for the prestigious honor.

A pace car was created with integrated light bars. At first, four strobes were added up front with seven in the rear spoiler. They were sent to the track for testing with drivers reporting

This 1993 pace car is identified with a modified sail panel that contains rear-facing strobe lights.

not being able to see it from behind. To add visibility, an additional five strobes were mounted in the B-pillar.

Chevrolet created another 125 festival cars that were used by the track during the weeks leading up to the race. Each car was numbered with graphics at the base of the windshield. Powertrain modifications were not made, which marked the first time that a Camaro's factory-installed engine was up to the task of pacing without additional alternations.

A replica package was available to customers and cost $995 (ordered under RPO B5A). Five hundred cars were produced, and all the cosmetics from the track pace car were included except the light bar. The cars were all automatic-equipped Z28 models with 275 hp and 325 ft-lbs of torque, and they came in a striking black and white paint scheme. The two-tone look was broken up by flowing celebrity bands of pink, purple, yellow, and teal ribbons on the vehicle's profile and hood. Originally slated to be all T-tops, manufacturing issues or part limitations at the beginning of production caused issues that led to only coupes being produced.

Other exterior additions included white painted wheels, front fender Indy graphics and special bronze badging on the hood, B-pillar, and rear bumper.

The interior matched the exterior, sporting white and black splattered Graphite Sport Cloth upholstery with the same multi-hued ribbons and confetti.

Chevrolet also offered the pace car's unique looks on the 1993 Fleetline pickup truck in both short- and long-bed configuration. The package was $606 and added the two-tone color scheme, five-color stripes, and Indy decal. The custom interior and exterior badging was not included. The look was also applied to Suburbans that were used as track support.

BONUS CONTENT

Scan to view the 1993 Indy 500 Camaro festival and dealer replica registry.

www.cartechbooks.com/ct658-qr23

In addition to offering the Camaro pace car replicas, Chevrolet offered a similar exterior package on both short- and long-bed C/K trucks. A total of 1,534 came equipped with the Indy Appearance Package (RPO 5S6), which cost $606.

The celebratory mood carried over to the interior, which featured multi-hued ribbons and confetti on the cloth seat covers and door panels. This example still retains its protective dealer-prep plastic.

During testing, drivers noted they couldn't see the seven strobe lights in the pace car's spoiler. As such, a new roof was fabricated containing five additional five strobe lights that were more visible.

A gold hood emblem was included in the package. It was one of the last times that an Indy-specific Camaro received three-dimensional badging.

1995 Indianapolis 500 Festival Camaro Z/28

For the 1995 Indianapolis 500, Chevrolet provided a Corvette pace car (in Dark Purple Metallic and Arctic White) along with 75 additional Corvettes for use by the track. In addition, 51 white 1995 Camaro Z/28 convertibles with beltline graphics were provided for festival use. A single black coupe was included, too, which was assigned to Jim Moss, who was Chevrolet's special vehicle manager.

The Camaros were then repurposed for that year's Brickyard race.

1995 Indianapolis 500 Festival Camaro Convertible Z/28: Registry								
#	Car #	VIN *	#	Car #	VIN *	#	Car #	VIN *
1	8	2S2162823	18	25	2S2164037	35	42	0S2165140
2	9	XS2162875	19	26	8S2164043	36	43	9S2165203
3	10	2S2162935	20	27	8S2164169	37	44	7S2165233
4	11	6S2163103	21	28	1S2164272	38	68	6S2165255
5	12	2S2163146	22	29	6S2164347	39	69	6S2165272
6	13	2S2163163	23	30	XS2164478	40	70	6S2165286
7	14	8S2163202	24	31	3S2164628	41	71	0S2165333
8	15	4S2163391	25	32	6S2164641	42	72	1S2165356
9	16	3S2163429	26	33	8S2164690	43	73	4S2165383
10	17	1S2163541	27	34	6S2164705	44	74	5S2165475
11	18	4S2163696	28	35	1S2164790	45	75	5S2165490
12	19	7S2163742	29	36	5S2164906	46	76	5S2165523
13	20	4S2163777	30	37	9S2164973	47	77	8S2165533
14	21	XS2163783	31	38	2S2164989	48	78	6S2165742
15	22	XS2163864	32	39	8S2165063	49	79	6S2166096
16	23	8S2163894	33	40	4S2165092	50	80	5S2166123
17	24	3S2164029	34	41	XS2165128	*	Following 2G1FP32P	

While all festival Camaros used at the 1995 Indy 500 received different graphics for use at that year's Brickyard 400 race, this example in the foreground, car #71, was later returned to its Indy-correct looks.

1998 Indianapolis 500 Festival Camaro Z/28

For the 1998 Indy 500, Chevrolet provided a 1998 Corvette (in Radar Blue with yellow-painted wheels) for use as the pace car along with 109 other examples for parade and track use. In addition, an unknown quantity of 1999 Arctic White Camaro Z28 convertibles were onsite as well. They featured an Arctic White leather interior, automatic transmission, and exterior graphics, including a prominent gold beltline stripe.

Upon the race's conclusion, nine Camaros received new graphics and were used at the 1998 Brickyard 400 race.

1999 Indianapolis 500 Festival Camaro Z28

For the 1999 Indianapolis 500, Chevrolet provided a Torch Red 2000 Monte Carlo as the pace car, which was joined by 52 1999 Camaro

1999 Indianapolis 500 Festival Camaro: Registry								
#	Car #	VIN*	#	Car #	VIN*	#	Car #	VIN*
1	1	3X2130606	23	23	5X2130889	44	44	6X2130903
2	2	9X2130832	24	24	7X2130537	45	45	5X2130603
3	3	1X2130810	25	25	8X2130806	46	46	2X2131076
4	4	9X2131124	26	26	0X2131030	47	47	6X2130741
5	5	1X2130760	27	27	6X2130819	48	48	2X2131157
6	6	9X2130961	28	28	5X2131007	49	49	2X2130610
7	7	4X2130933	29	29	8X2131020	50	50	8X2130563
8	8	6X2130769	30	30	3X2130986	51	51	6X2130965
9	9	XX213056	31	31	0X2131111	52	52	XX2131083
10	10	9X2130894	32	32	3X2131040	53	53	4X2130558
11	11	1X2130548	33	33	2X2130950	54	54	0X2130590
12	12	XX2130533	34	34	3X2131121	55	110	2X2116064
13	13	7X2115430	35	35	3X2131121	56	111	0X2115737
14	14	0X2130699	36	36	9X2130958	57	112	4X2115126
15	15	3X2130793	36	36	0X2130900	58	113	6X2115824
16	16	7X2130585	37	37	8X2130854	59	114	1X2115536
17	17	8X2130563	38	38	8X2130918	60	115	4X2115708
18	18	2X2130641	39	39	6X2131050	61	116	9X215526
19	19	XX2130810	40	40	3X2131023	62	117	8X2115386
20	20	XX2115079	41	41	2X2130685	63	118	3X2115649
21	21	XX2130757	42	42	9X2130846	64	5 *	3X2131278
22	22	3X2130860	43	43	4X2130950	*	Winners car: SS trim	

The 1999 Indy festival Z28s were painted Arctic White with a checkered flag beltline graphic.

The entire run of Z28 convertibles was equipped with optional chromed wheels, and beltline graphics were used.

Z28 convertibles for festival use. All were painted in Arctic White, were paired with a white top, and were equipped with optional 16-inch chrome-aluminum wheels. The interior was fitted with the optional Dark Gray leather.

The vehicles were marked with unique graphics on the door, beltline, rear fenders, and taillight panel. They were also numbered at the base of the windshield and behind the rear license plate.

Needing more vehicles at the track, an additional 11 white V-6 convertibles were procured from a promotion at the Lowe's Motor Speedway in Concord, North Carolina. Differing from the Z28s, these featured a white leather interior.

A SS Camaro convertible was awarded to driver Arie Luyendyk for winning that year's pole. It was labeled as #5 to correspond with the number on his race car.

2002 Indianapolis 500 Festival Camaro Z28 Convertible

For the 2002 Indy 500, held on May 26, Chevrolet provided a 2003 50th Anniversary Edition Corvette (in Red Tint Coat), along with 62 Z28 convertibles painted in Sebring Silver and

The pace cars' Silver Ice Metallic paint was broken up with "fractured" red graphics.

equipped with the optional 16-inch chromed cast-aluminum wheels and Ebony interiors. They also received special beltline and door graphics.

Upon the close of the event, 40 received different graphics and were used for parade and festival duties during that year's Brickyard 400 NASCAR race.

2002 Indianapolis 500: 2002 Festival Camaro Z/28 Convertible: Registry							
#	VIN	#	VIN	#	VIN	#	VIN
1	222140658	17	222140885	33	522140590	49	322140572
2	122142644	18	22140971	34	622140808	50	522140895
3	122141073	19	22140922	35	622141733	51	X22141105
4	022140562	20	22140917	36	022141100	52	022141016
5	722140946	21	22140614	37	922140933	53	622140758
6	122141395	22	222141728	38	822141166	54	022140836
7	322140698	23	022141078	39	G422140841	55	322141088
8	122140733	24	622141022	40	722140798	56	222141115
9	122140912	25	922141189	41	822140678	57	022140626
10	022141033	26	922141130	42	322140653	58	922141161
11	422141827	27	322140846	43	322140555	59	822140907
12	622141182	28	X22141637	44	522140783	60	322140703
13	X22141038	29	X22140648	45	522141125	61	222140773
14	022140979	30	722141028	46	122141011	62	X22141055
15	622141005	31	122141543	47	022141050		
16	622141151	32	122140831	48	922141323		

2010 Indianapolis 500 Festival Camaro (2009 Race)

In 2009, the Camaro was selected for the fifth time to pace the Indianapolis 500 race. The trio of cars were 2010 SS coupes in Silver Ice Metallic that were highlighted with "fractured" red accents.

As part of the festivities, 25 additional festival 2010 Camaros were produced along with an additional 35 festival Corvettes. Twenty-one of the Camaros were preproduction and were identified by the "900" in their VIN as opposed to production Camaro's "910."

The 2SS Camaros were all painted in Silver Ice Metallic with a black leather interior, and they

The festival Camaros had a similar motif to the Camaro pace car, featuring a red side spear with "fracturing" on the rear quarter panel.

came equipped with an automatic transmission. Foregoing the radical fractured red exterior accents of the pace cars, these festival vehicles had a more subdued look, which was highlighted primarily by a beltline spear graphic. There was no extra charge for the Indy package option.

One of the vehicles (#25) went to race winner Hélio Castroneves. Five others were later used at the 2009 Brickyard 400 NASCAR race with the same silver and red stripe design but with a new door Brickyard door graphic.

2010 Indianapolis 500 Centennial Edition Camaro

A limited run of 2010 Camaros were offered as part of the Speedway's Centennial Era celebration that ran from 2009 through 2011. Twenty-four 2010 Centennial Edition Indy 2SS/RS Camaros were built, and all came in Victory Red paint with a black interior, automatic transmission, and remote start. Inside, special door sill plates were added. The 6.2L V-8 received a GM Performance exhaust.

Cosmetically, the run received a graphics package, adding black stripes to the sides of the hood cowl and along the side of the vehicle. Callouts were included for the engine size, package name, and horsepower rating. The car also received the Speedway's special centennial era logo as an additional graphic on the front fenders and the rear panel. Each car cost $39,366.

	VIN		VIN
1	8A9127492	13	1A9127853
2	A9128213	14	4A9129645
3	5A9129279	15	6A9130023
4	XA9129620	16	2A9129613
5	8A9127591	17	4A9128348
6	8A9128966	18	8A9129809
7	3A9128969	19	8A9129673
8	21A9129943	20	1A9127266
9	4A9129080	21	3A9129975
10	6A9129520	22	2A9128459
11	1A9127402	23	0A9130243
12	9A9129267	24	2A9129840

2009 Indy 500: 2010 Camaro: Registry

Pace cars	#1	G1FT1EW190001EX		
	#2	G1FT1EWS9000016		
	#3	G1FT1EW190002EX		
Festival Camaros				
#	VIN		#	VIN
1	7A9000847		14	2A9100046
2	7A9101604		15 **	0A9000544
3	4A9000577		16	4A9000837
4	XA9000597		17	9A9000882
5 **	5A9000670		18	2A9000559
6 **	8A9000615		19 ••	5A9000832
7	8A9000789		20	0A9000754
8	6A9000869		21	XA9000681
9	3A9000747		22	8A9101069
10 **	8A9000873		23 ** •	2A9000870
11	8A9100325		24	6A9000757
12	1A9000813		25 * •	7A9000670
13	7A9000623			
Preproduction vehicles (ex. #2,11 and 22)				
*	Given to winner Hélio Castroneves			
**	Vehicle used at the 2009 Brickyard 400	#5 renumbered to #25		
		#6 renumbered to #38		
		#10 renumbered to #22		
		#15 renumbered to #21		
		#23 remained the same		
•	Repainted to mimic the pace car			
••	Vehicle now equipped with an Edelbrock E-Force supercharger			

All 24 Centennial Edition Camaros were painted Victory Red and used black graphics.

2010 Indianapolis 500 Pace Car Limited Edition Camaro (2010 Race)

Total	297	Pace cars	2
		Parade	50
		Replicas	201
		Canada	44

For 2010, the Camaro was once again selected to pace the Indianapolis 500. It was based on a 2010 2SS with the RS Appearance Package. The exterior drew inspiration from the 1969 pace car, inverting its iconic color scheme. As such, the vehicle featured Inferno Orange Metallic paint that was highlighted by full body White Pearl rally stripe decals.

Under the hood, the 6.2L V-8 (L99) engine, which produced 400 hp and 410 ft-lbs of torque, was topped with an Inferno Orange engine cover. The car came with a 6-speed automatic transmission and remote start.

On the exterior, the car received a body-color heritage grille insert, 20-inch polished aluminum wheels, and centennial fender badges and door decals.

On the exterior, the vehicles received elements such as a body-colored grille insert and centennial fender badges.

Inside, orange and black leather upholstery was highlighted with Inferno Orange accents on the door panels and dashboard insert. New floor mats boasted orange stitching, and the front seat headrests were embroidered.

The 2010 Camaro pace car inverted the colors of the 1969 Camaro pace car, being painted orange with white stripes.

Embroidered headrests were part of the cabin additions.

2010 Indianapolis 500 2SS Camaro: Pace and Parade Car Registry									
Pace car 1	2A9165429		Show car 1	8A9208266		Show car 3	9A9210446		
Pace car 2	1A9166183		Show car 2	9A9210771		Show car 4	9A9210415		
#	VIN	#	VIN	#	VIN	#	VIN	#	VIN
1	0A9210383	11	6A9210338	21	8A9204685	31	1A9208111	41	XA9207653
2 *	0A9210450	12	8A9210583	22	A9207934	32	2A9207646	42	XA9208950
3	1A9210571	13	UNK	23	7A9207979	33	2A9208277	43	2A9209767
4	8A9208266	14	XA9210407	24	7A9208310	34	4A9208409	44	2A9210028
5	9A9210415	15	0A9210741	25	8A9208123	35	6A9208069	45	3A9209454
6	-A9210446	16	2A9210711	26	8A9208154	36	7A9207755	46	4A9209849
7	2A9210286	17	1A9205077	27	9A9208115	37	8A9209062	47	6A9210193
8	3A9210247	18	2A9204617	28	0A9208195	38	8A9209126	48	8A9210034
9	2A92188??	19	8A9204637	29	1A9207993	39	2A9208960	49	9A9210057
10	1A9210599	20	1A9204642	30	1A9208058	40	3A9208997	50	4A9210175
*	Renumbered #51 after the race								

Two-hundred limited-edition replicas of the Indy pace car were available through 187 of the top-selling Camaro dealers based on 2009 retail sales. An additional 44 were available to the Canadian market.

2011 Indianapolis 500 Camaro SS Convertible

The 2011 Indianapolis 500 was the 100th anniversary of the race the 100th anniversary of Chevrolet, and the Camaro was chosen for the seventh time to pace the race. As part of the festivities, Chevrolet provided four 2010 Camaro SS pace cars that were painted Summit White along with 500 festival Camaro replicas. Fifty-one of those were used for festival and parade duties, and they were marked with stickers at the base of windshield and a graphic on the dash.

All 504 were convertibles and equipped with the 2SS with the RS package and 20-inch polished aluminum wheels. Drawing direct inspiration from the 1969 pace car, they were painted Summit White, which was highlighted by full-body Inferno Orange rally stripes, a body-color front grille insert, and door decals.

The orange and white look had a direct connection to the 1969 Camaro pace car.

The orange stripes carried over onto the dash insert, and the seats received Inferno Orange leather upholstery.

2011 Camaro SS Indy 500 Festival 2SS Convertible: Registry								
#	VIN	T	#	VIN	T	#	VIN	T
PC *	4B90035EX	A	1A/15 ****	8B9169080	A	35	2B9168801	A
PC3 *	6B9155999	A	16	7B9169765	A	36	XB9170666	A
PC2 *	4B9156617	A	17	3B9169167	A	37	XB9169047	A
PC1 *	9B9156015	A	18	7B9171046	A	38	6B9170695	A
1/15 ****	5B9164709	A	19	7B9169169	A	39	8B9171847	A
1	0B9163421	A	20	5B9170333	A	40	XB9169968	A
1/15 ****	8B9169080	A	21	1B9170152	A	41	8B9170858	A
2	XB9165130	A	22	XB9169808	A	42	9B9170805	A
3	0B9163421	A	23	8B9170097	A	43	5B9169926	A
4	3B9171836	A	24	XB9171042	A	44	XB9171819	A
5	6B9169496	A	25	1B9169096	A	45	5B9170882	A
6	-B9170247	A	26	1B9168997	A	46	6B9170311	M
7	6B9170339	A	27	8B9169936	A	47	2B9165082	M
8	4B9170761	A	28	0B9170367	A	48	1B9165610	M
9	XB9169677	A	29	4B9170212	A	49 ••	6B9168728	M
10 •••	1B89172032	A	30	XB9170474	A	50 **	4B9169500	A
11	7B9170916	A	31	8B9169953	A	51 •	9B9172733	A
12	1B9169583	A	32	7B9170852	A	52 ***	3B9163206	A
13	1B9169535	A	33	0B9170577	A	53 ***	8B9127494	A
14	1B9168944	M	34	3B9169066	A	T	Transmission	
*	Pace Car		**	Winner's Car		***	Dealer coupes	**** Exact data unknown
•	Sold new to Jon Bon Jovi				••	Equipped with optional Hurst shifter handle		
•••	Vehicle used for press photos in Trump Tower with former President Donald Trump, who was selected to drive the pace car for the race. He was replaced by A.J. Foyt.							

Inside the cabin, there was an Inferno Orange–accented leather upholstery, unique sill plates, and embossed front seat headrests. A unique touch was the continuation of the exterior stripes on the center dashboard trim, which was white along with the door panels. Premium floor mats as well as footwell and cupholder lighting were also included.

Under the hood, most of the vehicles were equipped with the 6.2L V-8 (L99 with 400 hp and 410 ft-lbs of torque) paired with an automatic transmission. A smaller number were equipped with the 6.2L V-8 (LS3 with 426 hp and 410 ft-lbs of torque) paired with a manual transmission. An Inferno Orange engine cover was included, and the package costed $6,500.

2012 Indianapolis 500 Camaro 2SS Festival Camaros

For the 2012 Indianapolis 500, Chevrolet provided 53 2012 2SS Camaros for festival and parade duties along with a 2013 Corvette ZR1 in Arctic White for pacing duties.

The 2012 Indy festival Camaro harkened back to the appearance of the 1967 Camaro pace car.

All were painted in Summit White with a black leather interior and automatic transmission. Inspired by the 1967 Camaro pace car, they featured blue stripes and unique graphics. There was no extra charge for the Indy 500 package.

2013 Indianapolis 500 Festival Camaro 2SS Convertible Hot Wheels Edition

For the 2013 Indianapolis 500, Chevrolet provided a fleet of 52 2013 Camaros that were used for festival and parade duties. A 2014 Corvette Stingray in Laguna Blue was provided for pacing duties.

All Camaros were Hot Wheels Edition convertibles, and, as such, they were painted Kinetic Blue Metallic highlighted with a black center stripe. Each was equipped with the L99 V-8

The 2013 Indy festival Camaro convertibles received the Hot Wheels package, adding elements sourced from the top-tier ZL1, such as the front grille and rear spoiler.

2012 Indianapolis 500 Festival Camaro 2SS: Registry									
#	VIN	#	VIN	#	VIN	#	VIN	#	VIN
1	9186514	12	9188536	23	9187462	34	9186222	45	9187621
2	9188030	13	9187132	24	9186455	35	9188096	46	9188313
3	9188171	14	9186837	25	9187909	36	9188021	47	9189173
4	9188631	15*	9103034	26	9188500	37	9188484	48	9187990
5	9188234	16	9188003	27	9187625	38	9186108	49	9186316
6	9187754	17	9186605	28	9188719	39	9186976	51	9187941
7*	9146899	18*	9180357	29	9188443	40	9188048	53*•	9149368
8	9188015	19	9187693	30	9187589	41	9187477	54*•	9147223
9	9187118	20	9188391	31	9186895	42	9188242	55	918864
10	9188238	21	9188436	32	9188173	43	9188218	*	RS trim
11	9187615	22	9188534	33	9187432	44	9188888	•	Coupe
Note: Cars #50 and #52 were skipped									

that produced 400 hp and 410 ft-lbs of torque and was paired to an automatic transmission.

New additions for race duties were limited primarily to door and windshield banner graphics.

2013 Indy 500 Festival Camaro 2SS Hot Wheels: Registry					
	VIN	Role		VIN	Role
1	9D9206169	IMS	27	5D9206590	Fest. 9
2	9D9206592	IMS	28	6D9207053	Fest. 10
3	7D9205411	IMS	29	2D9207051	Fest. 11
4	1D9207252	IMS	30	8D9206454	Fest. 12
5	8D9206972	IMS	31	4D9206869	Fest. 13
6	0D9206061	IMS	32	XD9206729	Fest. 14
7	2D9206160	IMS	33	4D9205527	Fest. 15
8	5D9206668	IMS	34	3D9204742	Fest. 16
9	8D9205837	IMS	35	3D9206779	Fest. 17
10	3D9205809	IMS	36	3D9207060	Fest. 18
11	5D9205620	IMS	37	5D9205908	Fest. 19
12	2D9205428	IMS	38	6D9205867	Fest. 20
13	6D9206520	Fest. 33	39	8D9205966	Fest. 21
14	7D9204744	IMS	40	3D9207138	Fest. 22
15	7D9205117	IMS	41	8D9205174	Fest. 23
16	8D9209550	IMS	42	2D9205946	Fest. 24
17	7D9208244	IMS	43	3D9204885	Fest. 25
18	XD9209985	IMS	44	3D9210167	Fest. 26
19	5D9209344	Fest. 1	45	5D9209800	Fest. 27
20	0D9207534	Fest. 2	46	7D9209281	Fest. 28
21	0D9209638	Fest. 3	47	7D9209331	Fest. 29
22	3D9209925	Fest. 4	48	7D9208440	Fest. 30
23	8D9209080	Fest. 5	49	3D9210007	Fest. 31
24	6D9207819	Fest. 6	50	7D9209555	Winner
25	7D9205652	Fest. 7	51	9D9210139	Fest. 32
26	6D9205772	Fest. 8	52	2D9208636	IMS

2014 Indianapolis 500 Festival Camaro SS Convertible

For the 2014 Indianapolis 500, the 98th running of the event, Chevrolet provided three 2014 Camaro Z/28 coupes for pacing duties (painted black), marking the model's eighth time of having the honor.

2014 Indianapolis 500 Festival Camaro SS Convertible: Registry							
#	VIN	#	VIN	#	VIN	#	VIN
1	2E9278753	12	9E9279334	23	XE9279410	34	7E9278294
2	9E9279401	13	6E9278870	24	XE9278614	35	6E9279307
3	3E9278499	14	7E9279249	25	2E9279241	36	1E9279263
4	7E9278974	15	6E9279128	26	6E9278285	37	3E9279488
5	1E9279327	16	5E9278326	27	6E9278853	38	6E9279274
6	8E9279471	17	1E9279134	28	0E9278492	39	7E9278800
7	1E9278095	18	5E9279282	29	2E9278770	40	9E9278250
8	6E9278531	19	8E9279173	30	0E9278945	41	XE9278984
9	2E9278459	20	XE9278807	31	0E9279299	42	0E9279318
10	8E9278725	21	9E9278409	32	6E9279209	43	1E9279201
11	2E9279112	22	0E9278623	33	2E9279224	44	2E9279031

The 2014 Indy 500 pace car was this track-oriented 2014 Camaro Z/28 coupe.

The 2014 festival Camaros weren't Z/28 trim but instead were SS convertibles. Their wheels were painted black to complete the look.

Joining the activities was a fleet of 44 2014 Camaro SS convertibles that were used for festival and parade duties. Power came from the L99 6.2L V-8 and an automatic transmission.

To mirror the pace car, they were painted black and came equipped with a black convertible top. They also included the optional 20-inch forged-aluminum five-spoke wheels, but instead of Bright Silver, they were painted black to match the Z/28's black wheels. Inside was black leather upholstery. Final cosmetic touches included unique graphics and a windshield banner.

2015 Indianapolis 500 Festival Camaro SS

For the 2015 Indianapolis 500, the 99th running of the event, Chevrolet provided a 2015 Corvette Z06 painted Arctic White as the pace car. It also provided a fleet of 100 2015 Camaro 2SS convertibles for fleet and parade use with the L99 6.2L V-8 engine that produced 400 hp and 410 ft-lbs of torque. Thirty-three were used by festival officials, 17 were used by the track, and the rest were used by Indiana Chevrolet dealer representatives.

The Camaros were all commemorative editions (costing $1,995), and they were equipped with an automatic transmission. They all were painted in Summit White and highlighted with a variation of the edition's stripe. Instead of silver, it was black with a red accent outline. Inside, the vehicles featured the commemorative special edition's exclusive Adrenaline Red leather interior.

The Special Indy 500 option package cost an additional $2,995. It brought Indy 500 decals and ground effects as well as a red engine cover and premium Camaro floor mats, both of which were installed by dealers.

As part of the promotion, 50 Camaros were provided to Chevrolet dealers across the state and were made available for purchase prior to the race.

2015 Indianapolis 500 Festival Camaro SS: Registry							
#	VIN	#	VIN	#	VIN	#	VIN
1	1F9229836	26	0F9231335	51	2F9231451	76	1F9234048
2	6F9230822	27	5F9230536	52	XF9231052	77	8F9232877
3	0F9235403	28	7F9233728	53	0F9231853	78	6F9231078
4	2F9230204	29	1F9232929	54	8F9229509	79	1F9231179
5	5F9230195	30	7F9229369	55	7F9231655	80	6F9229380
6	6F9232196	31	4F9234531	56	5F9231556	81	0F9231481
7	4F9231807	32	1F9230744	57	8F9233267	82	6F9229928
8	3F9230308	33	9F9229633	58	3F9229658	83	5F9232383
9	7F9233809	34	5F9233534	59	5F9232559	84	3F9229689
10	7F9231610	35	3F9229935	60	5F9232660	85	7F9232885
11	1F9229481	36	6F9230545	61	4F9233461	86	7F9232286
12	2F9233412	37	4F9230348	62	5F9231962	87	XF9230659
13	5F9233713	38	1F9230453	63	7F9230263	88	4F9229488
14	8F9232314	39	XF9233139	64	3F9234164	89	7F9229789
15	7F9233275	40	6F9232439	65	7F9231588	90	8F9233690
16	4F9233816	41	2F9230722	66	6F9231677	91	5F9230780
17	0F9231867	42	5F9232142	67	7F9230067	92	2F9231790
18	4F9231418	43	9F9233043	68	3F9231877	93	2F9232096
19	3F9231619	44	9F9232944	69	1F9230369	94	6F9233994
20	3F9232320	45	XF9230645	70	3F9231698	95	7F9230795
21	7F9223331	46	8F9233446	71	1F9233188	96	0F9233196
22	6F9232022	47	1F9230159	72	5F9232772	97	5F9232397
23	6F9232523	48	6F9231548	73	XF9231973	98	3F9224380
24	9F9231124	49	1F9232249	74	5F9229516	99	4F9232780
25	1F9232428	50	6F9231260	75	1F9233675	100	0F9230900

The Commemorative Edition stripe was altered to be black with a red outline.

The run consisted of convertibles with Adrenaline Red leather interiors.

The cars were equipped with ground effects and some additional race graphics.

2016 Indianapolis 500 Parade Camaro SS Convertible

For the 2016 Indianapolis 500, the 100th running of the event, Chevrolet provided four 2017 Camaro coupes to be used as pace cars along with a fleet of 54 2016 Camaro 2SS convertibles for fleet and parade use.

While the four pace cars were based off the forthcoming 2017 50th Anniversary Edition motif, instead of being painted Nightfall Gray Metallic, they were painted Abalone White, which was a color sourced from Cadillac.

The parade cars were visually different. They were painted Hyper Blue Metallic and accented with White Pearl rally stripes. They received a black convertible top and Jet Black leather interior. As part of the Festival Package (costing $5,750), they also received Indy 500 decals, an 8-speed automatic transmission with remote start, 5-spoke 20-inch bright-silver-painted aluminum wheels, dual-mode performance exhaust,

the MyLink audio system, and magnetic ride control. Each was equipped with the 6.2L V-8 LT1 engine that produced 455 hp and 455 ft-lbs of torque. The total cost was $55,045 per vehicle.

They were sequentially numbered with numeral graphics at the base of the windshield and on a sticker inside the driver's doorjamb.

#	VIN	#	VIN	#	VIN	#	VIN
1	8G0148783	15	3G0149226	29	4G0149140	43	0G0148681
2	2G0149122	16	1G0149158	30	5G0149146	44	1G0148687
3	2G0149220	17	2G0148777	31	8G0148699	45	2G0149718
4	9G0148789	18	1G0149208	32	4G0148795	46	0G0149250
5	9G0149618	19	5G0148675	33	6G0148801	47	8G0149724
6	8G0149674	20	3G0149582	34	6G0148717	48	XG0148705
7	7G0148693	21	4G0149588	35	0G0149152	49	XG0148669
8	XG0149238	22	XG0149594	36	3G0149128	50	1G0149256
9	7G0149116	23	1G0149600	37	7G0148807	51	7G0149570
10	5G0149244	24	9G0149134	38	5G0149700	52	8G0149576
11	3G0149680	25	2G0149606	39	6G0149708	53	6G0149110
12	1G0149712	26	9G0149232	40	2G0148813	54	5G0148711
13	4G0149686	27	7G0149214	41	3G0148819		
14	XG0149692	28	8G0149612	42	9G0148825		

Table: 2016 Indianapolis 500 Parade Camaro SS Convertible: Registry

The four pace cars came equipped as 50th Anniversary Editions but were painted Abalone White, a Cadillac color.

Inside, all festival Camaros were equipped with Jet Black interiors and 8-speed automatic transmissions.

The 2016 festival Camaros were painted Hyper Blue Metallic with White Pearl rally stripes.

Each vehicle received this numbered graphic inside the driver's doorjamb.

2017 Indianapolis 500 Festival Camaro

For the 2017 Indianapolis 500, Chevrolet provided a 2017 Corvette Grand Sport (painted Arctic White) along with a fleet of 50 2017 Camaro 2SS convertibles for festival use. An additional 51 Camaros were made available for Indianapolis-area dealer sales.

The Camaros were created under the unique RPO code of Z4Z and were painted Summit White, receiving a black convertible top and Adrenaline Red leather interior. All were equipped with an 8-speed automatic transmission and paired to the LT1 6.2L V-8 with 455 hp and 455 ft-lbs of torque with remote start and dual-mode exhaust.

They received a combination of dealer-installed Chevrolet accessories, including a front splitter, an SS lower grille with red accents, Red Hot hash-mark fender decals, black bowtie emblems, premium floor mats, and SS wheel center caps.

The package cost $6,995 and included a center stripe in an exclusive blue that featured a ghosted Indy logo on the driver's side. Other additions included a blacked-out rear graphic with an Indianapolis Motor Speedway logo on the driver's side as well as a lower black and red side stripe that featured a repeating "Z4Z" pattern. Red and blue Indy 500 door decals completed the look.

Each vehicle cost $55,895 and was numbered with graphics at the base of the windshield and inside the driver's doorjamb.

2017 Indianapolis 500 Festival Camaro: Registry

#	VIN	#	VIN	#	VIN	#	VIN
1	XH0186601	26	0H0187126	51	3H0186651	76	5H0187476
2	2H0186902	27	6H0186627	52	5H0187882	77	6H0188247
3	7H0186703	28	5H0186828	53	2H0187953	78	1H0187278
4	9H0187304	29	0H0187529	54	6H0186854	79	5H0187557
5	8H0187665	30	8H0186810	55	1H0188155	80	1H0187670
6	3H0188206	31	9H0186931	56	2H0186947	81	5H0186800
7	9H0187027	32	4H0187632	57	7H0187057	82	4H0187582
8	6H0187728	33	7H0187723	58	2H0187158	83	5H0186800
9	8H0187309	34	7H0187334	59	6H0187759	84	5H0186800
10	1H0186910	35	5H0187655	60	9H0187660	85	2H0187385
11	7H0186331	36	8H0187536	61	4H0187131	86	4H0187100
12	9H0187612	37	3H0187637	62	8H0187262	87	5H0187087
13	4H0187713	38	8H0187438	63	6H0186465	88	6H0187888
14	3H0186844	39	3H0187329	64	XH0187764	89	6H0187809
15	2H0187015	40	6H0188040	65	4H0186965	90	9H0187190
16	7H0187916	41	1H0186731	66	2H0188066	91	5H0187865
17	8H0187617	42	5H0187042	67	8H0187567	92	3H0186892
18	6H0186918	43	6H0187843	68	1H0187457	93	0H0187854
19	4H0187260	44	2H0186544	69	9H0187769	94	7H0187494
20	5H0187820	45	1H0187345	70	0H0187370	95	6H0187695
21	1H0187121	46	8H0187116	71	1H0187071	96	4H0187548
22	1H0187622	47	8H0187147	72	7H0188242	97	2H0186897
23	6H0186823	48	3H0187718	73	3H0187380	98	7H0187897
24	XH0187294	49	2H0186849	74	8H0187178	99	9H0187299
25	3H0187945	50	1H0187250	75	XH0187375	100	5H0186800
						101	0H0187627

The 2017 Indy festival Camaros utilized a combination of Chevrolet accessories with a red, white, and blue theme.

The lower rocker graphic featured a repeating Z4Z pattern, which was the unique RPO code assigned to the vehicle.

Premium floor mats were included in the Adrenaline Red interior. All the vehicles featured remote start and dual-mode exhaust.

The 2018 festival Camaros came painted in Crush when equipped with the Hot Wheels package.

Each vehicle was marked with this numbered graphic inside the driver's doorjamb.

2018 Indianapolis 500 Hot Wheels Camaro Parade Car

Joining the orange Hot Wheels festival Camaros were six Hyper Blue Metallic convertibles.

For the 2018 Indianapolis 500, the 102nd running of the event, Chevrolet provided a 2019 Corvette ZR1 coupe painted Long Beach Red for use as the pace car. It also provided a fleet of 51 2018 Camaro 2SS convertibles for fleet and parade use that were equipped with the LT1 6.2L V-8 with 455 hp and 455 ft-lbs of torque. These Camaros were all equipped with the Hot Wheels Special Edition package, which was $4,955, and they were all painted Crush Orange.

Unique content was limited to door graphics, coming in graphite and black to match the Hot Wheels look. Each vehicle was numbered at the base of the windshield. There was no charge for the graphics.

An additional six Hyper Blue Metallic 2SS Camaro convertibles were ordered (not with the other run), and while they were not assigned to anyone, they were used for track duties.

2018 Indianapolis 500 Hot Wheels Camaro Parade Car: Registry									
#	VIN	#	VIN	#	VIN	#	VIN	#	VIN
1	XJ0155466	11	6J0156372	21	7J0155456	31	5J0156377	41	8J0156034
2	7J0155893	12	9J0156253	22	6J0155898	32	7J0156090	42	1J0156022
3	7J0156039	13	4J0156421	23	2J0155963	33	4J0156564	43	XJ0155631
4	4J0155883	14	3J0156779	24	8J0155451	34	3J0156930	44	8J0156017
5	9J0157080	15	6J0155481	25	0J0155721	35	1J0156876	45	3J0155888
6	2J0156367	16	5J0155486	26	9J0155958	36	5J0156699	46	7J0155537
7	3J0156524	17	7J0155604	27	3J0156085	37	0J0156660	47	6J0155612
8	4J0156080	18	7J0155599	28	5J0156914	38	3J0155471	48	3J0156796
9	8J0156549	19	XJ0155953	29	0J0156531	39	0J0155461	49	2J0156241
10	XJ0156942	20	9J0155569	30	0J0156514	40	2J0155476	50	3J0157110
								51	3J0156362

2020 Indianapolis 500 Camaro Parade Car

For the 2020 Indianapolis 500, the 104th running of the event, Chevrolet provided a Torch Red 2020 Corvette Stingray coupe for use as the pace car along with a fleet of 50 2020 Camaro 2SS convertibles for fleet and parade use. Each car was painted Red Hot and given red-painted brake calipers and Adrenaline Red leather upholstery. Each car was equipped with the LT1 6.2L V-8 that produced 455 hp and 455 ft-lbs of torque with an automatic transmission.

The cars were also equipped with a collection of Chevrolet accessories, including 20-inch polished forged wheels,

2020 Indianapolis 500 Camaro Parade Car: Registry					
#	VIN	#	VIN	#	VIN
1	2L0133500	18	7L0133492	35	2L0133870
2	4L0133420	19	4L0133496	36	2L0133853
3	2L0133416	20	9L0133865	37	9L0133882
4	1L0133424	21	1L0133472	38	4L0133837
5	8L0133436	22	7L0133508	39	5L0133829
6	0L0133432	23	6L0133886	40	1L0133813
7	XL0133440	24	8L0133890	41	0L0133821
8	3L0133456	25	1L0133861	42	XL0133809
9	5L0133460	26	9L0133428	43	6L0133841
10	2L0133464	27	XL0133504	44	7L0133833
11	XL0133468	28	9L0133512	45	8L0133825
12	7L0133444	29	9L0133476	46	7L0133878
13	4L0133448	30	6L0133516	47	XL0133874
14	6L0133452	31	XL0133857	48	7L0133895
15	0L0133480	32	9L0133817	49	8L0134182
16	8L0133484	33	3L0133845	50	6L0134178
17	5L0133488	34	0L0133849	L-38*	5L0134186
				*	For long-term use

The 2020 festival Camaros were equipped with 20-inch polished forged wheels, red-painted brake calipers, and ground effects.

black bowtie emblems, White Pearl Rally stripes (highlighted with "104th Running" callouts on the driver's side), and a carbon flash metallic ground effects package. They also received a blacked-out rear taillight graphic that was accented with an "NTT INDYCAR Series" logo on the driver's side.

Additional unique content included door and rear quarter-panel graphics. Each was numbered at the base of the windshield.

2021 Indianapolis 500 Camaro Parade Car

The 105th running of the Indianapolis 500 on May 30, 2021, featured a 2021 Corvette painted Arctic White as the official pace car.

An additional 50 2021 Camaro 2SS (specially ordered under RPO Z4C) convertibles were provided as parade cars. All cars came with the Shock and Steel Special Edition package, which included 20-inch blade-design aluminum wheels with summer-only tires, a fuel-filler door in black with a visible carbon-fiber insert, premium carpeted floor mats with the Camaro logo, yellow-painted brake calipers, and black suede interior knee pads. The yellow hood cowl graphics featured the speedway's logo and the race callout.

They also all came fitted with the accessory second-generation ground effects in Carbon Flash Metallic. A bespoke touch at the rear of the vehicle was the inclusion of the Indy logo in the taillight blackout panel.

The vehicles were painted in two different colors: cars numbered 1 through 15 were painted Summit White, while

The 2021 festival Camaros came in both Summit White and Satin Steel Gray Metallic of the Shock and Steel package.

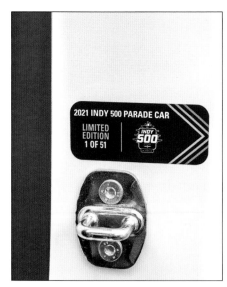

Each vehicle was marked with this numbered graphic inside the driver's doorjamb.

2021 Indianapolis 500 Camaro Parade Car: Registry								
#	VIN	Paint	#	VIN	Paint	#	VIN	Paint
1	77M0128049	SW	18	76M0127961	SS	35	7XM0129339	SS
2	71M0128225	SW	19	75M0127949	SS	36	70M0129480	SS
3	71M0128239	SW	20	70M0127955	SS	37	78M0129887	SS
4	74M0128266	SW	21	75M0127966	SS	38	73M0130039	SS
5	70M0128345	SW	22	78M0128092	SS	39	78M0129999	SS
6	76M0128396	SW	23	72M0128248	SS	40	78M0129114	SS
7	76M0128494	SW	24	77M0128486	SS	41	75M0129040	SS
8	72M0128556	SW	25	75M0128616	SS	42	79M0129199	SS
9	75M0128728	SW	26	76M0128639	SS	43	73M0129490	SS
10	75M0128955	SW	27	71M0128645	SS	44	75M0129510	SS
11*	77M0129852	SW	28	70M0128832	SS	45	76M0129502	SS
12	73M0129845	SW	29	71M0129004	SS	46	74M0129899	SS
13	77M0129945	SW	30	76M0129015	SS	47	70M0129981	SS
14	77M0130755	SW	31	70M0129026	SS	48	76M0130049	SS
15	77M0129153	SW	32	72M0129187	SS	49	72M0130226	SS
16	77M0127578	SS	33	72M0129173	SS	50	79M0130613	SS
17	75M0127935	SS	34	75M0129331	SS			
Paint	W	Summit White	*	Equipped with a 6-speed for IMS Track President Doug Boles				
	SS	Satin Steel						

Neon accents (part of the Shock and Steel Special Edition package) can be seen in the interior on the door sills and base of the steering wheel.

cars numbered 16 through 50 were painted in Satin Steel Gray Metallic. Each car was identified with a numeral graphic at the base of the windshield on the driver's side.

All cars received a black interior and black Indy door and rear fender graphics along with a numbered graphic inside the driver's doorjamb. Each car in the run was equipped with an automatic transmission except for car #11, which had a 6-speed transmission. It was requested by IMS Track President, Doug Boles.

2022 Indianapolis 500 Camaro Parade Car

The 106th running of the Indianapolis 500 on May 29, 2022, featured two 2023 Corvette Z06s painted White Pearl Metallic with the 70th Anniversary Edition package as the official pace car.

An additional 50 2022 Camaro 2SS convertibles (ordered under RPO Z4C) were provided as parade cars. All were painted Wild Cherry, which was highlighted with a central black graphic stripe. It was bordered with smaller white graphics that included the speedway's logo and callout on the hood cowl. A bespoke

The 2022 festival Camaros featured a similar motif to the 2021 festival Camaros but were painted Wild Cherry.

touch at the rear of the vehicle was the inclusion of the speedway's logo in the added taillight blackout panel.

Other exterior cosmetic details included large door graphics along with a smaller graphic on the rear quarter panel. The 20-inch, 5-spoke aluminum wheels were painted Carbon Flash, and a Brembo brake upgrade with red calipers was added. Each car came fitted with ground effects in Carbon Flash Metallic and dual-mode exhaust. A numeral graphic at the base of the windshield on the driver's side identified the car.

The cabins all came with a Ceramic White interior and a numbered identification graphic inside the driver's doorjamb.

2022 Indianapolis 500 Camaro Parade Car: Registry					
#	VIN*	#	VIN*	#	VIN*
1	XN0110100	18	2N0112522	35	1N0113497
2	2N0111743	19	5N0112501	36	1N0113550
3	5N0111719	20	4N0112506	37	18N0113531
4	7N0111902	21	4N0112618	38	4N0113607
5	1N0111975	22	5N0112756	39	9N0113618
6	1N0112060	23	6N0112832	40	3N0113596
7	1N0111992	24	XN0113160	41	5N0113602
8	2N0112066	25	4N0113185	42	2N0113623
9	9N0112078	26	8NO114095	43	4N0113641
10	4N0112084	27	5N0113339	44	9N0113652
11•	7N0111515	28	7N0113357	45	8N0113657
12	3N0112044	29	0N0113345	46	0N0113667
13	XN0112378	30	6N0113351	47	1N0113662
14	2N0112388	31	9N0113375	48	9N0113800
15	6N0112393	32	4N0113381	49	9N0113828
16	5N0112496	33	5N0113387	50	1N0114022
17	3N0112481	34	4N0113591		
*	All vehicles (except #11) equipped with automatic transmission.				
•	Equipped with a 6-speed for IMS Track President Doug Boles, the 11th track president. VIN start: 1G1FG3D7				

Brickyard 400

This section features details about 10 Brickyard 400–edition Camaros from 1995, 1997 (two), 1998, 1999, 2000, 2002 (three), and 2010.

1995 Brickyard 400 Festival Camaro Z/28

For the 1995 Brickyard 400 race, held August 5, 1995, Chevrolet provided a 1995 C/K 1500 pickup truck that was painted teal with purple stripes as the pace vehicle. It also repurposed the 50 1995 Camaro Z/28s (equipped with an automatic transmission and painted Arctic White) that had been in use at the year's previous Indianapolis 500 race. For this second event, they received turquoise beltline graphics, a windshield banner, and door decals.

After being used at the Indy 500, 50 Camaro Z28s were given new graphics and used at the Brickyard 400 race.

1997 Brickyard 400 Festival 35th Anniversary Camaro Z/28

For the 1996 Brickyard 400 NASCAR race, Chevrolet provided four 1996 Camaro T-top Z/28s that were painted Arctic White with orange stripes for the pace cars along with 50 additional 1997 Z/28 convertibles for festival use. The latter featured factory upgrades including digital odometer readings (instead of analog), and because they were so early in the production run, there was a conscious effort to match the last digits of the VIN with the plate number.

All Camaros were painted Arctic White and came equipped with the 30th Anniversary Package (RPO Z4C), an automatic transmission, Arctic White leather interior with Houndstooth inserts, and blue and gold graphics on the doors. The convertibles received white tops and Indianapolis Motor Speedway graphics on the rear quarter panels. The pace cars had the graphics mounted on the B-pillar.

Complementing the 30th Anniversary Package (RPO Z4C) stripes, these 54 Camaros received blue and gold door graphics for the 1996 Brickyard race.

1997 Brickyard 400 Festival 35th Anniversary Camaro Z/28: Registry									
#	VIN	#	VIN	#	VIN	#	VIN	#	VIN
1	3V2100061	11	6V2100054	21	2V2100021	31	5V2100031	41	8V2100041
2	5V2100062	12	8V2100055	22	4V2100022	32	7V2100032	42	XV2100042
3	7V2100063	13	XV2100056	23	7V2100080	33	9V2100033	43	1V2100043
4	8V2100072	14	1V2100057	24	8V2100024	34	3V2100075	44	3V2100044
5	0V2100065	15	7V2100015	25	XV2100073	35	2V2100035	45	5V2100045
6*	2V2100066	16	9V2100016	26	1V2100026	36	4V2100036	46	7V2100046
7	4V2100067	17	5V2100059	27	2V2100052	37	6V2100037	47	9V2100047
8	6V2100068	18	1V2100060	28	5V2100028	38	9V2100078	48	0V2100048
9	8V2100069	19	0V2100079	29	7V2100029	39	XV2100039	49	2V2100049
10	4V2100070	20	0V2100020	30	3V2100030	40	6V2100040	50	9V2100050
*	Given to race winner								

1997 Brickyard 400 Festival Camaro Z/28

For the 1997 Brickyard 400 NASCAR race, Chevrolet provided several 1998 Monte Carlo Z34s that were painted Yellow and Bright White to be pace cars along with 50 additional 1997 Z/28 convertibles.

All vehicles were painted in Arctic White and were equipped with a white top, chrome 16-inch five-spoke aluminum wheels, a Dark Gray leather interior, and an automatic transmission. They were marked with a colorful yellow, red, blue, and green beltline graphic and door and fender decals.

1997 Brickyard 400 Festival Camaro Z/28: Registry									
#	VIN	#	VIN	#	VIN	#	VIN	#	VIN
1	3576	11	4024	21	4260	31	4728	41	4731
2	4469	12	4677	22	4333	32	5110	42	5788
3	3807	13	4393	23	3881	33	5141	43	3576
4	3950	14	4384	24	5216	34	5294	44	5706
5	4699	15	4345	25	5677	35	6206	45	5849
6	3848	16	3479	26	5616	36	5902	46	5085
7	4320	17	4048	27	5882	37	5051	47	6343
8	3902	18	3594	28	4933	38	5899	48	4841
9	UK	19	4192	29	4947	39	5526	49	5498
10	UK	20	3978	30	9061	40	5315	50	UK

Fifty Arctic White convertibles were provided for use at the 1997 Brickyard 400 NASCAR race.

1998 Brickyard 400 Festival Camaro

For the 1998 NASCAR Brickyard 400 race, Chevrolet provided a Bright White with Lime graphics Monte Carlo Z34 to be the pace car. For use as track support and as parade vehicles, Chevrolet also provided 50 1998 Camaro SS convertibles and 9 Z28 convertibles that had been used at that year's Indy 500. They were all painted in Arctic White with Arctic White leather interior and a white top. All came equipped with an automatic transmission, and all received unique graphics with a green beltline stripe.

After the race, the vehicles were used at other GM sponsored automotive events. Cars #1 and #2 were used at the NHRA's US Nationals, while 20 more (#8 through #27) were sent to the Bristol Motor Speedway in Tennessee. Later, a large group of vehicles were stripped of their graphics and sent in November to Las Vegas to be used as courtesy cars at that year's Specialty Equipment Market Association (SEMA) show.

1999 Brickyard 400 Camaro

For the 1999 Brickyard 400, Chevrolet provided a 2000 Torch Red Monte Carlo SS as the pace car along with 56 1999 Camaro convertibles for festival and promotional use.

The Camaros were all painted Arctic White with a white top and dark gray leather interior. On the side, the vehicles were marked with a checkered-flag stripe and large door graphics. Additional IMS logo graphics were mounted on the rear quarter panels and the center of the rear decklid.

Forty-eight Z28s were used as festival vehicles (#1–44,

1998 Brickyard 400 Camaro SS Registry									
#	VIN	#	VIN	#	VIN	#	VIN	#	VIN
1	49016	11	48636	21	52589	31	51489	41	51657
2	49559	12	49812	22	51537	32	52151	42	51714
3	49915	13	49007	23	52128	33	52754	43	51905
4	48938	14	49241	24	52071	34	52598	44	52920
5	50103	15	49517	25	51662	35	51896	45	51641
6	47753	16	52179	26	52064	36	52244	46	51763
7	48377	17	49331	27	52647	37	51547	47	51988
8	49949	18	49484	28	51558	38	52458	48	52142
9	49540	19	49552	29	51964	39	52515	49*	51745
10	47905	20	49826	30	52462	40	51733	50	52583
*	Vehicle featured in the 2000 Camaro brochure (pages 28 and 29)								

Z/28 Registry			
87	2846	92	2559
88	3631	93	3354
89	2785	94	3172
90	2569	95	3572
91	3467		

For the 1998 Brickyard 400, Chevrolet provided 50 Camaro SS convertibles. The last time the performance trim had been used for Indy 500 festivities was in 1969.

#	VIN	#	VIN	#	VIN	#	VIN	#		VIN	#	VIN
1	8669	11	9226	22	8653	32	9222	42		9269	112 *	5126
2	9050	12	8930	23	8717	33	9477	43		9601	113 *	5824
3	8865	14	8791	24	8947	34	8586	44		8854	114	0616
4	9057	15	8730	25	8095	35	9061	45		9697	115	9658
5	8489	16	8107	26	9051	36	8082	91 **		8875	116	0761
6	9167	17	8433	27	9450	37	8454	92 **		8939	117	0933
7	8329	18	8770	28	8448	38	8595	93 **		9069	118	9689
8	8280	19	8857	29	8310	39	8153	99 ***		1003	Note: #13 not used	
9	9046	20	8845	30	0582	40	8438	110 *		6064		
10	9212	21	8975	31	1111	41	9400	111 *		5737		
#1-44,114-118	Z28	*	Admin, V-6	**	Lowe's Promotion, V-6	***	Winner SS					

Both Z28 and V-6 Camaros that were used at the 1999 Brickyard 400 were equipped with optional 16-inch chrome aluminum wheels.

skipping #13, and #114–#118). Four V-6 convertibles with the Sport Appearance package were used for administrative duties (identified as #110–113), while three more (#91–93) were part of a promotion with home-improvement retailer Lowes.

A white SS convertible (identified as car #99 to correlate with the year) was awarded to that year's race winner, Dale Jarrett.

2000 Brickyard 400 Festival Camaro SS

For the 2000 NASCAR Brickyard 400, Chevrolet provided a 2001 Monte Carlo SS that was painted black along with 55 2000 Camaro SS convertibles for use as track support and parade vehicles. All came painted in Arctic White and were equipped with a black top, Ebony interiors, and an automatic transmission.

2000 Brickyard 400 Camaro: SS Registry

#	VIN	#	VIN	#	VIN	#	VIN	#	VIN	#	VIN
1	2136	10	1759	20	2574	29	1969	38	1750	47	4922
2	1757	11	1894	21	1804	30	1557	39	1790	48	5645
3	1680	12	1796	22	1732	31	1878	40	2412	49	7270
4	1572	14	2055	23	1670	32	2128	41	1779	50	1996
5	2065	15	2207	24	2141	33	2027	42	3163	51	2091
6	1852	16	2342	25	1469	34	2156	43	1991	52	7015
7	2179	17	1809	26	2192	35	1884	44	2277	Note:	
8	2162	18	1658	27	1600	36	UK	45	2287	Car #13 was not	
9	1862	19	2367	28	1929	37	UK	46	4877	used	

Z28 Registry

Pewter with Black Top	
	VIN*
288	46656
289	46680
290	26080
White with White Top (Carried over from 1999 race)	
291	39384
294	39649
295	38348
296	39726
297	39930
298	39881
299	39294

They received a unique purple beltline and door graphics along with a 42-inch red bowtie graphic on the hood. There was no charge for the special package.

2002 Brickyard 400 Camaro 35th Anniversary SS

2002 Brickyard 400 Camaro 35th Ann. SS Registry				
Parade	Convertible	VIN	222100001	
lap	Coupe	VIN	122100002	
Festival Vehicles				
#	VIN	#	VIN	#	VIN
1	522100378	16	722100446	31	022100482
2	522100498	17	322100248	32	322100654
3	522100514	18	922100271	33	X22100490
4	522100326	19	322100458	34	222100645
5	522100840	20	922100738	35	622100678
6	522100510	21	122100426	36	422100310
7	522100430	22	022100708	37	222100466
8	522100633	23	422100209	38	322101514
9	522100354	24	X22100442	39	X22100280
10	522100462	25	G022100689	40	522100221
11	522100398	26	022100336	41	222100239
12	522100478	27	622100454	42	522100669
13	522100494	28	222100502	43	222100306
14	522100474	29	822100200	44	522100297
15	522100362	30	822100438	45	422100257

For the 2001 Brickyard 400 NASCAR race on August 5th, Chevrolet provided a 2001 Monte Carlo SS that was painted Competition Yellow for pace car duties along with 45 2002 35th Anniversary Camaro SS convertibles for festival and parade use.

Two more anniversary Camaros with a manual transmission (one convertible and one with T-tops) led an opening parade lap in front of the pace car and race field prior to the start of the race. Both cars were equipped with strobe lights in the headlights.

All Camaros were painted in the 35th Anniversary's Rally Red and retained the silver checkered flag rally stripes along with the package's unique wheels, badging, and interior treatment. New content included door and fender graphics and numbers at the base of the windshield. The pair of parade vehicles was not numbered. The vehicles cost $36,540 each.

Camaros provided for the 2001 Brickyard 400 NASCAR race were optioned with the 35th Anniversary Edition Package and painted Rally Red.

2002 Brickyard 400 Camaro

Total	97	Role	Total	Build Date	Car #	
SS *	57	Pilot car	1	3/18/02	1	
		Driver intro	43	5/27/02	2-43,45	
		Pace car	1		44	
		Central office	13		51-62	
Z/28	40	VIP and pre-race laps	12	2/26/02	2,3,7,9,16,17,26, 27, 28,30,31,44	
					Backup	47
		Other duties	28		--	
Camaro SS: Transmission Breakdown •						
6-speed manual (MN6)			5	#	1,51,52,53,60	
Automatic (MXO)			52	#	2-50,54-57,59,61,62 **	
*	Vehicles receiving RPO Z7D – Brickyard 400 package					
**	Renumbered to #12	•	Excluding the pilot car			

Both Z28 and SS Camaros were present at the 2002 Brickyard 400 race. All of them were painted in Sebring Silver Metallic paint, which was complemented with flowing colorful beltline graphics.

The SS vehicles were unique and were ordered under RPO code Z7D, which equipped the cars with the 35th Anniversary Edition's 10-spoke wheels.

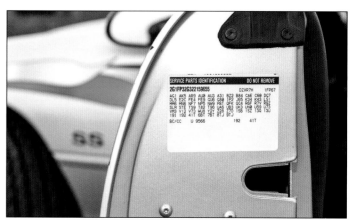

For the 2002 Brickyard 400 NASCAR race on August 2, Chevrolet provided a 2002 Monte Carlo SS, which was painted Superior Blue, for pace car duties along with 57 Sebring Silver SS convertibles for use as festival vehicles.

An additional 40 Sebring Silver 2002 Camaro Z/28s were repurposed from the duties at that year's Indy 500 race and used for parade and festival duties.

2002 Brickyard 400 Camaro: RPO Z7D

The SS vehicles were ordered under RPO Z7D, which costed $650 and added the 10-spoke wheels from the 35th Anniversary Package. All were painted in Sebring Silver and fully loaded, including the optional leather upholstery for $500 and the accelerate slip regulation, which cost $450. The 12-disc CD changer was left off due to concerns of theft.

A pilot car was built in March before the rest of the batch which was all built on May 27. The run featured "North Central Region Cars," which included 43 vehicles that were used for the driver introductions at the race.

They were part of a Dealer Drive-Away promotion in which Chevrolet dealers could win an all-expense paid trip to the race by winning a sales contest. This promotion also included the chance to purchase one of the vehicles through a lottery drawing.

On race day, the vehicles were used for driver introductions and bore the drivers' name in large vinyl graphics on the passenger's side of the hood. The drivers also signed the original window sticker of the vehicles. Each SS was numbered at the base of the windshield and behind the rear license plate.

The second batch, which is referred to as the central office cars, contained 12 additional cars that were used for additional festival and race duties.

All cars (SS Z7D and Z28) were given unique graphics by Graphik Concepts Inc. of Farming Hills, Michigan, that were very similar to those used at the previous Indy 500 race.

Because of time constraints, the anniversary edition's two-tone leather seats were not included, and as such, the cars received ebony interiors.

Graphik Concepts Inc. in Farmington Hills, Michigan, fitted the cars with the graphics.

2002 Brickyard 400 Camaro SS Z7D: Registry

#	VIN	Driver	#	VIN	Driver	#	VIN	Driver
2	567	Bill Elliot	17	009	Dale Jarrett	32	358	Bobby Hamilton
3	599	Dale Earnhardt Jr.	18	014	Matt Kenseth	33	363	Dave Blaney
4	625	Robby Gordon	19	089	Ward Burton	34	379	Jerry Nadeau
5	740	Ryan Newman	20	109	Todd Bodine	35	384	Rusty Wallace
6	750	Steve Park	21	124	Jeff Gordon	36	444	Ted Musgrave
7	776	Kevin Harvick	22	149	Ricky Craven	37	459	Jimmie Johnson
8	806	Sterling Marlin	23	179	Jeff Burton	38	464	Kurt Busch
9	827	Mark Martin	24	195	Geoffrey Bodine	39	469	Elliot Sadler
10	832	Joe Nemechek	25	215	Ricky Rudd	40	489	Bobby Labonte
11	857	Johnny Benson	26	266	Kenny Wallace	41	529	Hut Stricklin
12	911	Jeremy Mayfield	27	272	Kyle Petty	42	570	Brett Bodine
13	926	Mike Skinner	28	277	Casey Atwood	43	603	Mike Wallace
14	936	Michael Waltrip	29	302	Jeff Green	44	608	Kim Smith (pace car)
15	961	Jimmy Spencer	30	312	Ken Schrader	45	662	Tony Stewart
16	987	John Andretti	31	128	Terry Labonte			

Central Office Cars

#	VIN	Role/Used by	T
1	592	Pilot Car	6
51	655	Corvette Museum	6
52	509	Corvette Museum	6
53	019	Jim Perkins	6
54	725	Corvette Museum	A
55	484	Corvette Museum	A
56	347	Corvette Museum	A

Central Office Cars

#	VIN	Role/Used by	T
57	129	Corvette Museum	A
58	931	Used on Race Day	A
59	169	Corvette Museum	A
60	099	Howard Kirchenbauer	6
61	404	Chevrolet Brand Team	A
62	434	Camaro Legends Tour	A

#	VIN	Role on Race Day	#	VIN	Role on Race Day
2002 Brickyard 400 Camaro Z28: Registry *					
1	140658	IMS/not used	32	140831	Not present
2	142644	IMS/used	33 **	140590	Festival board
3	141073	IMS/used	34	140808	Not present
4	140562	IMS/not used	35	141733	Not present ••
5	140946	IMS/not used	36	141100	Not present ••
6	141395	Mayor (Indy)	37	140933	Not present ••
7	140698	IMS/used	38	141166	Not present ••
8	140733	IMS/not used	39 **	140841	IMS/not used
9	140912	IMS/used	40 **	140798	Festival board
10	141033	IMS/not used	41 **	140678	IMS/used
11	141827	IMS/not used	42 ** •	140653	Renumbered to #14
12	141182	IMS/not used	43 **	140555	Festival board
13	141038	IMS/not used	44 **	140783	IMS/used
14	140979	IMS/not used	45 **	141125	Festival board
15	141005	IMS/not used	46 **	141011	Festival board
16	141151	IMS/used	47 **	141050	IMS/used
17	140885	IMS/used	48	141323	Festival board
18	140971	IMS/not used	49	140572	Festival board
19	140922	IMS/not used	50 ** •	140895	Renumbered to #16
20	140917	IMS/not used	51	141105	Not present ••
21	140614	IMS/used	52	141016	Not present ••
22	141728	IMS/not used	53	140758	Not present ••
23	141078	IMS/not used	54	140836	Not present ••
24	141022	IMS/not used	55 ** •	141088	Renumbered to #22
25 **	141189	IMS/not used	56 ** •	141115	Renumbered to #10
26 **	141130	IMS/used	57 ** •	140626	Renumbered to #10
27 **	140846	IMS/used	58	141161	Not present ••
28 **	141637	IMS/used	59	140907	Not present ••
29 ••	140648	Not present ••	60	140703	Not present ••
30 **	141028	IMS/used	61	140773	Not present ••
31 **	141543	IMS/used	62	141055	Renumbered to #12

*	Master list for vehicles present at either the Indy 500 or Brickyard 400				
**	Vehicle used by festival members		••		Vehicle sold after Indy 500
•	Vehicle renumbered (From the Indy 500 assignment to the Brickyard 400 assignment)		#42 to #14		
			#50 to #16		
			#55 to #22		
			#56 to #10		
			#57 to #10		
			#62 to #12		

2010 Brickyard 400 Camaro

For the 2009 Brickyard 400 NASCAR race on July 26, Chevrolet provided a 2009 Corvette Z06 for pacing duties that was painted Victory Red. The brand also repurposed five 2010 Camaros that were used at that year's Indianapolis 500.

All were 2SS trim and were painted Silver Ice Metallic with a black leather interior and automatic transmission. The red fractured side graphic applied for Indy was retained, but new door graphics were added.

#	VIN
21	0A9000544
22	8A9000873
23	2A9000870
25	5A9000670
38	8A9000615

Five Camaros were repurposed and renumbered from that year's Indy 500 for use at the 2009 Brickyard 400. This is vehicle #25, which was #5 at Indy.

## CHAPTER 3

ANNIVERSARY EDITIONS

It wasn't long after the Camaro's 1967 launch that it became apparent that it would be a permanent pillar of affordable performance in the Chevrolet lineup. Year after year, it was made available for driving enthusiasts, and soon the decades of production started to pile up.

Wanting to celebrate the model's milestones, Chevrolet offered anniversary editions, beginning with a 20th edition and continuing with new anniversaries being celebrated every five years.

1987 20th Anniversary Edition Camaro

		LT	1
Total	1,007	Sport Coupe	262
		Z28	11
		IROC	733

The first anniversary-edition Camaro arrived in 1987, which marked 20 years of the iconic model. It was only available as a convertible, which was a bodystyle that had been absent from the factory lineup since 1969.

This drop-top alteration wasn't handled in-house by General Motors but rather through a partnership with the Automobile Specialty Company (ASC), which was a division of the American Sunroof Company and was headquartered in Livonia, Michigan. The specialty firm had a close working relationship with Chevrolet, having contracts to convert four General Motors models as well as to manufacture the soft tops and 190 parts for the roadster Corvette that ASC helped design.

For years, market demand for a convertible Camaro had been high, as was evidenced in the wide assortment of third-party vendors around the country. Those third-party

The 1987 20th Anniversary Edition Camaro lacked any kind of special exterior markings or badging. The sole giveaway to the package is the convertible bodystyle.

vendors included Auto Form in Elkhart, Indiana; Matrix3 in Costa Mesa, California, and Jacksonville Florida; and American Custom Coachworks in Beverly Hills, California. These companies offered conversion kits that sported a variety of final looks and appearances. Some of them courted Chevrolet, showing off their handiwork to secure the contract to be the authorized upfitter.

Aware of this and the trend, Chevrolet designers tried mocking up an iteration of their own converted droptop, bringing in consultants from ASC to help dial in the render. Despite the efforts, they never could convince upper management to approve the concept. ASC took it upon itself to fully flesh out the idea and rolled out its own kit and conversion in 1986.

1986–1987 ASC Special Edition

Upon arriving at their facility, the roof and B-pillar hoop were cut and removed. Next, additional galvanized reinforcements and supports were added to the floorpan, quarter panels, and cowl. The manually folding top mechanism and a vinyl top (in either black or tan) was mounted and covered by painted components, such as the trunk lid and rear quarter-panel caps that flowed to a rear spoiler. The look of the final flush boot was striking, seamless, and well executed (whether up or down).

Several hundred were created, and to mark their work, a numbered special-edition plaque was mounted on the passenger's side of the dashboard under the factory badge. In addition, with the removal of the factory rear defrost (the soft top window lacked the feature), the switch on the dash was typically covered with a blank plate that featured an ASC logo.

Conversion Process: 20th Anniversary Edition

Impressed and ready to change its stance, Chevrolet offered a factory convertible in 1987 complete with a warranty. The contract was given to ASC to handle the builds.

As opposed to the ASC office, customers could now order the option under RPO Z08 Convertible Equipment through select Chevrolet dealers. It was limited due to those that were not prepared to properly handle warranty claims. The option was available on all four available Camaro models (the IROC-Z, Z28, LT, and Sport Coupe), but the cars needed to be ordered with T-tops (RPO CC1), which had additional structural bracing compared to the coupe counterpart.

Vehicles destined to become convertibles at ASC left Chevrolet's Norwood, Ohio, and Van Nuys, California, factories lacking items such as the hatch panel and some rear interior trim, which helped to streamline the process. The cars had to be equipped with a 305-ci V-8 with a 4-barrel carburetor (LG4) or TPI (LB9, Z28, and IROC only), and they were available with either an automatic or manual transmission. Cars ordered in this fashion received a unique VIN, bearing a "3" as the sixth digit, designating it as a two-door convertible.

As in the year prior, ASC carried out the same steps with a few slight changes. The soft vinyl top was only available in black. It was listed as RPO 19T. The numbered dash badge was exchanged for an added leatherette map pouch that had an anniversary logo. There was no additional option for the cosmetic touch.

Seeking that factory appearance, the dash defrost button plate was still installed but without the ASC marking. It did show up on a sticker on the driver's doorjamb that also contained the month and year of the vehicle's conversion. While the final look was seamless, it didn't come cheap, boasting a

Third-party automotive vendor Automobile Specialty Company handled the convertible conversion. To mark their work, this sticker was added to the driver's door.

A leatherette map pouch with anniversary embroidery was added on the passenger's side of the dash. It's the only callout to the 20th Anniversary Edition.

hefty conversion charge of nearly $5,000. As such, only 1,007 units were sold.

ASC continued to offer the setup for dealers and customers who didn't order through the factory system. These conversions would be completed the same way but lacked the map pouch. Instead, they received ASC's numbered special-edition badging from the year before. Besides this touch, these cars were differentiated from the factory-ordered convertibles in that they still retained the "2" in the sixth digit in the VIN. This calls it out as a two-door hatchback. Another distinction between the two is the presentation of the trunk.

1992 Anniversary Heritage Edition Camaro

Total	7,144	Hardtop/T-Top		6,606	
		Convertible		538	
		Hardtop/T-Top		**Convertible**	
Paint Color		Z28	RS	Z28	RS
Arctic White		322	1,576	86	64
Black		248	1,061	50	28
Polo Green II Met.		0	498	0	40
Bright Red		430	1,094	114	107
Purple Haze Met.		55	512	16	33
Total		1,055	4,741	266	272

In 1992, Chevrolet took greater steps to expand its Camaro anniversary celebration, which now commemorated 25 years of the motoring icon. All models produced that year featured a special badge on the passenger's side of the dash. This tradition was carried over to subsequent anniversary years (1997, 2002, 2014, and 2017) with the anniversary callout being on the dashboard or at the base of the steering wheel.

Regardless of the year, the brand offered smaller batches that sported additional cosmetic touches and labeled them as anniversary editions.

For 1992, the 25th Anniversary Edition was ordered under RPO Z03, the Heritage Appearance Package.

Configuration

In 1992, customers could opt for the Heritage Appearance Package, which was labeled as RPO Z03. Costing $175, it was available on RS and Z28 as both a coupe or convertible. It came in select colors, being available on Camaros painted in Arctic White, Black, Bright Red and the new colors for 1992, which were Polo Green II Metallic and Purple Haze Metallic.

The purely cosmetic package brought a unique cloisonné badge to the rear decklid, black headlamp pockets, and heritage rally stripes on the hood, decklid, and spoiler. A body-color grille was included except on cars painted in Polo Green II Metallic and Purple Haze Metallic. Those vehicles received black grilles.

The 1992 Anniversary Edition received this exterior anniversary badge mounted on the decklid.

All Camaros produced in 1992 had this celebratory dash-mounted anniversary plaque, but only those equipped with RPO Z03 are anniversary editions.

Rally stripes were included in the anniversary package, coming in red, black, silver, or gold depending on the car's paint color.

The 1997 30th Anniversary color scheme harkened back to the iconic orange and white design of the 1969 Indy 500 Camaro Pace Car. Painted white wheels or optional chrome wheels (like those shown) were available.

All 25th Anniversary Edition Camaros received painted wheels that featured red, white, silver, or gold accents based on the vehicle's exterior paint color.

BONUS CONTENT

Scan to view the color configuration data.

www.cartechbooks.com/ct658-qr24

1997 30th Anniversary Edition Camaro Z/28

Total	4,534	Convt.	1,001	Auto	684
				Man	317
		Coupe	3,299	Auto	1,802
		T-Top		Man	1,497

To celebrate the Camaro's 30th anniversary, Chevrolet released an anniversary edition in 1997 that featured distinct colors that paid tribute to the iconic 1969 Indianapolis 500 Camaro Z/28 pace car.

Exterior

The new appearance package (ordered through RPO Z4C) cost $575 and was available on Z28 coupes and convertibles that were equipped with the LT1 V-8 engine that produced 285 hp and 325 ft-lbs of torque. It featured a monochromatic Arctic White exterior, including a white front foglamp surround fascia (instead of the Z28's black unit), white mirrors, white door handles (black door handles were standard), and a white roof hoop (on coupes). Convertibles received an Arctic White top.

The stark look was highlighted with dual vinyl Hugger Orange rally stripes. Matching the white scheme, the stock five-spoke 16x8 aluminum wheels were painted white. Customers could select the model's optional 16x8 chrome aluminum wheels.

Interior

Inside, there was an Arctic White leather interior with black and white houndstooth cloth inserts. All-white leather seats were optional for $499.

All Camaros produced in 1997 had a 30th anniversary logo embroidered on the front headrests and in center of the rear seat, but for this special package, it was embroidered in five-color stitching. The front floor mats also received embroidered logos in silver stitching.

1997 30th Anniversary Edition Camaro Z/28: Package Contents (RPO Z4C Appearance Package 30th Anniversary)	
Exterior	• Arctic White Paint • Arctic White foglamp surround • Arctic White rearview mirror caps • Arctic White door handles • Arctic White roof (Coupes) • White soft top (Convertibles) • Hugger Orange rally stripes
Wheels	• Stock five-spoke 16x8-inch painted white • Optional: 16x8-inch chrome aluminum wheels

Interior	• Arctic White leather seats
	  • Black and white houndstooth cloth inserts
	  • Optional: All-white leather ($499)
	• Seat headrests (front and center rear) embroidery in five-color stitching
	• Embroidered floor mats with silver stitching

Package Price	$575

Embroidered floor mats were part of the package along with black and white houndstooth cloth seat inserts.

All Camaros produced in 1997 had this embroidery in the seats, but only the anniversary editions had it in five-color stitching.

SS, LT4, and Race Duties

For customers who wanted more, SLP Engineering offered its SS upgrades to the 30th Anniversary Edition. The company also offered the rarest version of the 30th Anniversary Edition Camaro in the form of an LT4 version.

To harken back to its 1969 pace car predecessor and to build excitement, four 30th Anniversary Edition Camaros were built in the early summer of 1996 for pacing duties at the 1996 Brickyard 400 race at the Indianapolis Motor Speedway on August 3, 1996. Because of their early assembly, the group used the 1996 platform, which is readily identifiable by the different dashboard.

In addition, 50 convertibles built on the 1997 platform were also given the anniversary treatment and provided by Chevrolet for use as event festival cars.

2002 Camaro SS 35th Anniversary Edition

2002 Camaro SS 35th Anniversary Edition: Production and Package Contents						
Total	3,369	US 3,000	Coupe	1,971	Auto	934
					Man	1,037
		Canada 369	Convt.	1,398	Auto	789
					Man	609
Package Contents (RPO Z4C)			Package Price		$2,500	
Exterior		• Bright Rally Red paint • Checkered flag–style stripes • Hood scoop blackout graphic • Black SS wheels with machined edge • Fender badges • Anodized brake calipers				
Interior		• Ebony/Pewter leather seating surfaces • Embroidered front seat headrests				
Other		• Trophy mat (Ebony vinyl) • Owner's portfolio (booklet, pen, patch, pin, letter opener, key chain, ID card, and paper pad)				

Camaro's 35th anniversary was celebrated in 2002 with a special cosmetic package on both T-top and convertible SS models. It was ordered through option RPO Z4C. The cars were equipped with the LS1 V-8 that produced 325 hp and 350 ft-lbs of torque.

Under a revived D82 option that called for a monochromatic roof, coupes received body-colored mirrors (body-colored mirrors were standard) and roof hoops. Convertibles received black canvass tops. The stock SS powertrain was retained and was mated to the automatic transmission or the optional 6-speed manual at no extra cost.

The 35th Anniversary Edition featured Bright Rally Red paint and rippling checkered-flag stripe graphics.

Design Alterations

The original plan was for the cars to be painted Sebring Silver. Scott Settlemire, a Camaro assistant brand manager, had Kay Automotive, the automaker's graphics supplier, create a few design proposals based around a silver vehicle.

The renderings were shown to a focus group of Camaro enthusiasts who unanimously selected their pick for the anniversary package as a silver car highlighted with red, white, and blue graphics.

Despite the positive feedback, Jim Campbell, the brand manager for the Camaro and Corvette, felt that color scheme did not do the iconic car justice. He tasked Settlemire with finding a suitable replacement, who then selected Bright Rally Red. Variants of the hue had been offered since the model's release in 1967 and consistently were the top-selling colors in all generations. Black was a close second, but it was passed over because it wasn't available on the model in the early 1970s.

A revised graphic scheme was created by John Cafaro, a GM designer, and featured rippling checkered race flag stripes. Cafaro also developed the black hood inlay graphic set ahead of the hood scoop.

Other exterior highlights included anniversary fender badges and silver debossed "CAMARO" lettering in the front grille insert and the rear panel.

Inside, the Ebony seats received pewter gray inserts and an embroidered anniversary logo on the front headrests. The cloisonné above the radio is not unique to the package, as all trims of 2002 Camaros received it, paying tribute to the model's milestone.

Wheels

With the program approved so late in the production cycle, there was little time to tool and engineer a new wheel design. Stuck with the stock 17-inch cast-aluminum SS wheels, it was proposed to paint them gray with a machine-finished edge as a tribute to the ones used on the third generation IROC Camaro. Mockups were created but the gray paint on the recesses didn't show up. The team moved forward with painting those areas solid black, and the look was well-received. To achieve an even more distinct look, Settlemire proposed painting the center black too.

While attractive, focus groups preferred the machined-finish center, which is ultimately what was used on the final vehicles. The wheels were wrapped in P275/40Z-17 Goodyear Eagle F1 tires, and the brake calipers were anodized black.

Owner's Portfolio

The anniversary package came with many accessories, including a trophy mat with an embroidered logo. It was stored in the rear cargo area and matched the rest of the Ebony interior. New owners also received an owner's portfolio, including the car's manual, a pen, tire pressure gauge, tire-tread depth gauge, key chain, notepad, cloisonné pin, patch, and Camaro history booklet.

While originally intended to be placed in the vehicles, the kit was not approved until early January, which was after the first 1,500-or-so cars had been produced and shipped. The packages were then mailed to owners or dealerships that still recorded vehicles in stock.

All Camaros produced in 2002 received the center anniversary cloisonné, but only those with RPO Z4C are anniversary editions.

A trophy mat that features the anniversary logo was a special inclusion.

Pricing and Distribution

The 35th Anniversary Package cost $2,500, and Street Legal Performance (SLP) handled the conversion of the vehicles.

Special badges were mounted on the fenders, and the stock SS wheels were painted black with a machined finish.

The interior only came in Jet Black with white door and dash inserts. Embroidered floor mats and unique door sill plates were also included.

2012 Camaro 45th Anniversary Edition

Total	8,283	V-6	2,915
		V-8	5,368
V-6	Coupe	Man.	269
		Auto	1,942
	Convt.	Man.	66
		Auto	638
V-8	Coupe	Man.	1,525
		Auto	2,216
	Convt.	Man.	524
		Auto	1,103

Package Contents (RPO H45)	
Exterior	
• Carbon Flash Metallic paint • RS package • Deep Silver DRL and taillamp bezels • Rear spoiler • Medium Charcoal and Brilliant Red inlay stripes • 20-inch Deep Silver–painted aluminum wheels • Fender badges	
Interior	
• Jet Black with white door and dash inserts • Red, white, and blue stitching • Steering wheel anniversary logo • Anniversary logo on dashboard • Anniversary sill plates • Embroidered floor mats • Embroidered seat backs	
Package Price	$1,375

Ordered under RPO H45, the 45th Anniversary Edition came in an exclusive Carbon Flash Metallic paint.

This anniversary logo was included on the dash insert.

In 2012, Camaro's 45th anniversary was celebrated with a special edition. It was offered on coupe and convertible body-styles in both 2LT V-6 and 2SS V-8 form. It cost $1,375. Under RPO H45, the exterior received Carbon Flash Metallic paint and featured a unique variant of the factory rally striping. On the driver's side, the Medium Charcoal stripe was interrupted with a Brilliant Red inlay, and the hood cowl featured the numeral 45. A stripe delete option was available. Special red, white, and blue badging was mounted on the front fenders, and the fog lamp and taillamp bezels were finished in Deep Silver. This matched the exclusive and newly designed five-spoke 20-inch Deep Silver painted aluminum wheels.

The anniversary package included the RS package, which brought HID headlamps with LED halo rings, a body-color shark-fin antenna, and body-color roof ditch moldings. A standard rear spoiler was also included. A sunroof was available on coupes, while convertible models had a black top.

Inside, there was a Jet Black interior featuring leather-trimmed seats with embroidered "45th Anniversary" logos on the front seat headrests and front floor mats. The dashboard and door trim inserts were white with the anniversary logo included on the passenger's side of the dash. Red, white, and blue stitching was used on the seats, steering wheel, shift knob and boot, door armrests, and the center console lid. Finally, the anniversary logo was featured on the steering wheel and special sill plates.

2017 Camaro 50th Anniversary Edition

Total	5,982	Coupe	4,649	Convt.	1,333
Package Contents (RPO H50)				Package Price	$1,795

- Nightfall Gray Metallic Paint
- Matte black stripe with orange accents
- 20-inch machined face wheels with exclusive center caps
- Summer tires
- Front splitter
- Fender badges
- Rear panel blackout graphic with anniversary logo
- 50th anniversary front grille
- Orange Brembo brake calipers
- Black/Gray Interior with orange accent stitching
- Steering wheel anniversary logo
- Dash "FIFTY" detailing
- Embroidered front seat headrests
- Illuminated sill plates

In 2017, Camaro celebrated its 50th anniversary. The resulting special edition was subtle and refined, as it was available in Nightfall Gray Metallic paint.

Celebrating five decades of the Camaro in 2017, Chevrolet released the 50th Anniversary Edition under RPO H50. The cosmetic package was offered on coupes and convertibles in both 2LT and 2SS trims and with 4-, 6- and 8-cylinder powertrains paired to both manual and automatic transmissions.

The cars were painted in Nightfall Gray Metallic and featured a body-colored front splitter, 50th Anniversary front grille, and satin chrome accents. In a subtle nod to the 1969 Pace Car Z/28, the included special matte black center stripe was highlighted with orange accent stripes that matched the orange Brembo calipers. On LT trims, only the front brake calipers were orange.

Other additions included "FIFTY" fender badges and unique 20-inch machined-face wheels with exclusive center caps. On SS trims, they were wrapped in summer-only, run-flat tires with the standard-equipment tire sealant and inflator kit deleted.

Inside, the package included Jet Black leather-appointed seats with Dark Gray suede inserts and orange accent stitching. Other "FIFTY" touches were found on the sill plates and debossed seat headrests. The anniversary logo also appeared on the center console, steering wheel, and dashboard. Embroidered floor mats were available as a dealer installed option, costing $160.

The seats came with Dark Gray suede inserts while the dash design incorporated a special "FIFTY" addition.

2017 50th Anniversary Edition Camaro Production

	Coupe		Convertible		
	2LT	2SS	2LT	2SS	Total
Total	1,042	3,607	255	1,078	5,982
4-cylinder man.	43	0	5	0	48
4-cylinder auto.	269	0	56	0	345
6-cylinder man.	98	0	25	0	123
6-cylinder auto.	632	0	169	0	801
8-cylinder man.	0	855	0	188	1,043
8-cylinder auto. M5U	0	2,752	0	890	3,642
US Market					
Total	860	2,824	226	875	4,785
4-cylinder man.	40	0	4	0	44
4-cylinder auto.	174	0	42	0	216
6-cylinder man.	91	0	25	0	116
6-cylinder auto.	555	0	155	0	710
8-cylinder man.	0	699	0	158	857
8-cylinder auto. M5U	0	2,125	0	717	2,842
Canadian Market					
Total	53	244	17	102	416
4-cylinder man.	3	0	1	0	4
4-cylinder auto.	7	0	2	0	9
6-cylinder man.	7	0	0	0	7
6-cylinder auto.	36	0	14	0	50
8-cylinder man.	0	93	0	22	115
8-cylinder auto. M5U	0	151	0	80	231

## CHAPTER 4

FACTORY COSMETIC SPECIAL EDITIONS

In addition to motoring fun, the Camaro has always been about personalization. With a foundation that suits a wide array of preferences, Chevrolet has offered a wild assortment of factory cosmetic-focused special editions. These cars have marked all kinds of occasions, presenting drivers with pop-culture tie-ins and head-turning packages that deliver unique looks and appearances.

From celebrating major sporting events and highlighting starring roles in major motion pictures to returning to the childhood wonder of toy cars, there's been a special Camaro to feed and fuel every enthusiast's drive to stand out.

1984 Camaro Olympic Edition

Chevrolet signed on to be the official US cars and trucks of the 1984 Winter Olympics that were in Sarajevo, Yugoslavia.

The marketing push included the Chevrolet releasing an Olympic trim package that was available on the Camaro, Cavalier Type 10 coupe and hatchback, S-10 Blazer, and C/K 10 truck.

The package was applied to the Camaro Sport coupe, and all cars were painted in the stock enamel white (code 11), which was referred to in marketing as Winter White. Also included were the optional Rally wheels (RPO ZJ7) that were painted body color and featured a black cap and bright trim ring. A rear spoiler (RPO D80) was part of the package along with sport mirrors (RPO D35).

The appearance-focused package brought orange and blue (the official colors of the 1984 Winter Olympics) highlights in the form of stripes around the lower edges of the vehicle, with another running from the nose, along the beltline, and up the door frame. The official Olympic rings and Sarajevo emblem were mounted on a special graphic on the B-pillars. Inside, the cars were equipped with a Dark Royal Blue interior. A total of 3,722 Camaros received the package.

The Olympics Edition was part of Chevrolet's sponsorship as the Official US Cars and Trucks of the 1984 Winter Olympics.

The logo of the Olympics, along with the orange and blue striping, was added to the B-pillars.

Rally wheels were included along with a rear spoiler and sport mirrors.

The interiors were Dark Royal Blue, which contrasted with the white exterior.

2010 Transformers Special Edition

		US	Global
1LT/2LT	Man.	72	0
	Auto.	331	14
1SS/2SS	Man.	542	3
	Auto.	808	14
	Total	1,753	31
	Total	1,784	

One of the greatest boosts to the popularity of the fifth-generation Camaro was its starring role in the block-buster *Transformers* movie franchise.

In the first *Transformers* movie, which was in theaters in 2007, Bumblebee, who was one of the hero robots, was shown in the guise of a worn-out 1977 Camaro. Halfway through the film, he morphed into a modern—soon to be fifth-generation—version, two years before the production version went on sale for the first time to the public.

The car and character returned for the film's 2009 sequel, *Transformers: Revenge of the Fallen*, which opened a few months after the vehicle (as a 2010 model) had become available for purchase in dealership showrooms.

Enthusiasts buzzed with excitement, and Chevrolet rolled out a Transformers Special Edition. It was shown for the first time at the 2009 Comic-Con convention in San Diego, California.

The package, which cost $995 and was available under RPO CTH, could be added to LT or SS models with or without the optional RS Appearance Package. To mimic the exterior appearance of the hero car, the vehicles were painted in Rally Yellow with gloss black rally stripes. Subtle "Transformers" script adorned both sides of the hood cowl and was included on unique sill plates.

The hero character's "Autobot" shield logo was used for front fender badges and on the wheel center caps, and it was embroidered on the cabin's center console lid.

In 2010, Chevrolet offered the Transformers Special Edition Camaro, capitalizing on the popularity of the Transformers movie.

Subtle Transformers script was used on both sides of the hood cowl in the glossy black rally stripes.

Special additions to the cabin included special sill plates and an embroidered center console.

Only available in Rally Yellow paint, the package included Autobot fender badges.

2012 Transformers Special Edition

2LT	Auto.	464	
	Man.	49	
2SS	Auto.	527	
	Man.	371	
Total	1,411	US	1,093
		Canada	51
		Other	267

In 2012, Chevrolet offered a second Transformers Special Edition package, this time in conjunction with the third installment in the movie franchise, *Transformers: Dark of the Moon*, which again featured a yellow Camaro SS that transformed into the Bumblebee "Autobot" character.

The Transformers Edition returned in 2012, this time costing more but adding features such as a rear spoiler and two-tone effect stripes.

Factory Options and Accessory Content

The special edition was $3,000 and could be added to 2LT and 2SS coupes. It required Rally Yellow Paint (a $325 option) and a black interior with black door and dash inserts. It was ordered under RPO CTH.

The content from the RS Appearance Package (HID headlamps with LED halo rings, a body-color shark fin, and body-color roof ditch moldings) was included along with its 20-inch aluminum wheels. The wheels were painted gloss black instead of Midnight Silver. The accessory high-wing spoiler and gill stripe decals were also part of the Transformers package.

Original designs called for the package to include the Chevrolet Accessories ground effects (in black, not the typical body color) and larger optional 21-inch wheels, that mimicked the look of the screen-used vehicle. To keep the retail cost down and have the car be more attainable, they were not included but were offered as dealer-installed options.

Exclusive Package Content

To save on development costs, content from the 2010 Transformers package content was carried over, including the fender badges, sill plates, wheel center caps, and embroidered center console lid. Exclusive interior content included yellow accent stitching and embroidered front-seat headrests.

Exclusive exterior content included black rally stripes that, like the movie car, didn't run down the center of the vehicle but rather were pushed out to the outer edges of the hood, roof, decklid, and rear spoiler. The stripes had a two-tone effect with a solid inner edge that highlighted the carbon-fiber weave effect. The front fascia received a blacked-out graphic with subtle "Cybertonian" glyphs from the movie that spelled "Transformers" on the passenger side. The same glyphs were also included in the stripe on the driver's side of the rear spoiler.

The package was only offered in Rally Yellow paint that was accented with various black components.

2011 Camaro Neiman Marcus Edition

In 2010, luxury retailer Neiman Marcus approached Chevrolet about offering a special vehicle through its long-running annual Christmas Book holiday catalog. A similar partnership had been formed in 2003 when a limited run of 101 2004 Cadillac XLRs had been offered in the same way. Chevrolet agreed and offered a special-edition Camaro convertible as that year's automotive "fantasy gift."

While 100 were slated to be built, only 75 production units (and one pilot vehicle) were completed, preceded by the creation of a pilot car. The 76 cars were 2SS models painted black and equipped with every option and the RS Appearance Package. They were ordered under RPO API.

Inside the cabin, the black leather seats received amber-colored leather inserts and red stitching that was also used on the center console, steering wheel, and shift knob. The door panel inserts and dash panel matched the exterior's Deep Bordeaux color.

Included in the front blackout graphic and on the rear spoiler are "Cybertonian" glyphs that spell out "Transformers."

The 2010 Transformers Edition's sill plates and embroidered center console lid were carried over. New for 2012 was yellow accent stitching and embroidered headrests.

Just 75 Neiman Marcus Edition Camaros were sold. They were ordered under RPO API.

The cabin received amber-colored leather inserts, red stitching, and Bordeaux dash and door inserts.

In addition to the painted silver windshield frame, another striking element was the color-matched Bordeaux convertible top.

The edition received 21-inch, polished aluminum wheels that were found on other special editions, such as the 2011 Synergy Series Camaro.

After assembly, they were then shipped to a special facility in Sterling Heights, Michigan, where they received additional enhancements. All were repainted in a Deep Bordeaux metallic paint that was accented by black ghost rally stripes, and the cars were given a color-matched fabric top and a painted matte silver windshield frame.

The limited-edition vehicle was $75,000 and officially debuted on October 19, 2010. An example was highlighted on NBC's *Today Show* and was on display at Neiman Marcus's flagship store in Dallas, Texas. They were available through a dedicated phone reservation line and sold out in 3 minutes.

2013 Camaro Hot Wheels Special Edition

Total	1,524	Coupe	1,210		
		Convt.	310		
Trim	**Style**	**Total**	**T**	**Total**	
2LT (3.6L V-6)	Coupe	297	A	263	
			6	34	
	Convt.	54	A	46	
			6	8	
2SS (6.2L V-8)	Coupe	913	A	559	
			6	354	
	Convt.	260	A	203	
			6	57	
US	1,284	Coupe	974		
		Convt.	310		
Canada	36	Coupe	32		
		Convt.	4		
Mexico	96	Coupe	96		
Europe	108	Coupe	108		

When Hot Wheels rolled out its radical 1/64-scale toy cars in 1968, its first "Sweet Sixteen" lineup included a "Custom Camaro" that was modeled after a modified 1967 Camaro. In 2011, Chevrolet teamed with Hot Wheels to begin the process of producing a life-size version.

The 2013 Hot Wheels Special Edition came in Kinetic Blue Metallic paint and had a wide single stripe.

2011 SEMA Show Car

The first step was showing a radical concept at that year's SEMA Show that attempted to capture the toy's unique Spectraflame metallic paint. Coming in a variety of colors, its candied look was achieved through a transparent lacquer tint applied over a polished zinc plated casting.

Bringing that kind of radiant finish to a full-size vehicle proved difficult, but Chevrolet painters achieved it by using two primers, three color coats, and three final clear coats to achieve the final Vegas Green color. In addition, the vehicle received other touches from the toy car, including a custom hood with eight air extractors and a headlight and grille surround painted black.

Launch and Rollout

In 2013, marking the 45th anniversary of the toy's launch, Chevrolet offered the Hot Wheels Special Edition. It was available to order from January through June 2013 with no set minimum or maximum quantity.

It included the RS Appearance Package and was available on coupes and convertibles in either 2LT or 2SS trims. Much of the show car was retained, but a few major changes were made.

The wild chrome paint seen at SEMA was impossible to replicate, failing the validation process and thus being canceled. Still wanting the cars to stand out, the Camaro team dug into the GM archives and repurposed a blue that was slated to be used on a special-edition Saturn Sky roadster. Applied to the Hot Wheels vehicles, it was rebranded as Kinetic Blue Metallic and became the package's exclusive color. Chevrolet returned to SEMA in 2012 with a production version bearing that color before the run of vehicles went on sale in 2013.

The black interior featured red stitching and (upon arrival at dealerships) red-edge floor mats that the dealerships installed onsite.

Large Hot Wheels logos were embroidered into the seat backs.

The iconic Hot Wheels lick of flame logo was featured on fender badges and on a rear decklid badge.

Exclusive Changes

Exclusive exterior adornments featured a black center stripe with a large matte center section that was outlined by a satin edge. It ran on the hood, roof (on coupes), and rear decklid. To mirror that appearance, convertibles had a small section applied to the top center section of the windshield frame.

One of the stripe's unique aspects was its overall fit and finish. It wrapped over the individual body panels, including tucking behind the leading edge of the hood and behind the windshield in true custom-car fashion. That extended to include other black graphics that were added for styling emphasis: one ahead of the grille on the front fascia that was highlighted with a red outer stripe and one on the rear panel that was positioned between the taillights. That extreme attention to detail was made possible due to installation by an outside stage-two supplier that came to the Oshawa Assembly Plant, in Oshawa, Ontario, Canada, to complete the assembly on the Camaros.

Another distinct touch was graphics flaring over the rear quarter panels. This culminated in licks of Hot Wheels-esque fire. The translucent decal was specifically designed to achieve a custom ghost-flames effect that allowed the special blue paint to read partially through, making the illusion work.

The vehicle's front fenders were adorned with Hot Wheels badges that matched one on the rear decklid. More logos were added inside the cabin: at the base of the steering wheel, embroidered on the front seats, and on unique sill plates.

ZL1 and Factory Accessory Add-Ons

Part of the package's charm of exclusivity was its inclusion of many components from the top-tier ZL1. This included its black lower rocker panels, rear spoiler (coupes only), and distinct grille. Naturally, the chrome and red ZL1 badging was left off the driver's side, and the embossed imprint that was left behind was covered with a plastic plate bearing the Hot Wheels logo.

Red interior stitching in 2013 was another ZL1 exclusive, but it was included on the Hot Wheels black leather upholstery, which was further highlighted with Carbon Flash metallic–colored door and dash panel inserts.

The package included factory accessories, such as a front splitter, rear diffuser, and the accessory 21-inch five-spoke wheels, which were the largest factory offering that year. Normally, the cars were painted silver, but the ones included on the Hot Wheels edition were painted gloss black and featured a machined-cut mill face. Both sets featured a red outer flange but were made more appropriate on the Hot Wheels edition, as it further harkened back to the iconic toys red-line tires.

Upon arriving to dealerships, three additional Chevrolet accessory items were installed: red-edged floor mats, a black engine cover, and decals to darken the exterior side gills on the quarter panels.

After purchase, Chevrolet sent original owners an email with instructions on how to print a certificate with details that included the VIN and purchase date of the car.

The red wheel outline mimicked the look of the retro Hot Wheels toys.

Indy 500 Festival Cars

For the 2013 Indianapolis 500, Chevrolet made 52 Hot Wheels Edition convertibles available that spring for use by race directors. These festival cars received additional cosmetic touches, such as graphics on the doors, rear fenders, and windshield.

Collectible 1/64-Scale Versions

As part of the promotion and fanfare, Hot Wheels released a 1/64-scale version that mimicked the look of the full-size car. Two separate versions were created.

The more exclusive version was given away at the 2012 SEMA Show. In the spirit of the 1968 originals, it featured Spectraflame flames and came in an acrylic display case.

2013 Camaro Hot Wheels Edition: Package Additions			
Package Price	$6,995		
Factory Options	• RS appearance package • ZL1 lower rocker panels, rear spoiler (coupes only) and grille		
Paint	Kinetic Blue Metallic	Interior	Black
Wheels	21-inch black-painted aluminum with red outline		
Exterior	Graphics	• Center black two-tone stripe • Grille graphic with red outline • Beltline ghost flame stripe • Tail panel blackout graphic	
	Badges	Grille, fenders, and decklid	
Interior	• Sill plates • Embroidered seat inserts • Red stitching • Carbon Flash Metallic inserts • Steering wheel badge • Red-edged floor mats* • Painted black engine cover* • Sill gill decals*		

*Dealer-installed

As to be expected, 1/64-scale versions were created by Hot Wheels and were given away at the SEMA Show in Las Vegas and sold in stores. The ultra-large blister card was hung on the rearview mirror of cars that were displayed in showrooms.

The other version came on Hot Wheels's traditional blister card. Examples were given away at new car auto shows around the country. It was later offered under the HW Showroom line and was available in green too. A second green version was released through the company's HW Dream Garage series, but the looks differ from the full-size vehicle.

2018 Camaro Hot Wheels Edition

Building on the 2013 Hot Wheels Special Edition, Chevrolet and Hot Wheels teamed up again in 2018 to celebrate the toy company's 50th Anniversary with a second special edition. As with the first, it was available on 2LT and 2SS coupes and convertibles.

Originally, design plans called for a white vehicle paired with red accents that would have paired well with the distinct red Hot Wheels logo. At the time, a second special Camaro was being put together that featured Crush Orange paint and accents. To streamline marketing efforts, the Hot Wheels package was wrapped up into that effort.

Exclusive Content

All the vehicles were painted in an exclusive Crush Orange paint that mimicked the orange color on the iconic plastic tracks used by Hot Wheels 1/64-scale toy cars for decades. Orange was also a Spectraflame color offered in 1968.

Total	1,676	Coupe		1,477	
		Convt.		384	
		Coupe		Convt.		Total
		2LT	2SS	2LT	2SS	
All Countries		359	1,118	54	330	1,861
4 cyl.	Manual	9	0	1	0	10
	Auto.	39	0	2	0	41
6 cyl.	Manual	32	0	3	0	35
	Auto.	279	0	48	0	327
8 cyl.	Manual	0	246	0	46	292
	Auto.	0	872	0	284	1156
US		340	1,005	52	279	1,676
4 cyl.	Manual	8	0	1	0	9
	Auto.	35	0	2	0	37
6 cyl.	Manual	31	0	3	0	34
	Auto.	266	0	46	0	312
8 cyl.	Manual	0	222	0	38	260
	Auto.	0	783	0	241	1,024
Canada		19	113	2	51	185
4 cyl.	Manual	1	0	0	0	1
	Auto.	4	0	0	0	4
6 cyl.	Manual	1	0	0	0	1
	Auto.	13	0	2	0	15
8 cyl.	Manual	0	24	0	8	32
	Auto.	0	89	0	43	132

The package included dual Satin Graphite stripes with Silver Ice Metallic accents. The stripe graphics wrapped over the leading edge of the hood, marking the first time for this effect

The Hot Wheels Edition returned in 2018, marking the toy company's 50th anniversary. It's exclusive "Crush" orange paint harkened to the color of the plastic track used by the 1/64-scale cars.

Special badges were mounted on the fenders with the "50th" section mimicking the iconic track loop section of the toy cars.

on a sixth-generation Camaro's stripes. While the 2013 Hot Wheels Edition Camaro featured a single stripe that ran on the roof (or windshield frame for convertibles), the 2018 version's stripes were left off there, harkening back to the Camaros of the 1960s. To accent the distinct look, the brake calipers were painted orange as well and received "CAMARO" script that color matched to the rest of the car.

The cabin matched the exterior, featuring a Jet Black interior with exclusive orange accents.

The Camaro's profile was embossed on the front-seat headrests.

A special "50th" anniversary badge was created and featured a subtle loop in the zero that mimicked the loops in the toy tracks. It was mounted on the front fenders and featured a black background that matched the car's center stripes.

The package included unique lightweight 20-inch Satin Graphite wheels that were based on one of the forged Chevrolet Accessories wheels but were given a unique spoke pattern with a milled face. On SS models, they were wrapped in summer tires. Satin Graphite center caps were included and featured "flow-ties" that matched the other outlined Chevrolet emblems in the grille and on the rear panel.

Inside the cabin, all cars received Jet Black leather-appointed interiors with exclusive orange seat inserts, seatbelts, accent stitching, and kneepads on the doors and center console.

Other content included illuminated sill plates, embossed front-seat headrests, and an anniversary Hot Wheels logo at the base of the steering wheel.

Factory Accessory Add-Ons

As with previous special-edition fifth- and sixth-generation Camaros, the 2018 Hot Wheels Camaros leveraged existing Chevrolet Accessories parts by including them in the package.

The blacked-out "alternative finish" taillamps, which were either an accessory or included in the ZL1 package, were standard. They were complemented with the accessory rear blackout panel, which did not wrap over as with the 2013 editions but instead cut short of the panel's radius. Other blacked-out options included the front and rear bowtie emblems.

The front accessory lower SS grille normally included body-color inserts and a red SS badge. In this case, it was painted and featured Galvano Chrome inserts and dark gray SS badging. The accessory ground effects kit was included but was painted Satin Graphite.

Inside, the premium carpeted floor mats in Jet Black were included but with orange stitching and no center logo. Another unique touch was the inclusion of suede inserts on the steering

Blacked-out taillamps were part of the package along with a center blacked-out graphic that had a Hot Wheels logo.

wheel, center console, dashboard, and doors. Usually, that feature was reserved for the ZL1 trim.

Commemorative Box Gift

Original owners received a special gift from Chevrolet shortly after the purchase in the form of a box set of orange Hot Wheels Camaro cars. The pair included a reproduced 1968 Redline version and the 2018 special edition. Also included was a metal data card that had individual vehicle specifications and its sequence number.

2018 Camaro Hot Wheels Special Edition: Package Additions			
Factory Options	• Blackout taillamps • Blacked-out bowtie emblems (front and rear) • Accessory SS lower grille with Galvano Chrome inserts and dark gray SS badges • Accessory ground effects kit (painted Satin Graphite) • ZL1 suede inserts (steering wheel, center console dash, and door)		
Paint	Insery (Orange)	Interior	Jet Black
Wheels	20-inch Satin Graphite with milled faces with matching center caps		
Brakes	Orange-painted calipers with "CAMARO" script		
Exterior	Graphics	• Satin Graphite Stripes with Silver Ice Metallic accents • Blackout tail panel graphic with "HW" logo	
	Fender badges		
Interior	• Orange accents: seat inserts, seatbelts, stitching, kneepads, and center console • Illuminated sill plates • Embossed front seat headrests • Steering-wheel badge		
Accessories	Commemorative gift box (personalized data card and pair of 1/64-scale Hot Wheels diecast cars)		
Package Price	$4,995		

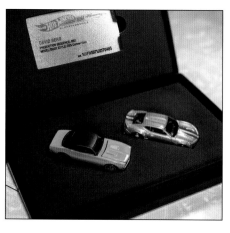

An exclusive touch was a commemorative gift box that contained two 1/64-scale Hot Wheels cars: a 1968 Redline version along with a modern version.

Indy 500

This edition was used in preparation for the 2018 Indianapolis 500 race as festival cars. Fifty 2SS convertibles were loaned out during the months of April and May. Along with the Hot Wheels additions, the cars also received unique fender and door graphics that were colored-keyed to the graphite and black colors of the Hot Wheels package.

COPO

For 2018, the option was given to apply the Hot Wheels package to the race-only COPO Camaro. Of the 69 built that year, 29 received the package. The vehicle on display at the SEMA Show was painted Supercrush Orange, which was a different hue from the rest of the run. The rest of the set reverted to receive the standard Crush Orange paint. The package also included up-level wheels in Matte Gray with Satin Graphite Metallic stripes that were painted on. It also included Silver Ice Metallic accent stripes in vinyl.

Both front and rear bowtie badges were black, the taillights and third brake light were darkened, and front and rear side-marker lamps used clear covers. Hot Wheels badges were mounted on the front fenders. The anniversary logo was also used on a large vinyl graphic on the rear quarter panels.

Inside, due to the vehicles being designed for competition, the sole additions were the special sill plates and steering-wheel logo.

	Serial	Engine	NA*	SC**		Serial	Engine	NA*	SC**
1•	1	350 SC	-	X	16	37	350 SC	-	X
2	2	427	X	-	17	38	350 SC	-	X
3	6	350 SC	-	X	18	40	427	X	-
4	11	350 SC	-	X	19	41	427	X	-
5	18	427	X	-	20	44	350 SC	-	X
6	20	350 SC	-	X	21	45	350 SC	-	X
7	21	427	X	-	21	46	427	-	-
8	22	350 SC	-	X	22	50	350 SC	-	X
9	23	350 SC	-	X	23	53	350 SC	-	X
10	26	350 SC	-	X	24	55	427	X	-
11	27	350 SC	-	X	25	56	350 SC	-	X
12	31	350 SC	-	X	26	57	350 SC	-	X
13	32	350 SC	-	X	27	59	350 SC	-	X
14	34	427	X	-	28	60	350 SC	-	X
15	35	427	X	-	29	69	350 SC	-	X
*	Racer's Package: Naturally aspirated engine ($2,100), included a weight box, dual batteries, carbon-fiber air intake, and parachute package.								
**	Racer's Package: Supercharged engine ($1,650), included a weight box, dual batteries, carbon-fiber air intake and intercooler quick-change coupling.								
•	2018 SEMA Show car with different orange paint.								

In 2018, a Hot Wheels package was offered on the race-only COPO Camaros. The vehicle that debuted at the SEMA Show wore a different paint hue that was labeled as Supercrush Orange.

The interior featured Dusk Mojave–colored leather paired to yellow stitching on the shift knob, center armrest, and steering wheel.

2013 Camaro Dusk Edition

Total	1,012		Coupe	854
			Convt.	158
2LT	Coupe		Auto.	318
			Man.	24
	Convt.		Auto.	56
			Man.	1
2SS	Coupe		Auto.	307
			Man.	205
	Convt.		Auto.	69
			Man.	32
			Total	1,012

The 2013 Dusk Edition Camaro was derived from a concept vehicle that Chevrolet displayed at the 2009 SEMA Show in Las Vegas, Nevada.

The cosmetic package was available on the 2LT and 2SS trims in the coupe and convertible (which received a blue top) bodystyles and came with the RS Appearance Package.

The vehicles were painted in an exclusive Blue Ray Metallic paint that was a brand-new color for 2013, and they were equipped with unique 21-inch Bright Silver painted wheels that were wrapped in low-profile summer tires.

The 2013 Dusk Edition added Blue Ray Mojave paint and blue convertible top. A total of 1,012 were built.

Inside the cabin, there was caramel-colored Dusk Mojave leather on the seats, door panels, and dashboard. Yellow stitching adorned the shift knob, center armrest, and steering wheel. Rounding out the package were Chevrolet Accessories premium floor mats, painted Blue Ray Metallic door inserts, and Ice Blue ambient lighting.

2015 Green Flash Edition

The 2015 Green Flash Edition was shown at the 2014 SEMA Show but left unnamed, being simply called the SS Special Edition. That was intentional because Chevrolet then invited enthusiasts to come up with an appropriate title. The winner was Green Flash.

The package was applied to 2SS trims with leather upholstery, and it came with the RS Appearance Package. It was available as a coupe or convertible.

It received Emerald Green Metallic paint (code G7J), which was exclusive but not new. The color had been rolled out in 2014 on the Corvette as Lime Rock Green. The special Camaros also received Cyber Gray stripes. Instead of being gloss black, the SS hood was painted in the green color, too, along with the lower ground effects, shark-fin antenna, and the ZL1 rear spoiler. The package's 21-inch wheel design was the same as found on the 2013 Dusk Edition but chromed.

A total of 811 cars were created: 729 coupes and 82 convertibles.

The 2015 Green Flash Edition featured Emerald Green paint (code G7J) and 21-inch chrome wheels.

CHAPTER 5

THE 1960s: DEALER PERFORMANCE PROGRAMS

After the Camaro's September 1966 launch and subsequent news that the 396-ci V-8 was the largest factory engine offering, it wasn't long before a dealer race was on.

Around the country, Chevrolet dealerships, realizing their easy accessibility (via their in-house parts department) to the larger 427ci V-8 engine that was found in Corvettes and full-size cars, such as the Biscayne and Impala, scrambled to get the engine installed in Camaros. It was filling a void in the marketplace because that's what lead-foot customers wanted and were willing to pay for.

The Motor Maverick: Dick Harrell

One of the leaders at the forefront of the emerging 1960s 427 conversion trend was Dick Harrell, who was a skilled driver, mechanic, and passionate enthusiast. Harrell's talent didn't go unnoticed. In late 1965, Chicago dealership Nickey Chevrolet offered him a full-time job as a performance advisor.

When the first few Camaros arrived to the Nickey lot in September 1966, Dick was immediately under their hoods. True to his nature, he wanted to make them faster and saw massive potential. In a short time, he developed the Nickey 427 Camaro.

BONUS CONTENT

Scan to view the prominent dealership players and partners of the 1960s 427 Camaro conversions.

www.cartechbooks.com/ ct658-qr25

BONUS CONTENT

Scan to view Harrell's 427-Camaro career path.

www.cartechbooks.com/ ct658-qr26

Nickey Chevrolet offered a range of performance modifications to Camaro customers. Traction bars and mag wheels were usual add-ons.

1967 Nickey 427 Camaro: Package Contents

The prepared package included three engine options with the flagship being the factory's forbidden fruit: an L72 427-ci V-8. It was available in two performance levels: 425-hp with a 4-barrel carburetor or 435 hp with three 2-barrel carburetors.

For customers working with smaller budgets, Harrell made a third option available by utilizing the stock 396 engine. All engines could receive a hotter cam or headers with other upgrades, including traction bars, an optional fiberglass hood and various rear-end gears. A heavy-duty Turbo Hydra-Matic 400 automatic transmission was available to be swapped in as well. For optimal performance, customers could have Harrell blueprint their engines.

From the get-go, Harrell set the cars up to run in AHRA classes with the organization approving them for competition use on October 9, 1966.

This is the site of Bill Thomas Race Cars at 510 E. Julianna St. in Anaheim, California. In addition to modifying Camaros, this is where Thomas and his crew assembled his unique Cheetah race cars.

offered a special deal. The company would pay for a customer's airline ticket from anywhere in the states to go to Chicago on his or her way to pick up a new 427 Camaro.

In addition to the engine swaps, Stage 1, Stage 2, and Stage 3 kits were offered to further boost performance on Camaros equipped with V-8 engines smaller than 350 ci. Assorted items were also available, such as a transparent distributor cap, exhaust headers, traction bars, and competition ring-and-pinion gearsets.

Like its contemporaries, Nickey would install whatever engine upgrades the customer was willing to pay for. In this case, an L88 was mounted under the hood. It can be identified by its "IT" stamping.

Partnering with Bill Thomas

Nickey introduced a third partner for its 427 Camaro venture in the form of Bill Thomas, who was a Corvette road race tuner and professional speed contractor. Besides utilizing some of his designed parts in the conversions, his race car shop in Anaheim, California, was set up in early 1967 as Nickey's west coast distribution center.

There, not only did they build Dick's 427 Camaros but they also carried the complete line of Nickey high-performance parts. Because of his connections, it's likely that Harrell facilitated the union. To create a splash in the marketplace, Nickey

The Hurst Super Shifter was added in the early 1970s by a previous owner, moving the manual shifter even closer to the driver.

Harrell Moves On

Despite the flurry of activity, Harrell didn't stay at Nickey long. Crafty Canonsburg, Pennsylvania, Chevrolet dealer Don Yenko caught wind of the activities, and in the spring of 1967, he swooped in and hired away the master motorsports mechanic.

Yenko was regrouping from a stalled partnership with Dana Chevrolet. Well-versed in road racing, straight-line speed wasn't fully Yenko's forte. As with his dealer peers, he also saw the lucrative potential in that kind of hot product. In late November 1966, Yenko and Dana formed an agreement and alliance. Dana, located in Southern California, was an early adopter of the 427-conversion program. It, too, had developed a hopped-up Camaro, and the dealership joined forces with Yenko in a reciprocal deal. In exchange for Yenko distributing the Dana 427 Camaro at Yenko's east coast location, Dana in turn sold Yenko's COPO Corvair Stinger in Southern California.

It had the makings of a deal made in hot rod heaven, but it was one that didn't last. Nearly as soon as it started, Yenko and Dana split ways. Yenko still wanted in on the 427 Camaro game, which made someone with Harrell's skill set a hot commodity.

Whatever sum or arrangement he offered Dick was enough to entice the veteran racer to leave Nickey, open his own shop, and build a new iteration of 427 Camaros.

Despite the legend's leaving, Nickey pressed on, leaning more on its relationship with Bill Thomas for proper know-how. This second iteration of vehicles was the called Nickey/Thomas 427 Camaros. Branding was simple and was typically limited to chrome Nickey lettering on the front fenders.

Conversions continued until the dealership's close in 1973. For the most part, the dealer's gamble paid off. Its performance parts business eclipsed expectations so much so that it forewent any dabbling in the subsequent COPO Camaros, seeing more value in upselling individual components than whole cars.

Nickey Performance: 2010–2023

In 2004, the Nickey name was revived and relaunched by Stefano Bimbi under the "Nickey Performance" name. No longer part of a dealership and now solely a performance tuner, operations were first based in St. Charles, Illinois, and then were moved to the current location in Loves Park, Illinois.

Joining in the effort was Don Swiatek, Nickey Chevrolet's high-performance cars and parts manager, and Ronnie Kaplan, the racing crew chief and engineer.

In the early days, this example was a regular at Great Lakes Dragaway in Union Grove, Wisconsin. It still resides in the Chicago area.

Since 2010, Nickey Performance has been crafting and creating performance-oriented Camaros imbued with a touch of retro flair.

In 2010, with the return of the fifth-generation Camaro, the shop developed three stages of performance that have carried on until today.

The shop was also called on to modify the 15 Camaros that were part of the 2014–2015 Hot Rod Edition.

Stages of Performance

The Stage I package typically involves external bolt-on components, such as upgraded exhaust and a high-flow cold-air intake system, as well as an engine tune. Nine vehicles have been created to date.

The Stage II builds on the Stage I packages and includes internal engine work, such as upgraded cylinder heads and camshafts. Fifty-seven vehicles have been created to date.

With plenty of power, modern Nickey Camaros pack serious straight-line capability.

Following the nomenclature of the 1960s, modern Nickey Camaros can be upgraded with Stage I, II, and III engine packages. This example is equipped with a ZL1 Stage I 900-hp option.

The top-tier Stage III is an engine swap using the LS7 427-ci Corvette-based LS engine. Customers can also add power adders, such as superchargers and twin turbochargers that receive S and TT to their designations. Eleven vehicles have been created to date.

General cosmetic additions for all three stages over the years have included a stinger-style hood, side stripes, embroidered front seat headrests, and door sill plates.

Vehicles are identified by a serialized plate that is riveted in the driver's doorjamb and with stickers at the base of the windshield.

1967 Yenko Super Camaro

In January 1967, the Harrells packed up and left Chicago, moving to Collinsville, Illinois. There, near the St. Louis International Raceway, Dick found a modest garage. At the end of spring, he opened the doors to his new Harrell Speed Center.

Interior additions can include items such as embroidered floor mats and front seat headrests as well as houndstooth seat inserts.

Like its contemporaries, the 1967 Yenko Camaro had a clean, understated exterior look. The fender badges are the same ones that were used on 427-equipped Impalas.

Dick Harrell helped Don Yenko develop his Camaro program's 427 conversion. This example, a YS-706, received the 450-hp package in July 1967.

The package added a lower gauge cluster and dash-mounted Stewart Warner tachometer in the cabin.

This Royal Plum example, YS-706, was sold new at Jay Kline Chevrolet, in Minneapolis Minnesota. It cost $4,214,95.

With Don Yenko trusting development of his new 427 Yenko Camaro to Harrell, the racer set to work. In short order, the master craftsman produced the Yenko Super Camaro. Power again came from a transplanted 427 short-block. It was available in both 410- and 450-hp variants, depending on if hydraulic or mechanical lifters were used.

As with Nickey's Camaro, other available upgrades included chrome valve covers, gauges, mag wheels, traction bars, exhaust headers, and a fiberglass Corvette stinger-style hood. As was common with his peers, Yenko occasionally raided his existing parts department for dress-up doodads. As such, items like Corvette "4-2-7" badge numerals were added to the front fenders.

In addition to a solid final product, Yenko benefited from Harrell's name recognition. In advertisements and marketing, he cited engineering credit to the straight-line hero who was well-known amongst enthusiasts. They also made personal appearances at dealerships together, with ads calling Harrell "Mr. Chevrolet of Drag Racing" and Yenko "Mr. Chevrolet of Sports Cars."

Things got off to a rolling start with Harrell's new team building cars from February into the summer, charging Yenko $91 in labor for each conversion. Twenty-two were completed before the pair had a financial disagreement that led to them parting ways in the fall of 1967.

Needing to continue to fulfill orders, Yenko converted the rest of his 1967 run back at his dealership. Some additional 60 cars received 427 engines. They were sold throughout Yenko's sprawling dealer network that now spanned as far south as Texas, as far west as Utah, and as far north as Ontario, Canada.

BONUS CONTENT

Scan to view 1967 Yenko Camaro production log.

www.cartechbooks.com/ ct658-qr27

Dick Harrell Performance Center: 1968–1970 Dick Harrell Super Camaros

Needing more space and being more than ready to scale his own ventures, Harrell moved again. This time, his family headed across the state, settling in Kansas City, Missouri. On January 1, 1968, he opened the Dick Harrell Performance Center, at 11114 Hickman Dr. The central location was ideal. Harrell could travel to national competitions while the larger building allowed an even bigger scale of the operations.

Lessons Learned Lead to Harrell Program

Speed equipment was sold in front, and out back, mechanics worked on the cars Harrell fielded in AHRA drag meets. By now, the team had grown to include 12 mechanics, parts specialists, machinists, and a painter nicknamed Oop.

While juggling a full-time racing career with a bustling speed shop and a joint ZL1 venture with Fred Gibb, Harrell found time to launch his own modified Super Camaro program.

From his experience working with Yenko, Harrell learned the ins and outs of a vehicle distribution program. As such, he applied those valuable lessons and established his own dealer network. The car he'd be delivering would be Harrell-branded Chevrolets. Harrell started with his new race sponsor, Courtesy Chevrolet, which had locations in Southern California as well as in Phoenix, Arizona. From there, he branched out further, connecting with dealers as far away as Florida, Michigan, Illinois, and Colorado. His closest dealership was Bill Allen Chevrolet in Kansas City, Missouri.

Those partners took orders and shipped stock SS 396 Camaros to Harrell's facility for modification. As he did before, Harrell removed the engine and exchanged it for a blueprinted 427 short-block. It was covered up with a custom fiberglass hood. Other touches included Cragar wheels, Sun gauges, and 427 emblems where the 396 ones were previously mounted.

Always one for more power, Harrell offered many other options. Items such as a Tri-Power intake, Holley carburetor, and exhaust headers could all be added. For the ultimate performance, an L88 427-ci V-8 could be installed. Stewart Warner gauges, traction bars, and both AHRA- and NHRA-approved scattershields were tacked on as well.

In 1970, Harrell rolled out a new program, installing LS6 454-ci V-8s under the hood of Camaros. Those and all other efforts halted with his sudden death in a Funny Car racing accident. At age 39, Dick died on September 12, 1971, at the Toronto International Dragway.

1967–1969 Yenko Camaro

After parting with Dick Harrell, Don Yenko brought his 427 Camaro program in-house. His team quickly got the hang of it, finishing strong and rolling out a robust program for 1968.

If his time with Harrell taught him one thing, it was the urgent need for streamlining the conversion process. Hiring technicians (whether inside or outside his organization) to remove the existing engine was labor intensive. It also resulted

Harrell tried various exterior treatments. This 1969 Camaro received a wide center stripe.

Harrell's Camaro program progressed into the model's second generation. This 1971 Tuxedo Black example was built in April 1971, exchanging its 396-ci V-8 for a 454-ci V-8.

Yenko's 1968 Camaro program quickly developed a more consistent look—as is shown on this example, a YS-8027.

in the hassle of selling the extracted 396-ci V-8s and any other swapped-out components.

1968 Yenko Camaro

Unlike his peers, Yenko was the first to the take the initiative to do something about it. His solution was to take on the impossible: convince Chevrolet to install the 427-ci V-8 right on the factory floor. Even though it wasn't offered through an existing RPO, Yenko had experience leveraging the system.

In 1966 and 1967, he created 125 race-ready Corvairs. Those came to fruition by using the overlooked Central Office Production Order. It had been in place since the close of World War II, and the paperwork was used for any out-of-the-ordinary new car requests. Until Yenko's Corvairs, it had been primarily used for fleet and commercial applications.

Yenko saw an opportunity to use it to skirt the company's mandated RPO rules to get a factory-created 427 Camaro. Approaching Vince Piggins and other GM contacts about the idea, Yenko's request was not approved. There was no doubt that Chevrolet liked the idea, but it remained cautious in its effort to avoid government intervention.

Still, all wasn't lost with the endeavor. Chevrolet granted Yenko the ability to alter some components on Camaros ordered through a COPO.

After arriving to Yenko Chevrolet, technicians would perform the short-block conversion, upgrading the L78 396 to the L72 427.

As part of COPO 9737, a 140-mph speedometer was installed.

an M21 4-speed manual transmission, a 4.10 Positraction rear differential, and a higher-CFM carburetor. Under the hood was a 396-ci V-8 engine, and all of his 1968 COPO Camaros received the special "Magic Mirror" trim tag that was often used on export Camaros.

All of this set them up nicely for the 427 short-block conversion that would come upon their arrival in Canonsburg. Seventy SS 396–equipped Camaros were ordered. A few cars received Yenko's cosmetic changes but retained the 396 engine.

The red, white, and blue Yenko crest was added to the front fenders next to the factory badging.

COPO 9737

Yenko took advantage of being able to alter some of the Camaro's components. Under COPO 9737, which was referred to as the Sports Car Conversion, his cars received a 140-mph speedometer (an upgrade over the factory 120-mph unit) and a larger 1-1/16-inch sway bar that required special mounting plates inside the frame.

The batch also received options such as front disc brakes,

1968 Yenko Camaro: Factory COPO 9737 Additions
Referred to as: Sports Car Conversion
• 140-mph speedometer
• 1-1/16-inch front sway bar (requiring special mounting plates inside the frame)
• Front disc brakes
• M21 4-speed manual transmission
• QD 4.10 Posi rear differential
• MV-coded L78 396-ci V-8
• Carburetor (part number 3935519 and sourced from 1968 L88)
• Magic-Mirror acrylic lacquer trim tag

Fiberglass Components

On the exterior, a fiberglass, dual-inlet hood was installed, and it was secured with hood pins. At the rear, several various decklid treatments were offered. Initially, a custom one-piece fiberglass decklid that incorporated a spoiler was created. A handful were installed on some of the early converted cars that hadn't been equipped with RPO D80 front and rear spoilers.

This type of decklid showed up on a brochure that advertised the 1968 Camaro, but it was readily apparent that it didn't fit well. It's likely that when Yenko ordered the cars, he was aware of the factory spoiler option. He likely figured that he'd create a superior lightweight custom-crafted unit to upsell to customers—just as he had with the Stinger. It wouldn't have taken long to see that getting them made, fitted properly, painted, and then installed back on each vehicle wasn't efficient or cost-effective.

For a sleeker look, the gas cap was painted matte black. It was then flanked by Yenko's custom badging.

This promotional photo clearly shows Yenko's second attempt at a spoiler. (Courtesy of the Barr Collection)

Scaling back on the second version, it was just a custom fiberglass lip spoiler that fit to the factory steel decklid. It mounted flush and peaked slightly higher in the center with the rear edge extending to and covering the rear edge of the factory decklid. It had wooden inserts and was attached with wood screws.

Finally, the third and more common option was for the cars to retain the factory D80 rear spoiler. The option also included a chin spoiler.

Rally II Wheels

To upgrade the stamped, base Camaro wheels, Yenko leveraged a friendship with a connection at nearby Arnold Pontiac in Houston, Pennsylvania. The dealership was less than a mile from his shop, and allegedly, the two swapped parts and extended deals and discounts regularly.

Pontiac had its steel mag-type 14x6 Rally II 14x6 wheel that was available on its pony car, the Firebird. Yenko purchased enough sets from Arnold to use them on all his incoming COPO Camaros. The SS Camaro's F-70-14 red-line tires were installed with them.

To cover Pontiac's black plastic disc center cap that read "PMD" for Pontiac Motor Division, Yenko overlaid it with a special emblem with a red letter "Y" for Yenko in a sans-serif font on a black background.

Yenko leveraged a relationship with nearby Arnold Pontiac in Houston, Pennsylvania, to source Pontiac mag-type Rally II wheels with unique center caps. They were wrapped with the SS Camaro's F-70-14 red-line tires.

1968 Yenko Camaro: Canonsburg Changes			
	Item	Description	Location/Notes
Engine	427-ci V-8	Short block conversion from 396-ci V-8	Engine bay
Exterior	Hood	Fiberglass with dual inlet and hood pins	Equipped with cold-air block-out plate and hood prop
	Decklid/ Spoiler	Fiberglass unit	Mounted on early cars; later cars utilized D80, which included a chin spoiler
	Gas Cap	Painted matte black	Center rear tail panel
Badging	427	Cast aluminum	Front fenders and rear panel (passenger's side)
	Yenko Crest	Red, white, and blue shield	Front fenders above factory "Camaro" script and on rear panel (driver's side)
	YS Serial Plate	Numbered metal plate	Riveted inside driver's doorjamb
Wheels	Rally II	Pontiac-sourced, used stock Camaro SS F-70-14 red-line tires	Center cap features red "Y" sticker
	Yenko Atlas (optional) Cast aluminum (14x6, 15x6)		
Interior	Tachometer	Stewart Warner	Screwed into dash to the right of the steering column
	Tri-cluster Gauges	Amps, oil pressure, and water temperature	Ahead of center console

An aftermarket Stewart Warner tachometer was mounted on the dash along with a tri-gauge cluster.

Badging and YS Tags

In 1968, building on strides from his 1967 Camaro program, Yenko began to give his cars a distinct brand identity. To diminish the impact of their SS foundation, the gas caps were painted flat black to cover up the silver "SS" letters. Special cast-aluminum "427" badging was installed on the front fenders to replace the stock "396" badging. One was also installed on the rear panel.

To mark each creation, Yenko's team affixed a metal tag to the driver-side doorjamb. It was mounted with small screws on several early examples, and rivets were used on later cars.

He carried over this measure from his Corvair Stinger project in which it was crucial to keep those cars straight, marking that 100 had been completed per SCCA road racing requirements. On the Camaro, following YS (for Yenko Sports Cars), the numbers picked up with "8" for the 1968 model year.

While no stipulation existed for the drag-race oriented Camaro, Yenko must have liked the idea and continued it. Later deeming it an unnecessary step, it was dropped on Camaros he modified in 1969.

Interior

Inside the car's cabin, black textured trim was the standard finish. A Stewart Warner tachometer was screwed into the dash along with a tri-gauge package that contained Stewart Warner gauges with a black dial and white font. These gauges displayed amperage readings, oil pressure, and coolant temperature, and they were installed down low ahead of the gear selector. The gauge faces were available in either white or black, and the surrounds were mostly chrome but some had wood-grain surrounds to match the walnut wood grain on the center console and ashtray door.

On some cars, the glove box Camaro script in the bottom right corner of the door was swapped for a Yenko crest emblem.

As with his COPO Corvair Stinger program, Yenko added these numbered door tags to his 1968 Super Camaros.

The fiberglass hood gave the cars a unique look, as is shown on a YS-8013. Hood pins were also part of the package.

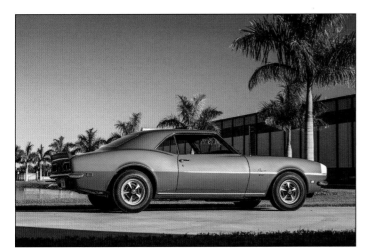

A few of Yenko's 1968 run, like this Rally Green example, received the cosmetics of the package but not the engine upgrade. Underhood is the L78 396-ci V-8.

1969 Yenko Camaro

For the 1969 model year, Yenko achieved what most thought would never happen: he worked with Chevrolet to have the factory install a 427-ci V-8 in the Camaro.

As his efforts grew more and more, Yenko defined success not as having his Camaros first in a straight line. Instead, he focused on making them first in the mind of consumers.

His solution was to deliver a clean, tidy package that could readily be scaled, scattered, and sold across his coast-to-coast dealer network. That came to fruition by finally getting Chevy to do the heavy lifting, utilizing the COPO system to get the job done.

In November 1968, corporate insider Vince Piggins gave the green light to what became COPO 9561. Camaro coupes

Part of Yenko's success with his 1969 Camaro program was his robust dealer network. This Dover White example was sold by Jack Douglass Chevrolet, in Chicago, Illinois.

ordered by Yenko would have the RPO L78 375-hp, 396-ci V-8 deleted and an L72 added—all at the Norwood plant.

That wouldn't be the only COPO these Camaros received. COPO 9737 was carried over from 1968, adding 15x7 Rally wheels with E70x15 wide tread tires, a 13/16-inch front sway bar, and a 140-mph speedometer. Out back, the cars received a 12-bolt differential housing (stamped with code BE) with 4.10 Positraction, and a heat-treated ring and pinion. There was also special shocks and a five-leaf-spring pack. The optional front disc brakes (RPO J50) were mandatory.

Two transmissions were available: an M21 4-speed manual or M40 Turbo 400 automatic. Six exterior paint colors were available: Daytona Yellow, Rally Green, Olympic Gold, Fathom Green, Lemans Blue, and Hugger Orange. Gold was dropped after the first run with only 10 being produced. All came in X66 trim.

Yenko hit paydirt for his 1969 Camaro program, getting cars delivered to his dealership already equipped with the L72 427-ci V-8. The only thing left for his team to add was a graphic on the radiator shroud.

The exterior graphics were bold yet simple, coming in either black or white. Custom 427 badges were added to either side of the hood cowl.

The cabin of these cars was clearly marked with these stickers on the front seat headrests.

The interiors were mostly left alone. The majority (171 cars) received the M-21 4-speed manual transmission.

With its mix of power and pleasing looks, the 1969 Yenko Camaro has become one of the icons of 1960s Camaro performance.

After leaving the factories, Chevy trucked them to Canonsburg. With the heavy lifting done, Yenko's team focused on branding. It applied the iconic side and hood stripes, the Yenko crest, and a new rendition of custom 427 badging. Inside, "sYc" graphics were applied to the front-seat headrests.

It was a major victory for Yenko and his efforts. Turnaround time was drastically reduced, which allowed completed vehicles to be shipped far quicker to Yenko's network of dealerships. For an all-too-brief season, Yenko was the exclusive recipient of these special vehicles. However, word leaked out. Much to his chagrin, other dealers began requesting their own special COPO Camaros.

In 1969, the COPO 9737 was carried over from year before, adding elements like a 140-mph speedometer.

1969 Yenko Camaro: Factory COPO Additions		
COPO 9561 High-Performance Unit		
RPO L72	427-ci V-8 (all built at Tonawanda, New York, plant and featured orange painted blocks, oil pans, and cylinder heads)	
RPO ZL2	Ducted cowl-induction hood	
RPO V48	Heavy-duty four-core Harrison radiator	
RPO F41	High-performance suspension with special springs and shocks	
COPO 9737 Sports Car Conversion		
15x7 Rally wheels with E70x15 wide tread tires		
140-mph speedometer		
13/16-inch front sway bar		
Mandatory Options		
RPO J50	Power front brakes	
RPO J52	Front disc brakes	

1981 Yenko Turbo-Z Camaro

Don Yenko's 1969 COPO Camaro program wasn't the last time he leveraged the central office to create small-batches of performance-oriented Chevrolets.

In 1971 and 1972, Yenko ordered a total of 400 Vegas. Reading the changing marketplace, he worked with Chevrolet to have them equipped at the factory with a turbocharger. Although that plan didn't materialize, he was able to roll that out as an in-house performance upgrade.

In 1981, still seeing the performance value in turbocharging and not being one to give up, he tried the plan again. By now, he had opened a new Chevrolet dealership at 960 Washington Rd. in McMurray, Pennsylvania, that was not far from his Canonsburg location.

Development began in late 1979, and this time, he moved back to modifying the Camaro. He didn't try to have Chevrolet install the turbos through channels such as the COPO but was going to again offer the upgrade as an in-house service. Unfortunately, he was plagued by similar woes that he encountered with his Vega Stinger project.

Inspired by its Cheverra Camaro race car, Yenko partnered with Cars and Concepts, in Brighton, Michigan, but then abandoned that plan. Further delaying the project was a change in turbocharger supplier. Initially, Yenko put together a deal with Martin, but then Martin went through financial hardship. In early 1981, Yenko turned to Turbo International in Garden Grove, California, to source his turbochargers. Boost on the final cars was set to around 6 to 7 pounds.

Further hindering progress was that any change required additional certification that created additional expense, so

Yenko was familiar with turbocharging, having already experimented with working it into a vehicle program in 1971 and 1972 with the COPO Vega Stinger.

Yenko's final modified Camaro program was working to turbocharge the model in the early 1980s.

Due to recertifying costs with the US Environmental Protection Agency, Yenko was prevented from offering a setup with a 4-speed manual transmission.

Yenko was prevented from offering a setup with a 4-speed transmission or even changing out the stock Z/28's 3.08 rear gearing.

Despite the setbacks, Yenko pressed forward. However, he fell short of his goal of building 200 cars and completed just 32, including 2 prototypes created in 1980. The package was available as Stage I and Stage II. Stage I added the turbocharger, wheels, and graphics. Stage II, which was not available with T-tops, brought additional upgrades that included a Racemark steering wheel, special floor mats, and Kamp Inc. leather seats. Both versions included "Yenko Sportscars" serial plates and were covered by GM's standard warranty and/or the turbo manufacturer's 12-month warranty. The cars were hard to sell, given their extremely high price tag.

No longer did Don adorn these Camaros with bold hood graphics like those seen on his Camaros in 1969. Instead, he went for a more subdued look. (Photo Courtesy The BC Collection)

As was his forte, Yenko branded these Camaros, foregoing exterior badging and instead just using graphics. (Photo Courtesy The BC Collection)

1967–1968 Dana 427 Camaro

Besides Dick Harrell, another early pioneer in the Camaro 427 conversions was the crew at Dana Chevrolet, which came out of the gate strong due to numerous figures who had racing backgrounds and former employment at Shelby American.

Dana Chevrolet was run by Paul Dombrowski and Peyton Cramer, who served as the location's general manager. Dombrowski and Cramer purchased Enoch Chevrolet at 8730 Long Beach Blvd. in South Gate, California. On August 26, 1966, they relaunched and opened their doors for business. Recognizing the potential, one of their first steps was getting right into racing.

Their strategy for speed included backing a Can-Am team, stocking Corvettes and developing their own 427 Camaro. By the end of October 1966, they had one together and began marketing.

For even wider distribution, they joined forces with Yenko Chevrolet in Canonsburg, Pennsylvania. A deal was inked where Dana would provide its 427 Camaro, and in return, it would carry Yenko's race-ready COPO Corvair Stinger. The arrangement fizzled out, but that didn't slow Dana's momentum.

Dana Camaros are easily recognized by their twin-inlet fiberglass hood. The option cost $125 and was made by Berry Plasti-Glass in Long Beach, California.

Dana's Hi-Performance Center: Race-Prep Services

After a full renovation, Dana Chevrolet opened a separate Hi-Performance Center on February 12, 1967. Located just a few blocks away at 9735 Long Beach Blvd., the 7,000-square-foot facility served as the flagship locale for all of Dana's performance, racing, and speed efforts.

Dana's race team was headquartered there and allotted 6 bay stalls. Another 12 stalls were set aside for customer builds, and, naturally, a fully stocked parts department was onsite.

Dana's performance center showroom is shown as it sits today in South Gate, California.

The new engine arrived without the carburetor, starter, alternator, pressure plate, clutch disc, and bellhousing. After the exchange, chrome valve covers and a chrome air cleaner were added along with Doug's racing headers. The transmission received a heavy-duty clutch disc, pressure plate, and scattershield bellhousing. Suspension stages could be tacked on along with a Sun tachometer and Stewart Warner lower gauging.

One of the unique options to Dana was a fiberglass twin-inlet hood. Made by Berry Plasti-Glass in Long Beach, California, and costing customers $125, it provided a unique and aggressive look. Chrome locking pins were optional. The overall branding on the cars was simple and usually featured chrome "DANA" letters on the front fenders.

In addition to the street version, a drag racing–oriented version was available as well that included components such as

In March 1967, veteran driver and former aerospace engineer Dick Guldstrand was hired as general manager of its operations. When the ace wheelman wasn't onsite, he would campaign his Camaro Z/28 in Trans Am competition. Meanwhile, Sales Manager Don McCain competed in a black 427 Camaro in drag racing to provide advertising for the Dana High-Performance Center.

The speed shop's services were ambitious and designed to be turnkey, offering customers a "you drive" system of racing that meant if the customer had the funds, all he or she had to do was drive. In addition to building and maintaining any kind of race vehicle (whether it was for the street, strip, slalom, or road racing), the center supplied a pit crew and transportation of vehicles to tracks. In addition, driver training was provided by one of Dana's expert racers.

The location also kept a full inventory of Corvettes and Camaro Z/28s for sale. Upon hearing of the news of the Z/28, an eager Cramer offered Chevrolet to buy all 1,000 of the proposed total that were to be built.

A customer brought this 1968 Camaro to Dana Chevrolet in April 1969 for modification, requesting a 427-ci conversion.

BONUS CONTENT

Scan to view Dana Chevrolet's key figures and roles.

www.cartechbooks.com/
ct658-qr28

427 Camaro Conversions

The facility was prime to handle 427 Camaro conversions, and they were overseen by McCain. The process included swapping the stock SS 350 and then 396 for an L72 427-ci V-8.

A Hurst shifter was installed in the cabin along with additional gauges.

a Sig Erson camshaft, Doug's headers, and heavy-duty traction bars. By April 1967, approximately 32 427-equipped Camaros had been assembled.

The Team Disbands

Despite the red-hot start, the efforts didn't last long. As fast as the team was assembled at Dana, they quickly moved on to other ventures. Guldstrand parted ways in October 1967, and he was followed by McCain in December. Next, following a fallout with Dombrowski, Cramer sold his interest in the company in February 1968 and moved on to open his own Lincoln-Mercury dealership.

With the key figures and experts gone, the efforts of the Dana High-Performance Center came to a screeching halt, and it closed in 1969. Dombrowski soldiered on but couldn't make it work. He closed the main location in the early summer of 1971.

Gorries marked its Black Panther Camaros with badges on the front fenders.

As opposed to branding, Dana's Camaro efforts mostly focused on performance modifications—building cars tailored to individual customer wants. This build included adding a spoiler.

1967 Black Panther Camaro

The craze for dealers to craft and concoct their own modified Camaros wasn't limited to the United States. Gorries Chevrolet Oldsmobile in downtown Toronto, Ontario, Canada, created its own package called the Black Panther.

Bob's wife, Lorraine, enjoyed driving the Black Panther around their home in Sault Ste. Marie, Ontario, Canada. Besides local drives, the couple vacationed in the car to cities such as Milwaukee, Wisconsin, and Traverse City, Michigan. (Photo Courtesy Simonen Family)

Bob Simonen, pictured here, was 26 years old when he purchased his Black Panther new from Gorries on April 7, 1967. (Photo Courtesy Simonen Family)

The massive three-story dealership at 28 Gerrard St. E. was the largest in Toronto. It historic ties to performance and race sponsorship. In marketing, the dealership claimed to be "Canada's Corvette Headquarters," keeping the "largest display" in stock. The man that buyers needed to see to get one was Jerry Coffey. Coffey, an enthusiastic salesman, stayed busy managing the dealership's high volume of high-performance inventory.

Besides the ready-to-roll offerings, Gorries staffed top-notch, competition-trained mechanics. One of those ace wrenches and service specialists was Doug Duncan. He was later inducted into the Canadian Motorsports Hall of Fame for his race car building prowess.

Creating the Perfect Package

Gorries management recognized and wanted to capitalize on the exploding market for tricked-out Camaros. After the car's introduction, the top staff assembled to discuss business strategies. The Black Panther was the result of their talks. It was a cosmetic package that possessed a set look and feel. In the spirit of the jungle cat name, the cars were painted black, which was accented with a gold interior and gold exterior highlights.

The name's origin is most likely tied to the fact that Chevrolet called the Camaro the Panther during development. A big-cat theme was certainly present in the 1967 model year, as rival Ford released its Mercury Cougar.

The Black Panthers were typically ordered as Sport coupes with gold Deluxe interiors and were optioned with RPO Z21 (Exterior Molding Group) and RPO Z23 (Interior Décor Group). The Deluxe interior fitted the cars with such items as

Gold Deluxe interiors were the norm, adding a striking contrast to the black exterior. Note the badge ahead of the gear selector.

If a 427-ci engine upgrade wasn't requested, the engine bay did not receive any additional items.

molded door panels, a trunk mat, seat trim, bright pedals, and roof rail moldings.

Under the hood, the vehicles usually received standard 210-hp 327-ci V-8s (LF7). This was paired to either the standard 3-speed manual transmission, an optional 4-speed manual, or an automatic.

With no hard-and-fast rules in place, RS and SS-350 Black Panthers were created as well, and even a convertible was made. At least one early car arrived at the dealership in a color that was not black, coming in Code S, Sierra Fawn. It was then painted black in the body shop. More than likely, most of the cars were ordered in Tuxedo Black (Code A), which streamlined the conversion process.

A Fancy Feline: Dealership Additions

Upon arriving at Gorries, the cars were sent directly to the dealership's body shop on the third floor where paint and body pros, such as Al Kenny, painted the gold highlights.

Up front, each car received a similar header treatment to the RPO D91 front accent band painted on Super Sport models and that year's Indianapolis pace car. As with the factory stripe, this new one was interrupted on both sides, making room for simple screwed-in black rectangle plastic badges that were adorned with chrome letters. That same badge was mounted on the passenger's side of the rear decklid under the Chevrolet badge. Another thick gold stripe (like those on Mustang GTs) was painted on the lower rocker panel.

When it was all said and done, the cars were quite attractive.

"The body shop worked extra hard buffing the black paint's acrylic lacquer finish," said Dave Hicks, who worked as a technician at the dealership from 1964 to 1967. "With the polished black paint and gold interior, they were sharp cars for the era."

Painted gold accents were added on the nose and lower rocker panels and with a pinstripe.

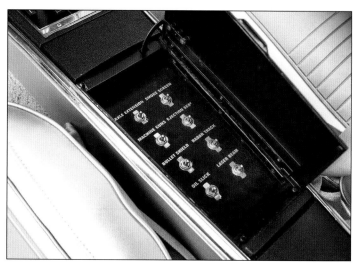

The "007" panel contained non-working switches but certainly was a conversation starter.

Other cosmetic touches included swapping the stock wheels for Magnum 500 14-inch mag-style wheels, which was a $207 option. Keeping the big-cat theme, the wheels were wrapped with Uniroyal Tiger Paw red-line tires, which was a $140 option.

All along, the planned intent was for Black Panthers to entice customers to add more go-fast parts that were available from the Gorries parts department. Those modifications were conducted on the second floor of the massive Gorries service center.

Cats On Track

To demonstrate the possibilities of their Camaro program, George Moss, one of the Gorries sales and performance managers, drove a Black Panther demonstrator with a 425-hp L72 427-ci engine. It had received a short-block conversion from the stock 396-ci V-8. The car received media attention, most notably a feature in the May 1967 edition of the *Canada Track & Traffic magazine*. While impressive, few other Black Panthers (if any) received that kind of powerplant. Many original owners were simply drawn to their cosmetic appeal and preferred to leave them as is.

BONUS CONTENT

Scan to view Gorries Chevrolet's key figures and roles.

www.cartechbooks.com/ct658-qr29

James Bond Panel

The "007 panel" was an unusual and quirky option. This surefire conversation starter cost $29 and reworked the center console into the ultimate spy-movie fanatic's fantasy.

When selected, technicians removed the stock console door. In its place, a piece of black plastic was fitted that had gold toggle switches. The non-functioning switchgear claimed to arm and deploy such high-tech spy gear as a laser beam, axle extensions, and an ejection seat. Covering the setup was a translucent acrylic panel that was attached with screws.

The whole gag was pitched by Graham Neale, a young insurance agent who hung around the dealership. While not an employee, Neale drove the blue and white 396-ci-equipped 1965 Nova Gasser that the dealership campaigned under the name "Grand Daddy Gorries."

The young gearhead was a fervent James Bond fan who never missed seeing the Sean Connery films on opening day. Besides his driving skills, he was also blessed with a persuasive gift of gab. One afternoon, Graham pitched his hair-brained idea. He sold it hard, charming dealership managers into going along with the outlandish idea.

Marketing and Distribution

Gorries heavily marketed the cars. Seeking to further expand the program, the dealership set up a franchise network. Other Chevrolet dealers in central and eastern Canada signed up to sell Black Panthers as well. Participating dealers included Myers Motors Co. in Ottawa, Ontario; Chevrolet Motor Sales of Montreal, Québec; Eastown Chevrolet, in London, Ontario; and Bob Johnson Chevrolet in Halifax, Nova Scotia.

In Windsor, not only did Webster Motors Ltd. sell the big cats but it built them too, applying the cosmetics in-house to a handful of cars. Reports of dealers in the United States selling Black Panthers have surfaced, but precise locations and quantities are unsubstantiated.

The Black Panther program was one of the first modified-Camaro programs to have a cohesive look and feel and a strong brand identity.

Legacy

Despite these and other bold marketing initiatives, the Black Panther never gained traction. The cosmetic draw to woo shoppers into showrooms worked beautifully, but the upselling initiative never materialized. Many area enthusiasts preferred to either build a high-performance Camaro themselves or recruit a full-blown race shop.

In addition, the dealership was transitioning to a new location, which pulled focus and resources away from the efforts. Gorries prime downtown location had become quite valuable. In early 1968, Gorries owner Bert Sykes sold the property to nearby Ryerson University. The staff, inventory, and operations combined with another location that Gorries owned called Golden Mile Chevrolet. This property was on Eglinton Avenue in the bustling Scarborough District of Toronto. The Black Panther was done by 1968.

While the time of the Black Panther was brief, its legacy lives on. It was one of the first dealer special-edition Camaros that possessed a distinct uniformity and brand identity. While not always fast, these cats were forward-thinking. The Gorries crew pioneered a well-rounded program that came within a whisker of scaling to unknown sales heights.

1967–1974 Baldwin Motion Camaro

Leaning on the more radical end of the spectrum were the Camaros produced in the service bays of the Motion Performance speed shop. It was located on the east coast at 598 Sunrise Hwy. in Baldwin, New York. Owner and racing enthusiast Joel Rosen wanted in on a custom Camaro. Needing a dealership partner to obtain new car inventory, Rosen teamed up with nearby Baldwin Chevrolet in Baldwin, Long Island, New York.

Initially, the young man's plan was to get Baldwin Chevrolet to sponsor him in a new 1967 Camaro set up for the Modified Production race class. It proved to be difficult, as Baldwin had no real background in speed or racing. Rosen and Baldwin Chevrolet struck a tentative deal that provided a gold Camaro for modification. Joel and his team swapped in an L-88 427-ci V-8 and put it use by competing on the track.

With that foundation, a larger roadmap was developed to scale the program. Camaros, followed by other Chevy vehicles, were sold at the dealership with financing available from General Motors Acceptance Corporation (GMAC). They'd

In New York, the Motion Performance speed shop partnered with nearby Baldwin Chevrolet to produce and sell modified Camaros.

This example received a Phase III L88 V-8 engine upgrade, fitted with aluminum cylinder heads and an aluminum high-rise intake manifold.

Many of the builds were bespoke—built to the taste, preference, and budget of a customer. As such, production was not uniform. One of Baldwin Motion's greatest assets was the relationship with Marty Schorr, a writer for *Cars* magazine, who helped with promotions and editorial content.

The conversion program continued into the Camaro's second-generation bodystyle, and like others, it was offered with 454-ci V-8 power. Eventually, the demand for extreme speed slowed, and work dried up. Baldwin Chevrolet closed in 1974, and the Motion Speed Shop carried on into the early 1980s, working on a variety of projects.

head less than a mile down the road to Motion for upgrades. Primarily, Camaros received 427 conversions. Motion also crafted custom bodywork and exterior design touches into its creations. One of its exterior hallmarks was the painted side spears that wrapped around to the rear.

The SS 427 Camaros were available in SS trim and rated at 425 hp. Starting in 1968, its Phase III version was released, which claimed more than 500 hp. It featured a Muncie 4-speed transmission and a heavy-duty suspension and radiator. Other hallmarks included red-line Wide Oval tires, chrome valve covers, striping, and emblems. It also received a Super-Bite suspension kit that was designed and engineered by Motion. It contained custom-valved shocks, front coil spring risers, and traction bars.

The Baldwin-Motion efforts continued into the model's second generation, as this 1970 example shows. As part of a Phase III upgrade, it received an LS6 454-ci V-8.

Traction bars were typically added on Camaro builds, helping to get the added power to the ground. Note the repurposed SS 427 badging that was sourced from the 1968 Impala.

## CHAPTER 6

CALLAWAY CARS

With a passion for racing and performance, Reeves Callaway spent time both as a driver and instructor before founding Callaway Cars in 1976. Focusing early on with forced induction, the team has partnered with a wide range of automotive brands, including General Motors, Land Rover, Aston Martin, and even Malibu Boats.

Over the years, Callaway Cars developed a worldwide reputation for producing limited runs of high-performance specialty vehicles with much of that spotlight on its Chevrolet sports car programs. Beginning with Corvettes in 1987, including the landmark C4 Twin Turbo Corvette known as the *Sledgehammer*, the team moved on to modify Camaros in 1993, launching its run of C8 Camaros.

Besides significant powertrain upgrades, its work typically involves radically altering the vehicle's exterior bodywork for improved aerodynamics and enhanced design. Each project undertaken is designated with "C" nomenclature followed with ascending numbers. More vehicles continue to be added to the lineup as Callaway continues to push the bounds of streetable performance.

1993–2002 Callaway SuperNatural

After years of success altering and modifying Corvettes, Callaway Cars, in Old Lyme, Connecticut, turned its attention in 1994 to the Camaro. What the company came up with was the SuperNatural C8, and the results were truly otherworldly.

This was the eighth project in the company's "C" line of vehicle projects, hence the C8 designation. A silver prototype was unveiled in January 1994 at the Los Angeles Auto Show with production beginning later that summer.

Both coupes and convertibles were offered on Z28s and then later on SS Camaros. The package was composed largely of two separate components: radical exterior bodywork known

Callaway's SuperNatural C8 featured radical bodywork and improved performance.

Only when a vehicle received both the CamAerobody and SuperNatural engine package would it became a Super-Natural C8 and receive this winged emblem on the nose panel.

as the CamAerobody and major mechanical upgrades to the engine called the SuperNatural package. Both were offered individually to customers, but when combined and installed by Callaway Cars, the complete package was called the Super-Natural C8. The cars were marked with a winged emblem on the front nose panel.

	C8	Supernatural	CamAerobody
Prototypes	1	0	0
Production	17	33	4

1993–2002 Callaway SuperNatural Camaro C8 Production			
	Type	Cpe.	Conv.
1993*	C8	2	0
	SuperNatural	4	2
1994	C8	4**	3
	SuperNatural	5	3
	CamAerobody	2	3
1995	C8	8	3
	SuperNatural	2	1
	CamAerobody	1	0
1996	C8	4	2
	SuperNatural	1	1
1997	CamAerobody	1	0
	SuperNatural	1	0
1998	C8	1	1
2002	C8***	1	1
C8	SuperNatural and CamAerobody upgrades, received winged hood badge		
SuperNatural	Engine upgrades only		
CamAerobody	Exterior body modifications only		
*	With the program rolling out in 1994, these vehicles were used cars brought to Callaway by customers for the conversions.		
**	Includes the 1994 L.A. Auto Show prototype		
***	Called a commemorative edition		
NOTE	While all the components were made available to customers for field installation, these production records are officially documented builds conducted by Callaway Cars at their Old Lyme, Connecticut, facility.		

Powertrain Upgrades

As part of the SuperNatural 400 upgrade (costing $9,965), the stock LT1 V-8 engine was stroked and overbored, increasing displacement from 350 to 383 ci. It received 10.5:1 forged alloy pistons, forged four-bolt main bearing caps, a forged nitride crankshaft, and forged H-beam connecting rods. Larger stainless-steel valves were installed in CNC-ported aluminum cylinder heads along with a roller lift camshaft. Polished aluminum valve covers engraved with large "CALLAWAY" script were optional for $388.

Callaway designed an exclusive Honker air intake option (costing $295 plus installation) that was paired with a K&N air filter. On stock engines, the special setup added 8 hp, and when paired with the SuperNatural engine upgrade, it added 19.

Callaway also offered a pair of tiered SuperNatural exhaust upgrades. The $695 cat-back option included a large-diameter intermediate pipe, dual-outlet mufflers and polished stainless-steel exhaust tips. All of that was included in the premium $1,986 package along with tubular stainless-steel Tri-Y 1-3/4-inch exhaust headers.

The engine was mated to the car's stock T-56 6-speed manual transmission. A heavy-duty Callaway shifter was optional. For $49, it was topped with a turned and anodized aluminum knob that was etched with Callaway's logo. The knob was available in colors including bright blue, red, silver, and black. With all of the upgrades, output was rated at 404 hp and 412 ft-lbs of torque. Original owners were given a lifetime warranty on the powertrain.

As part of the SuperNatural 400 upgrade, the stock engine was heavily modified to deliver 404 hp.

Suspension, Wheels, and Brake Upgrades

The vehicle's suspension received Eibach springs, adjustable Koni shocks, and a thicker front sway bar. A strut tower brace was also installed along with polyurethane bushings, trailing arms, and a tubular lateral link to stabilize the rear axle.

Three different wheel options were offered. First was 16-inch OZ Monte Carlo five-spoke wheels that accommodated the stock Z28 tires. The wheels could also be had in 17-inch sizes and then fitted with Corvette-sized GSC 275/40ZR17 tires. The premium option was a run-flat system that cost $6,067. It included cast-aluminum 17x9.5-inch Bridgestone three-spoke wheels with a bead retention wedge hump. The special wheels were first seen on the Callaway Corvette Speedster and wrapped in Expedia S-01A/M run-flat tires.

The system included low tire air pressure sensors and an available in-car warning system. Special adapters were created so that the wheels fit Chevrolet's hub bolt pattern. Less than a quarter of C8 production received the rare and forward-thinking option. For safety, the option was only installed by Callaway Cars or at an approved Callaway dealer. A fourth wheel option for OZ modular wheels with a staggered stance was shown on option sheets but never fully rolled out.

For brakes, a pair of Brembo kits was available with both exchanging the front calipers for Brembo 4-piston aluminum calipers, pads, brake lines, and vented rotors. The premium "F40" set cost $2,930 and required 17-inch wheels to accommodate 13.1-inch rotors. These were the same brakes found on Ferrari's F-40 super car, hence the option's name.

The $2,700 "Lotus" set brought 12.3-inch rotors and could be mounted with 16-inch wheels—either the stock Camaro alloy wheels or the optional OZ Monte Carlos. As the name implies, these brakes were the same ones found on the Lotus Esprit sports car. Callaway charged $455 for installation.

An available brake option (costing $2,930) added Brembo four-piston aluminum calipers and vented rotors. These were the same brake components that were on the Ferrari F40.

CamAerobody Additions

The radical performance alterations were paired to an equally striking exterior CamAerobody designed by Paul Deutschman. The fiberglass kit added a new elongated nose, rear bumper cover and side rocker panels with lower door overclads. While extreme, it was functional and improved aerodynamics, featuring elements such as stabilizing fins and flow-through side vents.

From a design perspective, the intention was to visually lengthen the front while shortening the tail. This was to balance out the visuals of the car to give it the appearance of a two-seater as opposed to the factory's 2+2 configuration. Clear headlight covers were initially installed but were soon deemed illegal for road use in many states. Callaway then included them in the car per "owner install" before eventually discontinuing them altogether. Despite the extreme bodywork, the stock lighting was retained, including the driving lights and front and rear side-marker lights.

Mounted on the vehicle, the CamAerobody cost $11,800 ($4,500 for the kit and $7,300 for installation and repainting). A color change added $1,200.

In addition to the elongated nose panel, the SuperNatural package brought fiberglass side rocker panels, door cladding, and a rear bumper cover.

Interior Additions

Inside, the car's stock fabric upholstery (leather wasn't a factory option until 1996) could be upgraded with front and rear Dove Gray leather seat covers and door panels. The setup cost $2,200. Customers could select color accent stripes in Azure Blue/Indigo, Charcoal/Yellow, and Red/Teal Green.

For $395, Rosewood or Carpathian Elm Burl wood accents were available on the center console around the shifter and on the door panels. A Callaway cloisonné signed by company founder Reeves Callaway was installed behind the shifter on cars equipped with the wood-grain accents. On all other SuperNatural-engined cars, it was mounted on the dashboard.

Available Callaway options inside the cabin included an anodized shift knob and wood accents. The Flame Red cloth inserts were a factory Chevrolet option.

A cloisonné signed by Reeves Callaway was mounted on the center console on vehicles equipped with the wood-grain option.

Pricing and Distribution

Callaway Cars worked closely with Bob Valenti Chevrolet in nearby Mystic, Connecticut, to procure cars for conversion. However, customers could also supply their own base vehicle. After a Z28's $24,000 price tag, the entire conversion cost around $31,500.

The SuperNatural C8's various components were modular and available piecemeal. This allowed customers to pick and choose individual enhancements for "field installation" by themselves, local garages, speed shops, dealers, and auto body shops.

Commemorative Editions

SuperNatural production continued into the Camaro's next phase: 1998–2002. A run of 10 commemorative editions were planned, but just two examples were created after faltering interest.

The Camaro's refresh included a revised front end with restyled headlights. Callaway Cars reworked the CamAerobody front clip to accommodate the design. Despite its best efforts, the final look wasn't as striking, but the company wanted to avoid the expense of recertifying new headlight designs. This was something it had already encountered with the Aerobody Corvette that featured Callaway-designed headlight lenses.

The Camaro's new generation also introduced the LS1 V-8 engine, which continued to respond very well to Callaway modifications. One example posted 500 hp with the SuperNatural modifications.

2010–Present Camaro SS Callaway Supercharged (SC) Series

2010–2020 Callaway SC Series Totals			
	Trim	Man.	Auto.
2010	SC552	0	13
	SC572	33	0
	HMS SC582	26	0
2011	SC552	0	13
	SC572	51	0
2012	SC552	0	10
	SC572	18	0
2013	SC552	0	3
	SC572	6	0
	SC582	1	0
2014	SC552	0	1
	SC572	1	0
	Z28 SC652	8	0
2015	Z28 SC652	3	0
2016	SC630	6	10
2017	SC630	2	7
	ZL1 SC750	3	6
2018	SC630	2	5
	ZL1 SC750	3	4
2019	SC630	0	0
	ZL1 SC750	3	9
2020	SC630	1	3
	ZL1 SC750	1	3
	HMS SC750	0	25

When the Camaro returned in 2010, Callaway responded quickly, developing a special SC-series package to improve performance. It soon carried over into the sixth generation. (Photo Courtesy Callaway Cars)

Camaro SS Callaway SC552 and SC572

With the return of the Camaro model in 2010, Callaway drew on its forced induction expertise and offered performance versions that were supercharged, hence the "SC" designations. It was followed a three-digit numeral that called out the horsepower rating. The package was available on SS trims in both coupe and convertible bodystyles and delivered two different performance levels. On vehicles with the LS3 V-8 and manual transmission, output was rated at 572 hp and 541 ft-lbs of torque. The L99 V-8 automatic had the same torque but only 552 hp.

Under the hood, the stock V-8 was given a Callaway TVS2300 supercharger and an intake manifold with an integrated intercooler. Callaway carbon-fiber injector covers, a Honker high-flow intake system and low-restriction exhaust system were included as well. A plaque with the vehicle's VIN number was mounted on the front core support. A second was fixed on the center of the dashboard.

Inside the cabin were embroidered floor mats, front seat headrests and anodized sill plates. Special key fobs were also part of the package. Exterior branding included chrome "CALLAWAY" lettering applied ahead of both rear wheels on the lower rocker panels and across the rear lower valence. On later model years, the script was moved up to the taillight panel, replacing the factory gold bowtie badge.

Callaway was commissioned by Hendrick Motorsports to build 26 Camaro SS coupes that featured 582 hp and 546 ft-lbs of torque. The run celebrated Hendrick Motorsports 25th anniversary and is covered in the Hendrick Motorsports chapter.

Optional Equipment

Customers could order additional cosmetic and performance options. The supercharger's standard black finish could be chrome-coated and further highlighted with a "Power Window" hood that was complete with chrome "Supercharged" script on the cowl for $3,950. On cars equipped with a manual transmission, a short-throw shifter could be installed for $495.

Two different tiers of suspension upgrades were available, and both utilized Eibach components. Level 1 was non-adjustable dampers and stabilizer bars for $2,990. It also included progressive-rate coil springs. Level 2 included double-adjustable dampers with external reservoirs and linear-rate coil springs. Callaway Le Mans GT (LMGT) brakes brought engraved calipers (6-piston up front, 4-piston calipers in the rear) along with larger rotors (355 x 32 mm). Nine-spoke alloy wheels were available in three finishes: chrome, Hyperblack, or Hypersilver. When selected, the original equipment tires were retained. A sport interior group was available along with an owner delivery experience.

As the model progressed, other options became available. This included an embroidered car cover, an extended powertrain warranty, and carbon-fiber ground effects designed by Callaway. This included rocker panels, a front splitter, a rear spoiler, an inlet duct, and rear diffuser with cutouts for quad exhaust. A separate option included the upgraded exhaust for the ground effects. While the pieces were available individually, the C18 Preferred Equipment Group option added the entire package.

2014: SC562, SC582, and SC652

In 2014, revamped versions were released, bumping output. Now, the manual transmission variant delivered 582 hp and 546 ft-lbs of torque. The automatic-equipped version was upgraded as well and was now rated at 562 hp and 526 ft-lbs of torque.

In addition, in response to Chevrolet offering a track-ready Z/28, Callaway offered the SC652 package, which, thanks to a TVS2300 supercharger, bumped the Z/28's output to 652 hp and 620 ft-lbs of torque. New items included larger fuel injectors along with a high-flow intake system and low-restriction exhaust. Production was limited to 11 units by 2015.

2016–2021: SC630

In 2016, Callaway unveiled the SC630 package that was available on the Camaro SS. At the core of the new Alpha upgrades were a Callaway designed, developed, and patented GenThree TVS2300 supercharger system, a TripleCooled intercooler system, and a low-restriction cold-air intake system.

With the updated equipment, output was rated at 630 hp and 610 ft-lbs of torque. The Callaway team also figured out

With the launch of the sixth-generation Camaro in 2016, Callaway debuted its SC630 package. (Photo Courtesy Callaway Cars)

The SC630's supercharged V-8 was rated at 630 hp and 610 ft-lbs of torque. (Photo Courtesy Callaway Cars)

how to deliver the same output on vehicles equipped with either the manual or automatic transmission.

Other items in the package included Callaway carbon-fiber engine mid-covers with emblems, the under-hood build plaque, door sill plates, and embroidered floor mats. The badging was restrained from previous years and was limited to an emblem in the front grille along with "CALLAWAY" script on the front fenders and across the taillight panel.

2017–2022: SC750

To continue raising the bar, in 2017, Callaway released the SC750 that was based on Chevrolet's latest ZL1. After receiving the Callaway's Alpha upgrades as the SC630, the package produced 750 hp and 739 ft-lbs of torque.

The SC750 package was based on Chevrolet's top-tier ZL1 trim. (Photo Courtesy Callaway Cars)

The SC750 engine was rated at 750 hp and 739 ft-lbs of torque. (Photo Courtesy Callaway Cars)

## CHAPTER 7

DALE EARNHARDT CHEVROLET

Few professional drivers kept it pedal to the metal and pushed the limits as hard as or fast as the legendary Dale Earnhardt. During his decades-long career, the veteran NASCAR competitor garnered an astonishing 76 career wins in the Cup Series alone, including 7 Winston Cup Championships.

Besides winning, Earnhardt became synonymous with his sinister black Chevrolet race cars and his "Intimidator" nickname. These elements were carried over into his street-going efforts, as he assembled several runs of small-batch modified Camaro programs and distributed them through his Chevrolet dealership in Newton, North Carolina.

1994 Dale Earnhardt Championship Series

	1994	1995
Total	6	7
Exterior Color	Black	
Interior Color	Graphite	
Bodystyle	T-Top	
Engine	5.7L LT1 V-8	
Output	275 hp	
Transmission	6-speed manual	
Championship Wins Celebrated	1980 1986 1987 1990 1991 1993	1980 1986 1987 1990 1991 1993 1994
Vehicle Price	$27,666	$29,325.31

Famed racecar driver Dale Earnhardt recognized the performance nature of Chevrolet's Camaro, offering several special editions through his North Carolina dealership.

The exterior was adorned with silver-painted ground effects and several graphic references to Earnhardt's race car.

All six vehicles were equipped with a 6-speed manual transmission. This example (#8100) bears autographs from both Dale Earnhardt Sr. and Dale Earnhardt Jr.

As part of the package, ground effects and a larger rear spoiler were added. The years presented on the rear panel are the six years Dale had won the NASCAR Winston Cup Championship.

In November 1993, Dale Earnhardt clinched his sixth NASCAR Winston Cup Championship. To celebrate, Earnhardt added a Camaro to his dealership's robust lineup of Signature Series vehicles. Focused on cosmetics, these were painted black and featured track-inspired graphics.

For 1994, the set included an S-10 pickup truck in both regular and extended cab form, a Monte Carlo, and an S-10 Blazer. Because of the win, the Camaros were classified in a subsection of the Signature Series called the Championship Series.

Six black Z28 Camaros with T-tops were ordered. They were equipped with the standard 6-speed manual transmission and Graphite cloth interiors. The vehicles received ground effects that were painted silver and a rear body-colored spoiler. Race-inspired vinyl graphics were mounted on the car, including the years of Dale's championships on the rear panel. The body kit was designed by Chevrolet designer Clay Dean for use on Lou Gigliotti's 1993–1996 ZR28 Special Edition Camaro that was assembled through his race shop, L.G. Motorsports.

Inside, the cabin received black leather seat covers in the front and back. The front headrests were adorned with unique stitching of Earnhardt's signature. The Camaros were available for general purchase through the racer's dealership, Dale Earnhardt Chevrolet, in Newton, North Carolina, on a first-come, first-serve basis.

Customers could also opt for a special weekend at the dealership's eighth-annual open house. Held the last weekend of September, the package cost $800 per couple and included lodging and dinner at the Speedway Club, which overlooked Charlotte Motor Speedway. Sunday's plans included admittance to the Tyson Holly Farm 400 race at the North Wilkesboro Speedway in nearby North Wilkesboro, North Carolina. Likely the highlight of the three days was a Monday morning autograph and photo session with Earnhardt at the dealership.

The getaway package continued to be offered in subsequent years with the exclusion of the race attendance, as the track closed in 1997.

1995 Dale Earnhardt Championship Series

In 1994, Earnhardt won NASCAR's Winston Cup Championship for the seventh time. With the victory, Earnhardt tied Richard Petty's record.

The Championship Series Camaro offering continued under the dealership's Signature Series line of vehicles. This time, seven black Z28 Camaros with T-tops were ordered. They were again equipped with the standard 6-speed manual transmission. They received ground effects and a spoiler, all of

After securing his seventh NASCAR Winston Cup Championship win, the exterior look of the latest special-edition Camaro was altered, replacing the lower silver paintwork with a checkered-flag design.

As with the previous year, all seven vehicles in the run were equipped with a manual transmission and T-tops.

With a seventh championship, room was made to add the "'94" graphic to the rear panel.

which were painted black, and they were again sourced from the L.G. Motorsports ZR28 Special Edition Camaro.

Similar vinyl graphics were applied to the exterior but with a new lower checkered band running around the vehicle. Inside, the Graphite cloth interior was upgraded with leather seat covers that sported a new checkered flag motif insert. Earnhardt's signature was still embroidered on the front headrests.

1996–2000 Dale Earnhardt Signature Series

1996–2000 Dale Earnhardt Signature Series Camaro Production						
Model Year	1996		1997	1998	1999	2000
Total	3	SS #0255	3	3	3	3
		SS #1731				
		SS # U/K				
Engine (V-8)	5.7L LT1			5.7L LS1		
Output	285 hp			320 hp		
Bodystyle	T-Top					
Paint Color	Black					
Transmission	6-speed manual					
Interior	Graphite leather					

In 1996, changes were made to Earnhardt's Championship Series Camaro program. With no championship at the end of the 1995 NASCAR season, the Championship Series name was dropped. The dealership team still went on to create decked-out Camaros but had them remain under the dealership's Signature Series line.

Production was also limited to just three Camaros, a nod to the iconic number on Earnhardt's race car. The three cars were ordered as Z28 SS models in black paint with the standard 6-speed manual transmission. They received lower ground effects and race livery–inspired vinyl graphics. A new addition

From 1996 through 2000, three Camaros were produced each year under Earnhardt Chevrolet's Signature Series.

was striking red accent pinstriping that outlined a lower silver border. Inside, the seats received the carried-over leather checkered-flag seat covers.

In 1997, another trio of black Camaro T-tops were ordered and given the same exterior and interior treatment. Customers received a special package for two at the dealership's 10th-annual Open House Weekend Celebration during the last weekend of September.

For 1998, three more SS Camaros were created, but they were now without the lower silver and red exterior band.

In 1999, three more black Camaro SS T-tops were ordered. Similar race-inspired graphics were applied with the 1996 version's striking red outlining. Inside, the seats received the leather checkered-flag covers. New this year was Earnhardt's signature logo embroidered on the door panels.

The look was carried over onto the 2000 edition, which again included three black SS Camaro T-tops. This was the final year for Earnhardt's Signature Series Camaros before he transitioned to a true performance-oriented Camaro package in the form of the GMMG-built 2001 Intimidator SS.

2001 Camaro Intimidator SS by GMMG

	2000	2001			2002
Prototypes	1	1			1
Production	0	82	T-Top	37	0
			Coupe	45	
Convertible	0	1			0

In 2001, with several special-edition Camaro programs under his belt, Dale Earnhardt sought to change both scale and performance capability. Instead of mere handfuls, the champion-winning driver sought a program that involved dozens of cars with horsepower and handling enhancements readily available for sale.

Another big departure from his prior ventures was making big improvements in performance. Past projects focused purely on cosmetics, but he now wanted a serious Camaro that could really perform.

After reaching out to Scott Settlemire, a plan was put in place (akin to that in use by Berger Chevrolet) to have the GMMG performance shop handle the assembly of the requested 100 special vehicles. (The origins and story of GMMG and its other efforts are covered in the chapter on Berger Chevrolet.)

These Earnhardt vehicles were called the Intimidator SS, which harkened back to the racer's track-earned nickname.

Ordering the Run and a Trio of Prototypes

Reflecting the racer's penchant for black, the entire batch came painted in Onyx Black and was equipped with the SS option and 6-speed manual transmission. Six cars (all T-tops) were ordered with the optional anti-slip regulation (ASR) traction control (cars PR1, 47, 51, 52, 54, and 55).

A pair of prototypes, both T-tops, were created. The first was built using a 2000 Camaro SS and was modified in July by GMMG. It was officially recorded as E-PR1 but is commonly referred to as PR2. It was delivered to the dealership in September and given to Dale Earnhardt Jr. in the spring. The second prototype, a 2001 Camaro SS, arrived at GMMG in September and was delivered to the dealership on November 22. It was officially recorded as E-PR01 but is commonly referred to as PR1. Earnhardt Sr. drove it regularly until his death in February 2001.

A final 2002 Intimidator Camaro was built for Earnhardt's oldest daughter, Kelly. It's often referred to as the third prototype (PR3). A single convertible (identified as car #13) was built by Murphy but not authorized by the dealership.

The first batch of production cars arrived to GMMG on November 28. The first vehicle that received modifications was car #3 in the run, which was built for Earnhardt Sr.

The 2001 Intimidator SS program was the final run of special Camaros commissioned and overseen by Dale Earnhardt Sr. In a departure from previous efforts, the design omitted any graphic references to his race cars and instead took on a sinister black and graphite look.

This Intimidator SS (identified as PR-1) was one of two prototypes created before the run. It was driven by Earnhardt Sr., who took ownership of car #03 of the run.

GMMG's back lot was full of black Camaros as well as Pontiac Trans Ams that were part of a separate dealer program. (Photo Courtesy GMMG Registry)

Camaros undergoing transformation to Intimidator SS status sit parked outside of GMMG's facility. (Photo Courtesy GMMG Registry)

Completed Intimidator SS Camaros arrive to Dale Earnhardt Chevrolet. (Photo Courtesy GMMG Registry)

To help keep track of its inventory, GMMG wrote large numbers on the windshield during the build process. (Photo Courtesy GMMG Registry)

Performance Upgrades

The cars received the GMMG's Phase 1 upgrades but claimed output was now rated at 381 hp. That number had a special meaning for Earnhardt. The race car he drove for Richard Childress Racing bore his iconic number 3. His son, Dale Earnhardt Jr., and Steve Park both drove for Earnhardt's team, piloting cars bearing the numbers 8 and 1.

A unique addition to the Intimidator SS cars was ball-milled brake rotors.

The fenders received the same badge as the rear panel. American Racing 200S alloy wheels were installed that featured painted Magnetallic Gray spokes. Ball-milled brake rotors were added as well.

All engines received GMMG's Phase 1 upgrades, bringing a new air-box lid complete with a special graphic.

Exterior Changes

The cosmetics of the Berger SS Appearance Package were applied to the run of vehicles. As with Tom Henry's Camaros, Earnhardt's cars had chromed infill "CAMARO" lettering applied to the painted satin black taillight panel. Special Intim-

idator SS badges were mounted on the front fenders and rear panel along with a numbered cloisonne mounted on the center console ashtray lid.

At each corner, 17x9.5 American Racing 200S alloy wheels with Magnetallic Gray spokes were installed with 275/40ZR17 Goodyear Eagle F1 tires. That distinct silver was also used on a hood stinger stripe that carried over to the roof (on coupes) and rear decklid.

Interior Changes

Inside the cabin, there was ebony leather upholstery and special embroidered floor mats. A Bright Argent silver gauge face was installed but lacked the usual dealer logo as seen on Berger and Tom Henry's cars. That was to make room for a personal autograph by Earnhardt.

The taillight panel was painted satin black and had chrome infill letters and GMMG and Intimidator SS badges. Also visible is GMMG's unique chambered exhaust and stainless tips.

Cabin touches included embroidered floor mats and a white shift-knob ball.

Each silver gauge cluster insert was to be signed by Earnhardt, but that plan was prevented by his untimely death. Thirty-three of the 86 vehicles received the special memento (cars #1–28, 46, 50, 52, and two prototypes).

A numbered cloisonné was mounted on the center console.

Serialized brass GMMG tags were riveted inside the driver's doorjamb.

Distribution

A special key fob and a fitted car cover with the Intimidator SS logo was included in the package. Each vehicle was marked with GMMG's brass tag in the driver's doorjamb.

Sadly, Earnhardt passed away mid-program right before the first batch of vehicles were delivered. He was tragically killed on February 18, 2001, on the final lap of the Daytona 500.

With the iconic figurehead gone and his team and family in mourning, the effort lost momentum. In the end, total production was cut short of the projected 100 vehicles, coming in at 82 production vehicles. Dale's sudden passing also cut short the rollout of the personalized gauges. Only 33 gauge clusters received his signature.

Another unique element cut short was the planned special Showroom Delivery Program. Under option ZE3, customers could pick up their car at Earnhardt's Mooresville, North Carolina, race facility while enjoying a behind-the-scenes tour and special dinner.

When it comes to the slew of special dealer program Camaros built by GMMG, the Dale Earnhardt Intimidator SS vehicles retain the most consistency in their appearance and uniform collection of options.

2001 Dale Earnhardt Intimidator SS Camaro by GMMG: Package Equipment				
Exterior	• Satin black painted rear panel • Chrome "Camaro" infill letters (rear panel) • Billet grille insert with "SS" emblem • Magnetallic Gray hood and decklid decal with hood cowl horsepower callouts • Power antenna			
Engine/ Powertrain	• Cat-back chambered exhaust • Underdrive crank pulley • Carbon fiber air box lid with "Intimidator SS" decal • Mobile 1 oil fill cap and badge (fixed on passenger-side strut tower)			
Suspension	Eibach 1.5-inch lowering springs	Brakes		Ball-milled rotors
Wheels	17x9.5 American Racing 200S alloy with Magnetallic Gray spokes			
Tires	275/40ZR17 Goodyear Eagle F1 tires			
Interior	• Bright Argent instrument panel insert (34 with Earnhardt signature) • Gentex rearview mirror with compass and auto dimmer • Intimidator SS floor mats • White Hurst ball shifter			
Badging/ID	Exterior	Fenders and rear panel		"Intimidator SS" badge
		Windshield base and rearview mirror		Numbered decals
	Interior	Center stack	Output data plaque	
		Console	Numbered cloisonné	
		Driver's doorjamb	GMMG brass door tag	
Accessories	• Numbered key fobs (x2) • Fitted car cover (with package logo)			
Package Pricing	$11,396-526	Vehicle Total		$41,376

The Intimidator SS could be had in both B4C coupe and T-top bodystyles.

2010 Dale Earnhardt Hall of Fame Edition Camaro

On May 23, 2010, Dale Earnhardt was posthumously inducted into the NASCAR Hall of Fame. To mark the occasion, his dealership team built a limited run of 10 special 2010 Dale Earnhardt Hall of Fame Camaros.

The tributes were built on 2SS coupes that were ordered with black paint. Five were equipped with an automatic transmission paired to the L99 engine, while five received a 6-speed manual transmission and the LS3 engine.

The cars were unveiled at Dale Earnhardt Inc. in Mooresville, North Carolina, on April 29, 2010, which was the racer's birthday.

Exterior and Interior

The cosmetics package featured a striking two-tone exterior effect, with Candy Apple Red paint being applied to the top half of the cars. Separating the look was a split silver metallic beltline pinstripe. The red was also painted on the rear taillight panel.

The edition's logo was applied on the hood cowl with a ghost effect. Other exterior highlights included black bowtie emblems, fender badges, and dealership badges mounted on the decklid and in the grille to replace the stock SS badge. A final touch featured graphics of Earnhardt's iconic "3" numeral on the outer lip of each of the wheels.

The engine cover was also painted in the Candy Apple Red with a pair of Earnhardt's ghosted-effect signatures.

Inside, the dash and door inserts and gauge surrounds were painted to match the red exterior. The door inserts were highlighted with large simulations of Earnhardt's signature applied in the same ghost-effect motif. The front-seat headrests and front and rear floor mats were embroidered with the edition's logo. A hall of fame badge was mounted on the passenger's side of the dashboard, and a sequentially numbered plaque was

In true Intimidator form, these Camaros were painted black with a Candy Apple Red top.

The Candy Apple Red paint was carried over to the cabin on the dash insert, door panels, and gauge surround.

mounted behind the ignition on the blank panel, which would be used on later models for heads-up display (HUD) controls. Machined sill plates were included along with machined inserts mounted on the underside of the trunk lid.

Final touches included a hall of fame logo key chain and a certificate of authenticity.

Each vehicle's number is showcased on this special data plate that is mounted by the ignition.

No modifications were made to the powertrain, but the engines received painted covers. The leading outer edges on both sides bear a simulated ghosted Earnhardt Sr. signature.

The two-tone paint was separated by twin silver pinstripes.

2010 Dale Earnhardt Hall of Fame Edition Camaro: Package Components and Alterations		
Paint and Body	• Candy Apple Red two-tone over stock Black • Split silver beltline pinstripe • HOF hood logo (ghost effect) • "3" numeral graphic (on each wheel) • Painted red stock engine cover with embossed Dale Earnhardt signature logo (ghost effect)	
Badging	• Black bowtie emblems (front and rear) • "HOF" fender emblems	
	DEC emblem	Grille and rear decklid
Uphol-stery	• Embroidered floor mats (front and rear) • Embroidered seat headrests (front)	
Painted Red Surfaces	• Dash insert • Gauge surround • Door panels with Earnhardt signature effect	
Badging	• HOF Edition emblem (on dash) • Numbered plaque (on HUD controls blank)	
Machined Inserts	• Sill plates • Trunk lid inserts (x2)	
Other	• HOF Edition key chain • Certificate of Authenticity	
Vehicle Price	$47,993	

2011 Dale Earnhardt Intimidator Historic Series Camaro

For years prior to his death, Dale Earnhardt dreamed of having his Newtown, North Carolina, Chevrolet dealership build high-performance street-going Camaros in the same vein as Don Yenko during the 1960s. The goal was partially accomplished with the 2001 Intimidator SS but built by outside vendor GMMG of Marietta, Georgia. Earnhardt wanted

Over the years, Earnhardt Chevrolet's runs of special-edition Camaros evolved, becoming more menacing in appearance and boasting improved performance capabilities.

to bring those kinds of fuel-fed ventures in-house. The veteran competitor didn't live to see that come to fruition, but his team carried on, releasing an updated Intimidator Camaro in 2011.

The car was bad to the bone with performance dialed up through the expertise of Earnhardt Racing Technologies. The run of 10 coupes was ordered in 2SS trim in black paint with a black interior. The cars came with a 6-speed manual transmission, the optional Hurst short-throw shifter ($380), and the RS package ($1,200).

2011 Dale Earnhardt Intimidator Historic Series Camaro: Package Components and Alterations	
Engine (704 hp/ 695 ft-lbs)	• Eaton 2300 Supercharger (11 psi) • Dual Intercooler with heat exchanger • High-flow cold-air intake box • Engraved aluminum engine cover • High-flow injectors • Electronically controlled return-less fuel pump system
Exhaust	• Stainless-steel system with ceramic-coated headers • High-flow catalytic converters • Intimidator badges on headers and exhaust tips
Suspension	• 1-inch-drop progressive-rate springs • Adjustable front and rear sway bars with polyurethane bushings • Subframe connectors
Wheels	Chrome-plated wheels with engraved Intimidator logo
Brakes	Cross-drilled rotors
Exterior	• Aluminum front splitter with support braces • Z-Force hood with silver Stinger graphic and ghosted Earnhardt simulated signature • Heritage grille with chrome plated Intimidator badge • Aluminum blade spoiler with support braces • Matte black rear panel • Fender badges and celebratory year decals • After-burner taillamps
Interior	• Painted checkered flag motif on door panels • Suede seat inserts (front) • Embroidered floor mats and front seat headrests • Custom racing one-piece shifter and knob • White-faced gauge inserts • Painted Earnhardt signature on dash insert • Trunk lid decorative plates
Other	• Monogrammed car cover • Certificate of authenticity
Vehicle Price	$85,993

Total Cars: 10	
Year	Celebrating
1979	Rookie of the Year
1980	Winston Cup Champion
1986	
1987	
1990	
1991	
1993	
1994	
2000	4-Time IROC Champion (1990, 1995, 1999, and 2000)
2001	Most Popular Driver Award

Performance Upgrades

The factory LS3 V-8 engine was equipped with an Edelbrock E-Force Gen IV 2300 TVS supercharger that had dual intercoolers and a high-capacity front-mounted water-to-air heat exchanger. A high-flow cold-air box was added along with a custom 3-inch stainless-steel exhaust system with 2-inch ceramic-coated long-tube headers and high-flow catalytic converters. "Intimidator" logos were engraved on the exhaust tips and on the exhaust headers. The fuel system was upgraded to an electronically controlled returnless setup with dual pumps and upgraded high-flow injectors.

With the supercharger set to 11 pounds of boost, each car was dyno tuned to deliver 704 hp and 695 ft-lbs of torque. To dress up the powerplant, an aluminum engine cover was installed with an engraved Intimidator logo on the top plate.

An Edelbrock supercharger boosted the car's output to 704 hp.

Suspension Upgrades

Eibach components were added to the suspension, including lowering springs, subframe connectors, and a rear cross-member tie bar. Other additions included adjustable front and rear sway bars with polyurethane bushings. Cross-drilled brake rotors were also installed.

Exterior and Interior Additions

Giving the car a unique, track-inspired look was a rear aluminum blade spoiler and front splitter. They both featured support braces for added downforce. Both were made by the Earnhardt Technologies Group. A painted heritage grille with chrome-plated Intimidator badge was mounted along with a new Z Force cowl-induction hood. The piece featured painted graphite accents that harkened back to the looks of the 2001 Intimidator SS Camaro. Earnhardt's simulated signature was also painted on the sides. Aftermarket "afterburner" taillights replaced the stock units.

The Earnhardt Technologies Group cut the Intimidator logo onto a spoke of each wheel and painted the inlay black. Chrome badging was applied to the rear panel and on the front fenders. Under the fender badge, the historic year that each car celebrated was painted on in Medium Gray Metallic.

Inside, the seats received suede leather inserts and an Intimidator logo embroidered on the headrests and floor mats. Retro white-faced gauges bearing a simulated Earnhardt signature on the tachometer were installed. A faux signature was also added to the dash. Painted highlights were added in the form of fading checkered race flags on both door panels. The finishing touch was a custom one-piece aluminum anodized black shift knob bearing Earnhardt's iconic number three. It

Painted door panels, suede seat inserts, and a custom one-piece shifter and knob were interior additions.

was made by Earnhardt Technology Group. The Intimidator logo was also engraved on the shaft.

Around back, the cargo area was accented with the underside of the trunk lid receiving laser-etched plaques with series graphics.

Sales and Distribution

The completed vehicles were unveiled on April 29, 2011, (Earnhardt's birthday) at Earnhardt Chevrolet. The original plan was for a two-part phased rollout. The first 10 cars would be designated as a special Historic Series. Each would be identified by 10 years, each commemorating a special accomplishment or milestone in Earnhardt's career. Besides painted callouts on the fenders, their official certificate of authenticity was marked. The set cost $85,993 each. After these special 10 were sold, the run of Intimidator Camaros resumed at a price of $79,993. Each came with a NASCAR-grade monogrammed car cover and certificate of authenticity. The second stage never came to fruition.

The first 9 cars were presold. The 10th was signed by members of the Earnhardt family and raffled off on April 29, 2012, at Earnhardt's dealership. The proceeds benefitted the Dale Earnhardt Foundation charity.

Each vehicle received a specific painted celebratory year that highlighted significant accomplishments from Earnhardt's storied career. This example marks Earnhardt's Winston Cup Championship win in 1990.

Afterburner taillights, an aluminum spoiler, and a chrome-plated Intimidator logo were added components that set the rear of the Historic Series apart from the rest.

## CHAPTER 8

STREET LEGAL PERFORMANCE AND SPECIALTY VEHICLE ENGINEERING

One of the major powerhouses of Camaro performance programs has come from the father-son duo of Ed and David Hamburger. With a decades long-history in the automotive business, they've impacted the model in major ways during two distinct operational phases. First, under their Street Legal Performance (SLP) division, they dominated the fourth generation Camaro scene, securing a partnership with Chevrolet as the official upfitter of factory top-tier trims, such as the wildly popular SS and LT4.

When the fifth-generation Camaro arrived, SLP dove in, drastically dialing up capabilities while reviving the storied ZL1 nameplate. The next chapter roared to life in 2015 when under their newly launched Specialty Vehicle Engineering, they breathed new life into a reimagined Yenko Camaro, and new models continue to be produced.

1996–2002 Camaro SS

1996–2002 Camaro SS Output				
	1996–1997	1997 LT4	1998–2000	2001–2002
HP	305/310*	330	320	325
TQ	325	340	345	350

*Equipped with optional Performance Exhaust

1996 Camaro SLP Z28 SS

1996 Camaro Z/28 SS			
Coupe	2,005	Auto.	673
		Man.	1,332
Convt.	264	Auto.	112
		Man.	152
Total	2,257		

The Camaro SS returned in 1996 with third-party upfitter, SLP, handling the modification. All fourth-generation versions can be readily identified by the composite hood (with scoop) and new decklid.

After a 24-year absence, the SS trim returned for the 1996 model year. Conversations began between Chevrolet and SLP Engineering in December 1993 regarding an up-level Z28 that could square off against Ford's Mustang GT and Cobra programs. The project was green-lit with SLP handling the authorized upfitting of what was called the Z28 SS. It was the first and only time both legendary Camaro performance trims would be combined in one model.

Completed Z28 Camaros left Chevrolet's Sainte-Thérèse, Quebec, Canada, plant and were transported to SLP's nearby Lasalle's facility. There, they received the additional upgrades and returned to Sainte-Thérèse for quality-control checks. After selecting RPO R7T, specifying the SS package, customers were then required to select RPO QLC ($132), which added the Z28's optional 245/50Z16 performance tires. Automatic transmission–equipped vehicles also required RPO GU5 ($250), which added the performance rear axle.

The SS package cost $3,999 and was available to order from any Chevrolet dealership on coupe, T-top, and convertible bodystyles. SLP provided a three-year/36,000-mile limited warranted on all of its modifications.

Customers could select from Arctic White, Black, Bright Red, Bright Teal, or Polo Green exterior paint colors. Those were paired to either a Graphite, Medium Gray, Neutral, or Flame Red interior.

Package Content

On the exterior, the package included a lightweight composite hood with a functional scoop that fed a forced air cleaner and induction system. Other body modifications included a revised decklid spoiler and exterior SS badging that replaced

Interior SS additions included embroidered floor mats— one of three areas on the vehicles bearing "Z28 SS."

all the Z28 pieces. At each corner, 17x9 Corvette ZR-1-styled cast-aluminum alloy wheels were mounted with 275/50 ZR 16 BFGoodrich Comp T/A tires. A larger front sway bar was installed, and the rear track bar was upgraded. Convertibles did not receive the suspension changes and received smaller 16x8 wheels and tires.

The Z28's 305-hp LT1 V-8 was retained but given Quaker State Synquest synthetic oil. Inside the cabin, a numbered commemorative cloisonné was installed on the center console.

The 1996 version is unique because it is the only year that a Camaro was a Z28 SS. It is called out on the air cleaner housing.

A center cloisonné identified the vehicle, including its production number.

1996 Camaro SS: Standard Equipment

RPO	R7T	Package Price	$3,999	
Body	• Composite hood with functional air scoop • Underhood forced air-induction system • Revised rear decklid spoiler			
Tires	BFGoodrich Comp T/A	Coupe/T-Top	275/40ZR17	
		Convertible	245/50ZR16	
Wheels	ZR1-style cast aluminum alloy	Coupe/T-Top	17x9 inch	
		Convertible	16x8 inch	
Suspension	Coupe/T-Top	Larger front sway bar		
		Revised rear track bar		
	Convertible	Stock Z28 components		
Engine	Synthetic oil			
Badging	"SS" replaces stock Z28 fender and decklid badges			
Other	• Numbered cloisonné (center console) • Numbered key fobs (x2) • Owner's manual supplement, owner's club, and wearables information			

Other Options

Additional options included a performance exhaust, a Level II Bilstein Sport Suspension Package, a Torsen limited-slip differential, and a Hurst 6-speed short-throw shifter. Track-focused R1 17-inch wheels and tires were available on coupes and T-top versions. The Synthetic Lubricants Package added premium synthetic engine oil filter, rear axle lubricant, and semisynthetic power-steering fluid.

Cosmetic options included embroidered front floor mats and a fitted cover that had the Z28 SS logo.

The package added SS badges on the front fenders and rear panel.

1997 Camaro SS

The package was again offered in 1997 with pricing remaining the same at $3,999. This year and moving forward, the Z28 was dropped from the name.

Sebring Silver was added to the list of available paint colors for the Camaro SS. The available options remained the same except for a new oil cooler that was $299.

Convertible				Coupe			T-Top		
Total	488	A	214	694	A	217	1,856	A	570
		M	274		M	477		M	1,286
Paint	A	M	Total	A	M	Total	A	M	Total
White	134	156	293	105	217	322	214	434	648
Silver	16	28	44	27	40	67	74	183	257
Black	31	50	81	47	109	156	126	371	497
Green	5	6	11	5	18	23	32	55	87
Red	28	31	59	33	93	126	124	243	367
Total	214	271	485	217	477	694	570	1,286	1,856

1997 30th Anniversary Camaro SS

Total	957	Auto.	438
		Man.	519
T-Top	466	Auto.	156
		Man.	310
Coupe	240	Auto.	73
		Man.	167
Convt.	251	Auto.	115
		Man.	136
Option take rate			
Level III suspension			58
R1 tires			25
Level III suspension and R1 tires			20
Leather interior			61
Cloth interior			39

In 1997, Chevrolet offered a 30th Anniversary Edition Camaro, and SLP created a special run of SS versions. Exclusive additions included a special dash plaque above the radio, a pair of key fobs, and a white car cover and tote bag.

One of the ultra-popular versions was the 1997 Camaro SS built on the 30th anniversary version (RPO Z4C).

Changes inside were minimal, with the anniversary edition bringing the Arctic White leather seats.

A unique anniversary cloisonné was installed on the center stack, replacing the standard "CAMARO" piece.

Package Price	$17,023

- 5.7L LT4 V-8 engine (330 hp/340 ft-lbs)
- 330-hp decal
- Dual exhaust with polished dual tips
- Stainless-steel exhaust manifolds
- Lightweight flywheel
- HP pressure plate
- Lightweight driveshaft
- High-strength ring and pinion gear set
- Hurst 6-speed short-throw shifter
- Engine oil cooler
- Torsen limited-slip differential with AAM cast-aluminum cover
- Quaker State Synquest synthetic lubricants
- Level II Bilstein sport suspension

These cars have multiple tiers of factory modifications: the 30th Anniversary Package (RPO Z4C), the SS Package, and the LT4 engine upgrade.

Mimicking Chevrolet's factory package, the SS cast-aluminum five-spoke wheels were painted Arctic White and were highlighted with an orange SS logo on the center cap. The exterior also included white and orange SS badging. The package was ordered under RPO Z4C, which costed $349 on top of the $3,999 SS option.

1997 30th Anniversary SLP Camaro SS LT4

In 1997, SLP brought Corvette power to the Camaro in the form of its LT4 Alteration Package. The upgrade was only available on 30th Anniversary coupes and cost $17,023 on top of the Camaro's base price.

The Corvette Grand Sport's LT4 engine is readily identified by the intake plate and the red-painted intake manifold.

The polished dual exhaust tips and "330 HP" graphic are the sole exterior indicators of the LT4 engine package.

Paint Color	Coupe			T-Top			Convertible			Total
	Auto	Man	Total	Auto	Man	Total	Auto	Man	Total	
Arctic White	30	63	93	143	161	304	81	35	116	513
Black	83	144	227	255	784	1,039	88	123	211	1,477
Bright Red	41	78	119	189	339	528	111	74	185	832
Bright Silver	15	27	42	38	104	142	27	14	41	225
Navy Blue Met.	44	90	134	117	235	352	32	37	69	555
Pewter Met.	54	76	130	280	313	593	69	48	117	840
Hugger Orange	11	54	65	75	174	249	26	35	61	375
Total	278	532	810	1,097	2,110	3,207	434	366	800	4,817

The package brought SS upgrades plus the 5.7L LT4 V-8 engine from the Corvette Grand Sport. After balancing and blueprinting, output was rated at 330 hp and 340 ft-lbs of torque. Other additions included stainless-steel exhaust manifolds, a lightweight flywheel, a high-performance pressure plate, an engine oil cooler, and dual exhaust with polished dual tips.

The transmission received a Hurst 6-speed short-throw shifter while the rest of the driveline was upgraded with a lightweight driveshaft and a high-strength ring-and-pinion gear. A Level II Bilstein Sport Suspension rounded out the kit.

A total of 108 cars were built: 2 prototypes and 106 production vehicles (100 for the US market and 6 for the Canadian market).

1998 Camaro SS

In 1998, the Camaro SS was equipped with an LS1 V-8 that had 320 hp and 345 ft-lbs of torque. The other change was switching to Goodyear Eagle F1 GS tires.

	Coupe		Convertible	
	Man.	Auto.	Man.	Auto.
Total	1,485	912	197	281
Red	598		144	
Black	967		109	
Navy	328		45	
Silver	316		58	
Gold	29		7	
White	248		114	
Convertible Top Colors				
Black	27			
Neutral	83			
White	123			

1999 Camaro SS

In 1999, several new paint color options were added to the Camaro SS lineup. A total of 4,817 cars were built, with 4,595 being sold in the US and 222 being sold in Canada.

2000 Camaro SS

In 2000, the SS package included 17-inch cast-aluminum wheels.

	Coupe		Convertible	
	Man.	Auto.	Man.	Auto.
Total	4,772	2,569	802	770
Arctic White	378	327	48	146*
Light Pewter Met.	718	451	154	154
Sebring Silver Met.	619	308	93	101
Navy Blue Met.	573	306	88	66
Onyx Black	1,591	679	274	165
Sunset Orange Met.	1	—	1	1
Bright Rally Red	892	498	144	173
Convertible Top Colors				
Color	Man.	Auto.		
Black	688	619		
Neutral	56	126		
White	8	25		
Accent Interior	4	1		

2001 Camaro SS

In 2001, output on the Camaro SS was bumped slightly to 325 hp and 350 ft-lbs of torque.

	Coupe		Convertible	
	Man.	Auto.	Man.	Auto.
Total	3,512	1,956	411	453
Arctic White	325	265	42	67*
Light Pewter Met.	591	378	54	74
Navy Blue Met.	456	254	54	39
Onyx Black	1,359	530	144	112
Sunset Orange Met.	234	170	37	44
Bright Rally Red	547	359	80	117
Convertible Top Colors				
Top Color	Man.	Auto		
Black	326	295		
Neutral	76	140		
White	9	18		
Accent Interior	3	1		

*55 ordered for Brickyard 400 NASCAR race festival use

2002 Camaro SS

	Coupe		Convertible	
	Man.	Auto.	Man.	Auto.
Total	4,811	3,527	1,297	1,556
Arctic White	232	246	52	73
Light Pewter Met.	403	307	74	88
Sebring Silver Met.	465	306	78*	141**
Navy Blue Met.	482	297	66	59
Onyx Black	1349	645	227	174
Sunset Orange Met.	263	283	41	46
Bright Rally Red	1617	1,443	739	975

Convertible Top Colors		
Top Color	Man.	Auto
Black	1,164	1,410
Neutral	103	110
White	30	36

*5 with "Z7D" Brickyard 400 Package
**52 with "Z7D" Brickyard 400 Package

When the fifth-generation Camaro returned in 2010, SLP offered a ZL package that featured cosmetic and performance upgrades. It was available on a wide variety of trims and versions, including the Transformers Edition. Car #2 of the Transformers Edition is shown.

For 2002, the final year of the Camaro's fourth generation, the Camaro SS package carried on unchanged.

New this year was the addition of a special factory 35th Anniversary Package that was based on the SS platform. Initially, Chevrolet was sending completed cars to the SLP facility for SS conversion before returning back to the factory to receive the anniversary treatment. During the run, SLP took over the entire process.

2010–2013 Camaro SLP ZL Supercharged Series

2010-2013 Camaro SLP ZL Series: Supercharged					
	Series	Engine	Tran.	Output	
2010	ZL550	L99	Auto.	HP	550
				TQ	550
	ZL575	LS3 V-8	Man.	HP	575
				TQ	550
2011	ZL560	L99 V-8	Auto.	560 hp	
	ZL585	LS3 V-8	Man.	585 hp	
2012	ZL560	L99 V-8	Auto.	560 hp	
	ZL585	LS3 V-8	Man.	585 hp	
	ZL600	V-8	Man.	600 hp	
2013	ZL560	V-8	Auto.	560 hp	
	ZL585	V-8	Man.	585 hp	
	ZL600	V-8	Man.	600 hp	
	ZL700	V-8	Man.	700 hp	

With the return of the Camaro model in 2010, SLP jumped right into offering modified versions of this fifth-generation version. The company rolled out its ZL line, which contained performance and cosmetic equipment that could be applied to both V-6 and V-8 Camaros with either the automatic or manual transmission and in both coupe and convertible bodystyles.

Each series was designated with a horsepower rating ranging from the lower-end naturally aspirated V-6 called the ZL327 all the way to the top-tier ZL700 that featured a supercharged V-8. Each came with a warranty and could be ordered through SLP's dealer network.

Any of the factory paint colors was available, and several conversions were performed on factory special-edition models, including the Transformers Edition and the Indianapolis 500 parade car.

Performance Additions

For performance, the ZL supercharged package brought upgrades, including a Magnuson TVS 2300 Supercharger, a lowered suspension, SLP's PowerFlo axle-back exhaust

A Magnuson supercharger was added along with a Blackwing cold-air induction system. David Hamburger, the son of SLP's founder, signed this example's air box.

system, and Blackwing cold-air induction system. The stock engine cover received special badging in 2010 and in subsequent years received custom body-colored inserts.

In 2011 and moving forward, the series received body-colored inserts in the engine cover.

Cosmetic Additions

For a distinct appearance, an SLP RTM hood was installed along with a block-out panel for the front fascia and a rear spoiler. All were painted the body color. The taillight panel was painted gloss black (flat black on black cars), and the side body gills received graphics that faded from clear to black. Red and white badges were mounted on the front fenders ahead of the wheel opening and on the passenger's side of the rear decklid.

Inside, the package included embroidered floor mats, embroidered front seat headrests, a sequentially numbered dash plaque, and two key fobs. Also included was a portfolio, documentation, and a silver car cover.

An optional Katzkin leather interior kit that cost $1,795 added cloth houndstooth seat inserts with an embroidered bowtie emblem.

Optional Content

Various options could be added on, ranging from upgraded Brembo brakes to retro SS badges in the rear grille and on the rear panel. Those wanting different looks could select painted rally-style stripes or hockey-stick-stripe side graphics.

Inside, a Katzkin interior kit was available, which brought a variety of leather inserts to the front and rear seats. A cloth houndstooth insert was also available.

In 2012, the package price dropped, as several items, such as the special hood and five-spoke wheels, were no longer standard but were now optional. New items included in the package included horsepower graphic callouts on the hood cowl that were available a trio of color combinations and a center stripe graphic that was given a carbon-fiber effect.

The rear panel was painted black, extending between the taillamp housings. Other additions were a body-color painted rear spoiler and ZL-series badge.

Coupes or convertibles were available in the ZL series, such as this 2011 ZL 585 drop-top, which is car #5.

2010–2013 ZL Series: Naturally Aspirated Vehicles

While the primary focus was on the supercharged iterations, much of the package's content was available for naturally aspirated Camaros as well. Some versions were converted by dealerships, bypassing SLP's facility completely. They could be equipped with much of the ZL optional content.

BONUS CONTENT

Scan to view the 2012 ZL series production data.

www.cartechbooks.com/ ct658-qr32

2011 SLP Camaro ZL1

In 2011, SLP offered the one-year-only ZL1 Camaro that harkened back to the 1969 COPO ZL1 Camaro. Intending to match that predecessor, this new iteration (based on 2SS Camaros with a manual transmission) was limited to 69 units. With a high retail price, two demo vehicles were created, and they were followed by a production run of 30 cars. Unlike that predecessor, both coupe and convertibles were offered.

The ZL1 was at the top of SLP's ZL series of upfitted Camaros, boasting 750 hp. Added components included the engine valve cover inserts, the blacked-out tail panel, and the appearance of both the exterior badges and interior dash plaque.

The SLP ZL1 was only offered in 2011, harkening back to the legendary 1969 COPO Camaro ZL1. The modern version is readily identified with exterior elements such as the carbon-fiber hood with its wide and low scoop and cowl.

Powertrain Upgrades

Under the hood, a custom-built 427-ci engine was installed, featuring an aluminum block and cylinder heads. This was a fitting tribute to the 1969 ZL1 Camaro, which also featured an aluminum engine block and heads. The 2011 ZL1 version was supercharged and topped with a carbon-fiber finish inserts in the engine cover.

Other upgrades included an aluminum radiator, an SLP Blackwing cold-air intake, and SLP's PowerFlo exhaust with SLP long-tube headers, retaining the stock catalytic converters. After a custom tune, output was rated at 750 hp, and the vehicle's speed limiter was raised to 205 mph.

The stock manual transmission was given a ZR-1 clutch assembly with an SLP flywheel and a short-throw shifter that was topped with a ZL shift knob. The suspension received adjustable coilovers, sway bars, and heavy-duty half shafts.

The brakes were upgraded with Brembo brakes: six- and four-piston calipers and two-piece rotors. The stock wheels were exchanged for forged lightweight wheels with ZL1 center caps and had Michelin Sport PS2 tires.

The ZL1's custom-built 427-ci V-8 featured an aluminum engine block and cylinder heads just like the 1969 ZL1.

Exterior Upgrades

On the exterior, a new carbon-fiber hood with a functional scoop was added along with a new front fascia and grille and lower front splitter.

A new rear spoiler was installed. It was painted the body color and given a carbon-fiber finish stripe that extended to the rear decklid. It continued the effect from the hood's center section of exposed carbon fiber. A new rear diffuser was also added.

The rear panel between the taillights was painted black, and ZL1 badges were mounted on the front fenders (ahead of

Rear additions include a painted body-color rear spoiler and a blue insert in the rear bowtie emblem, matching those found on the 1969 Camaro ZL1.

In addition to embroidered floor mats, the interior received carbon-fiber accents in the gauge cluster surround and steering wheel.

the wheels) and on the rear decklid. Harkening back to those on the 1969 Camaro ZL1, the front and rear factory bowtie badges were given blue inserts.

Interior Upgrades

Embroidered ZL1 floor mats were added in the cabin along with a numbered dash plaque and pair of key fobs. Carbon-fiber-finish accents were installed in the steering wheel, center console, and around the gauge cluster.

An optional Katzkin interior trim package allowed customers to select from seven different leather colors or cloth houndstooth, which added inserts in both the front and rear seats and stitching on the center console and door arm rests. As part of the upgrade, the ZL1 logo was embroidered in the front seat headrests with Chevy's bowtie emblem embroidered in the front seat backs.

The ZL1 package was $80,000 (with several additional bespoke options available) on top of the price of the foundation Camaro. The final modified vehicle carried a warranty and came with a car cover.

2012–2014 Camaro SLP Supercharged Panther

2012 SLP Panther		
	Coupe	Convertible
560 hp	1	0
585 hp	1	0
600 hp	5	5
700 hp	0	1
US	9	
Canada	4	
Total	13	

In 2012, Chevrolet introduced its own ZL1 Camaro, causing SLP to pivot and introduce a Panther package to its ZL series of modified supercharged Camaros. It served as a

The Panther replaced SLP's top-tier ZL1, featuring looks modeled after the Gorries Chevrolet 1967 Black Panther Camaro program. This is car #1 of the run.

BONUS CONTENT

Scan to view the 2011 ZL1 performance content.

www.cartechbooks.com/ct658-qr33

BONUS CONTENT

Scan to view the 2011 ZL1 appearance content.

www.cartechbooks.com/ct658-qr34

replacement for its top-tier 2011 ZL1 Camaro, which delivered 700 hp. In 2013, it was joined by the ZL700, which also delivered 700 hp.

While the Panther utilized many components from the ZL series, it possessed a very distinct look with its blacked-out appearance modeled after the Camaros in Gorries Chevrolet's 1967 Black Panther program. As such, the vehicles only came painted in black that was highlighted with gold accents.

In addition to the 700-hp trim, the Panther package could be applied to the rest of SLP's supercharged ZL lineup (including 560-, 585-, and 600-hp variants) in the coupe and convertible bodystyle and with a manual or automatic transmission.

Performance Upgrades

Like the 2011 SLP ZL1 Camaro, the 700-hp Panther received an exclusive custom-built supercharged 427-ci V-8 with an aluminum block and aluminum cylinder heads. It was further equipped with items such as SLP's Blackwing cold-air induction system and either SLP's PowerFlo or Loud Mouth II axle-back exhaust system. The transmission was enhanced along with the suspension, and a Brembo GT brake package (with black calipers) was installed.

Lesser-horsepower Panther variants utilized the Camaro's stock 6.2L V-8 and could be optioned with some of the 700-hp content.

All cars could be equipped with an optional boost gauge, and manual-transmission cars could receive an optional SLP ZR1 dual-disc clutch and flywheel assembly.

The 700-hp version received a supercharged 427-ci V-8 that was topped with SLP's engine cover inserts that had gold painted accents.

Wheel Upgrades

At each corner, 700-hp Panthers received the 2011 ZL1's forged lightweight wheels, which were given an exclusive satin black finish and were accented with a gold stripe. They were wrapped in Michelin Super Sport tires.

Lower trims received the ZL-series 5-spoke wheels, which were given a black-chrome finish with a gold rim accent. Both sets of wheels featured Panther center caps.

Appearance Upgrades

On the exterior, 700-hp Panthers received exclusive additions in the form of SLP's RTM carbon-fiber hood, a heritage grille insert and a "427" rear decklid badge. Other content (some of which was optional on lesser trims) included SLP's front fascia splitter and rear diffuser.

Fender badges were added along with the ZL1-style forged wheels that were given a satin black finish with a gold stripe.

Chrome taillight bezels were added to the rear along with a diffuser and spoiler.

All Panthers received SLP's rear spoiler, black-chrome taillight bezels, side gill graphic inserts that faded from gold to black, and SLP's ZL-series center carbon-fiber-effect stripe with gold hood accents.

All cars received front and rear gold bowtie emblems with a black-chrome surround, and all were marked with Panther badges on the rear decklid and fenders that had "7.0 Liter" or "6.2 Liter" lettering.

Interior Upgrades

Inside, all Panther packages included embroidered floor mats and front-seat headrests. A numbered plaque was mounted on the dash that matched the two key fobs.

A boost gauge was optional and when equipped was installed on the steering column.

Accessories and Pricing

Each car came with a cover, assorted documentation, and a powertrain warranty. While 700-hp Panthers received shorter coverage, customers could add an optional extension.

Package pricing for the 700-hp version was $64,996 on top of the Camaro 2SS price of $36,995. The 600-hp version package cost $24,995.

BONUS CONTENT

Scan to view the 2012 Panther option take-rate data.

www.cartechbooks.com/ ct658-qr35

2014 Camaro SLP Panther 1LE

In 2014, the Panther package was applied to the Camaro SS 1LE. While most of the performance and appearance content was carried over, several notable changes were made mostly due to new factory parts content.

The 1LE hood, which had a matte black graphic and central heat extractor vent, was retained with the vent grilles being painted gold. The stock 1LE 20-inch black 10-spoke wheels were retained but were given the gold rim accent and Panther center caps.

Redesigned taillamps omitted the previous style's bezel, which meant that there was no longer any kind of black-chrome finish. In addition, the redesigned front grille and rear fascia meant the heritage grille and SLP rear diffuser were incompatible.

2015–2022 SVE Yenko/SC Camaro

In 2014, Street Legal Performance rebranded to become Specialty Vehicle Engineering (SVE). In 2015, SVE secured the rights from the estate of Don Yenko to be the licensed manufacturer of new Yenko Chevrolet vehicles.

From 2015 to today, the company has created a limited run of Yenko Camaros each year. They harken back to the original 1969 Yenko Camaro in both performance and appearance.

From their inception and for the first several years, the SVE Yenko Camaros utilized the stock Camaro SS V-8 engine stroked to 427 ci as a nod to the special COPO-sourced L72 iron-block 427-ci V-8s that were equipped in Don Yenko's special run of Camaros.

In addition, the SVE Yenko Camaros were given a modern interpretation of Yenko's cosmetic additions, including hood and side graphics and five-spoke Torq Thrust–style wheels. They also included incorporated the letters "sYc," which stood for Yenko Super Cars. This was used on items such as special wheel center caps and embroidered front-seat headrests.

The vehicles were available in all the stock paint colors. As part of the package, each year, the vehicle came with a faux

In 2015, the now rebranded Specialty Vehicle Engineering team resurrected an iconic name, offering a modern Yenko Camaro package.

leather–bound portfolio, owner's manual supplement, window sticker, and manufacturer's certificate of origin.

2015-2021 Yenko/SC Camaro: Engine Output							
2015	2016	2017	2018	2019	2020	2021	2022
			Stage I				
700 hp	700 hp	800 hp/ 750 ft-lbs	825 hp/ 760 ft-lbs	835 hp/ 770 ft-lbs	N/A*	1,000 hp/ 875 ft-lbs	1050 hp/ 900 ft-lbs
		Stage II					
		1,000 hp/ 875 ft-lbs				1,050 hp/ 900 ft-lbs	1,110 hp/ 910 ft-lbs
*	No Stage I offering this year					750 hp/ 710 ft-lbs **	
**	California Edition						

2015 SVE Yenko/SC 427 Supercharged Camaro

In 2015, the SVE Yenko Camaros used the contemporary Camaro ZL1 as the foundation. The cars were available as either a coupe or convertible. The Camaro ZL1's LSA small-block V-8 was exchanged for a custom-built supercharged LS7 427-ci V-8.

A custom-built LS7 427-ci V-8 was installed, producing 700 hp.

Exterior Additions

The cars received exterior additions such as a new hood, five-spoke wheels in a gunmetal finish, a heritage grille, and graphics available in nine different colors.

At the rear, the ZL1's spoiler was painted flat black and "YENKO" lettering was added to the brake calipers. The stock tires were retained, but in the spirit of the classic Camaros, they were given white lettering.

Badging that harkened back to the iconic red, white, and blue Yenko crest was added to the front fenders and decklid along with "427" numerals.

Interior Additions

Inside the cabin, new sill plates were added along with a Yenko emblem at the base of the steering wheel, a sequentially numbered dash plaque that matched one found under the hood, and embroidered floor mats.

An optional Katzkin leather package was available, bringing a selection of colored leather or houndstooth cloth inserts to the front and rear seats. When selected, the headrests and backrests were also embroidered with "sYc" lettering and a bowtie emblem. It was not available if customers selected the ZL1's optional Recaro sport seats.

2015 SVE Yenko/SC 427 Supercharged Camaro			
Foundation Vehicle	2015 Camaro ZL1		
Engine 427-ci LS7 V-8 (700 hp)	• TVS 2300 supercharger • Cold-air intake • 10.3:1 compression • Custom tune with 205-mph top speed • ZL-series engine cover		
Transmission	ZR-1 clutch assembly with flywheel (manual only)		
Wheels	20x10-inch gunmetal finish	Tires	Added white lettering
Body	• RTM hood • Heritage grille (with bowtie emblem delete) • ZL1 spoiler painted flat black		
Graphics	• Hood and side stripe (various colors) • Side gill inserts (flat or gloss black) • "YENKO" lettering on brake calipers		
Badging	Yenko crest and 427 numerals (front fenders and deck lid)		
Interior	• Yenko/SC sill plates • "YENKO" steering wheel badge • Numbered dash, under hood plaque and key fobs (x2) • Embroidered front floor mats • Embroidered front seat headrests (stock seats)		
Package Price	$43,500	Total Price	$99,005

2016 SVE Yenko 427 700-hp Camaro

In 2016, the Yenko 427 returned with major changes. It was no longer based on the ZL1 but now was based on the 1SS or 2SS trim. It was available as a coupe or convertible with either the automatic or manual transmission.

Under hood, the stock LT1 6.2L V-8 engine was not supercharged but was custom-built. The stock engine cover was retained but given badging. Other additions included a new body-painted carbon-fiber hood and still stock Goodyear Eagle F1 tires but in a larger size.

Because of the Camaro's refresh, the heritage grille was not included, and the badge placement was different on the rear panel.

For 2016, the Yenko Camaro was no longer based on the ZL1 but was available in 1SS or 2SS trims. The exterior design mimicked the appearance of 1969 Yenko Camaros.

After rebuilding the stock LT1 V-8 engine, it was topped with an updated Yenko crest and 427 badging.

A numbered cloisonné continued to be mounted on the dash.

The stock rear spoiler was painted flat black, and badging was added to lower rear panel.

2017 Yenko/SC Stage II Camaro

In 2017, the Yenko/SC Camaro received a big boost in power with the stock LT1 V-8 being equipped with a Whipple 2.9L supercharger.

Around back, the Yenko crest was moved to the center of the decklid, replacing the stock gold bowtie emblem. Another new item was the replacement of the 427 numeral badges with horsepower ratings in a chrome and red finish. They were mounted on the hood cowl and rear decklid.

The numbered plaque that was mounted on the dash and under the hood was revised in 2017. In addition to the vehicle's build number, it (and subsequent years) now included the horsepower and torque figures.

2018 Yenko/SC Stage II Camaro

In 2018, the Yenko/SC Camaro received more power and split into two different stages that offered 825 hp and 1,000 hp.

The 2018 Yenko Camaro debuted a revised side stripe that now featured larger text.

For Stage I, the stock LT-1 V-8 engine was upgraded and equipped with a Magnuson TVS2300 supercharger. It was topped with an aluminum black powder-coated cover with badges. It could be painted to match either the vehicle's paint color or the color of the exterior graphics.

The Stage II required the Camaro's 1LE option and a manual transmission. The engine was upgraded with the Stage I components plus a larger 2.9L Whipple supercharger, stainless-steel long-tube exhaust headers with high-flow catalytic converters, and an upgraded fuel system.

Stage II cars were equipped with the same five-spoke wheels, but instead of gunmetal, the spokes were painted gloss black. The vehicles also received a revised graphics design that featured enhancements such as larger letting on the quarter panels and individual "sYc" lettering ahead of the hood scoop. The Stage II cars did not have the rear spoiler painted black because it and the rearview mirrors came satin-black wrapped as part of the 1LE option.

A new cosmetic touch was the inclusion of the Yenko crest in the front grille and the availability for the horsepower and stage badging to come in gloss black in addition to a chrome finish. The color palate for the optional leather seat trim package was also revised with new names and colors.

In 2019, blue stripes were available, as are seen on the #4 car.

The Stage II's supercharger could be painted for $995.

BONUS CONTENT

Scan to view the 2018 Yenko package contents.

www.cartechbooks.com/ct658-qr38

2019 Yenko/SC Stage II Camaro

For 2019, the Stage I package was tweaked to deliver 835 hp. Output remained the same for Stage II versions, which were now marked with a decklid blackout graphic from Chevrolet Accessories.

A new addition to both stages was two new stripe colors: gray and blue.

Interior additions continued to be minimal with a dash cloisonné continuing to identify the vehicle.

BONUS CONTENT

Scan to view the 2019
Yenko package contents.

www.cartechbooks.com/
ct658-qr39

2020 Yenko/SC Stage II Camaro

In 2020, only the Stage II Yenko/SC Camaro was offered. It was available in coupes with the 1LE option and a manual transmission. New cosmetic additions included the option to leave the center hood stripe and "sYc" lettering as exposed carbon fiber. The default wheel finish was gunmetal with the gloss black finish optional as opposed to being standard Stage II content as it had been in years prior.

BONUS CONTENT

Scan to view the 2020
Yenko package contents.

www.cartechbooks.com/
ct658-qr40

A new addition for the 2020 model year was the option to leave the hood stripe and lettering as exposed carbon fiber. This is shown here on car #1.

The stock rear spoiler was painted flat black, and a blackout graphic was added to the rear panel.

2021 Yenko/SC Camaro

Two stages of performance returned in 2021. The differentiation in power being was based on the transmission that was used. Both cars were based on SS Camaro coupes that were equipped with the 1LE option. Stage I had the automatic transmission, and the engine was rated at 1,000 hp. Stage II had a the manual transmission, and the engine was rated slightly higher at 1,050 hp.

The previous retro five-spoke wheel was replaced with a more modern multi-spoke design that was available in either brushed aluminum or a matte black finish. The latter was also available with an optional red-line stripe. The exposed carbon-fiber hood stripe and lettering feature were standard.

For 2021, SVE introduced a new wheel design. It was available in brushed aluminum or matte black. This is car #1 of the run.

In addition to embroidered floor mats and door sill plates, the interior received a "YENKO" badge at the base of the steering wheel.

Two stages of performance were offered based on the transmission. The top-tier Stage II boasted 1,050 hp with the manual transmission.

2021 Yenko/SC Camaro California Edition

In 2021, joining the SVE lineup was the supercharged Yenko/SC California Edition Camaro. Based on 2021 LT1, 1SS, or 2SS Camaro models in both coupe and convertible form, the stock V-8 engine was blueprinted and supercharged to deliver 750 hp and 710 ft-lbs of torque.

With 50-state legal emissions calibration on 91-octane pump gas (previous packages recommended 93 octane fuel), the package was available in all 50 states as well as in Canada through the brand's network of GM dealers. Either the manual or automatic transmission was available.

The rest of the package included the exterior and interior elements of the 2021 Yenko/SC Camaro with the addition of California Edition badges in the grille and on the spoiler as well as "750 HP" badging on the hood cowl and spoiler.

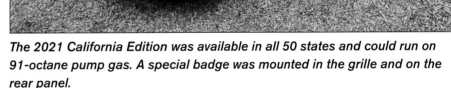

The 2021 California Edition was available in all 50 states and could run on 91-octane pump gas. A special badge was mounted in the grille and on the rear panel.

2022 Yenko/SC Camaro

Both stages returned in 2022. They now featured even higher output: Stage I was rated at 1,050 hp and 900 ft-lbs of torque, while the Stage II was rated at 1,100 hp and 910 ft-lbs of torque.

BONUS CONTENT

Scan to view the 2021 Yenko package contents.

www.cartechbooks.com/ct658-qr41

BONUS CONTENT

Scan to view the 2022 Yenko package contents.

www.cartechbooks.com/ct658-qr42

## CHAPTER 9

HENDRICK MOTORSPORTS

In 1984, after building a successful automotive dealership network, Rick Hendrick founded Hendrick Motorsports (HMS) in Concord, North Carolina. Out of the gate, there's been an ever-present drive toward checkered-flag finishes in wheel-to-wheel competition.

Over the past three decades, Hendrick's multiple Chevrolet teams have garnered a NASCAR record 16 national series owner's championships and 17 championships overall. The company has been behind top drivers including Terry Labonte, Jeff Gordon, Jimmie Johnson, Chase Elliot, and Kyle Larson. That passion for performance carried over from the banked turns of iconic tracks to produce numerous road-going special-edition Camaros that proudly bear the markings of HMS.

The silver and black motif of the Hendrick Motorsports 1997 SS Special Edition was revisited on the 2010 25th Anniversary Edition Camaro.

1997 Hendrick Motorsports SS Special Edition

Total	61	Auto.		16
		Man.		45
Coupe	7	Auto.		3
		Man.		4
T-Top	51	Auto.		12
		Man.		39
Convt.	3	Auto.		1
		Man.		2

In 1997, Hendrick Motorsports offered the Hendrick SS Special Edition, which was based on and utilized many of the components found on the Camaro SS. Sixty-one Z28s were modified for this HMS program by SLP. They were available in coupe, T-top, and convertible bodystyles. Each was sent to SLP and received a combined second sticker showing the SS and Hendrick SS–specific alterations in addition to the HMS SS build number.

On the exterior, all were painted in the SS's optional Sebring Silver Metallic paint (of which 368 were produced in total that year) and received dual black center rally stripes. A new set of chrome-plated American Racing 17x9-inch five-spoke wheels were added. These were also found on the 1996–2002 Pontiac Firehawk, which was another performance program that SLP had with GM. On the Hendrick Camaros, bowtie center caps were added, and tires were the standard Camaro SS tire: BFGoodrich Comp T/A 275/40ZR17s. Under the hood, each vehicle received the optional Camaro SS Performance exhaust, which raised the LT1 V-8's output from 305 to 310 hp.

Customers could then choose from four additional extra-cost SS options: the Torsen limited-slip differential, the Hurst 6-speed short-throw shifter with leather-wrapped shift knob, the Level II Bilstein Sport Suspension package (not offered on the SS convertible), and an engine oil cooler.

Special badges were applied on the B-pillar roof hoop (or on the front fenders of convertibles) along with a cloisonné on the center stack. Embroidered front floor mats and a car cover with locking cable and tote bag was also included (all of which were SS options repurposed for this package) along with a pair of key fobs bearing the Hendrick Motorsports logo.

The package retailed for $6,478 and was sold through the Hendrick Autogroup's eight Chevrolet dealerships scattered throughout North Carolina, and South Carolina, Kansas, and Virginia.

Special embroidered front floor mats were added to the cabin along with a dash cloisonné.

On T-tops and coupes, this special badge was mounted on the B-pillars, while convertibles had it located on the front fenders.

In addition to the SS-based cars, Hendrick Motorsports also offered a V-6-based special edition, which is in this second row of Camaros. The package featured similar cosmetics. (Photo Courtesy GMMG Registry)

1997 Hendrick Motorsports SS Special Edition: Package Contents		
Exterior	• Composite hood with cold-air induction* • Performance air induction with AC filter* • Revised rear deck lid spoiler* • Black SS fender badging* • Black center stripes	
HMS Badge	Coupe	B-Pillar roof hoop
	Convertible	Front fenders
Paint	Sebring Silver Metallic	
Engine	• Quaker State Synquest synthetic engine oil • Performance exhaust (dual exit with dual tips)	
Wheels	ARE 17x9-inch chrome 5-spoke with bowtie center cap	
Tires	275/40ZR17 BFGoodrich Comp TA*	
Interior	• Embroidered floor mats • Dash cloisonné	
Accessories	Car cover with locking cable, tote bag and key fobs (x2)	
Package Price	$6,478	

1997 Hendrick Motorsports SS Special Edition: Options Data						
		Trans.	TD*	HS**	SS•	EC••
Coupe	7	Auto.	3	0	0	0	1
		Man.	4	0	4	0	2
T-Top	51	Auto.	12	0	0	0	4
		Man.	39	6	39	9	25
Convertible	3	Auto.	1	0	0	0	1
		Man.	2	0	2	0	1
Total	61	Total		6	45	9	34

*	Torsen limited-slip differential	$999
**	Hurst ST shifter with leather-wrapped knob	$349
•	Level II Bilstein sport suspension package (N/A on convertibles)	$999
••	Engine oil cooler package	$299

The vehicles received SLP's dual/dual performance exhaust system that featured dual outlets and dual tips.

1997 Hendrick Motorsports LT4 Special Edition Coupe

Building on the 1997 Hendrick Motorsports SS Special Edition, the company offered similar cosmetic branding on the exclusive Camaro SS LT4—of which just 108 coupes were built by SLP and all had 30th Anniversary SS options. These vehicles were equipped with a 5.7L LT4 V-8 that produced 330 hp and 340 ft-lbs of torque.

Nine vehicles were created, and they were identified with special badging on the B-pillar roof hoop and a cloisonné on the center stack. Embroidered floor mats were included along with special key fobs and a car cover. All were equipped with a 6-speed manual transmission.

On top of the 30th Anniversary SS Package and the LT4

Completed HMS SS Camaros await final prep and delivery. (Photo Courtesy GMMG Registry)

Nine LT4 Special Edition cars were built. This example was delivered new through Performance Chevrolet.

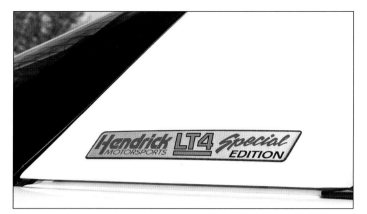

As with the 1997 Hendrick SS, the LT4 Special Edition received a similar B-pillar badge.

Special embroidered floor mats and a dash cloisonné were added to the cabin. This example is 1 of 7 equipped with the houndstooth seat inserts.

Hendrick Motorsports took advantage of the small-batch Camaro SS LT4, creating its own even more exclusive version.

was there along with a pair of SLP employees: Reg Harris and Matt Murphy, who later built his own dealer program Camaros through his GMMG performance shop.

1997 Hendrick Motorsports SS Special Edition LT4: Sales Distribution				
Car #	LT4 #	Dealership	Location	Seat Configuration
1*	1	City Chevrolet	Charlotte, North Carolina	Houndstooth Insert
2	3	City Chevrolet	Charlotte, North Carolina	Houndstooth Insert
3	4	Rick Hendrick Chevrolet	Durham, North Carolina	Houndstooth Insert
4	5	Hendrick Automall	Cary, North Carolina	Houndstooth Insert
5	6	Performance Chevrolet	Chapel Hill, North Carolina	Houndstooth Insert
6	16	Colonial Chevrolet	Virginia Beach, Virginia	Houndstooth Insert
7	23	Superior Chevrolet	Merriam, Kansas	All White
8	43	Rick Hendrick Chevrolet	Charleston, South Carolina	Houndstooth Insert
9**	71	Quality Chevrolet	Olathe, Kansas	All White
*	Rick Hendrick's personal car	**	Signatures on exterior of the hood	

alteration, the HMS Special Edition included the Level III Bilstein Ultra Sport Suspension, a signed certificate of authenticity, a case of Quaker State Synquest synthetic motor oil, a Quaker State duffle bag, and an HMS team baseball cap. The package cost $17,023.

Car #1 went to Rick Hendrick, and the remaining eight were sold through Hendrick Autogroup's eight Chevrolet dealers.

The vehicles were delivered in the summer of 1997 during a special presentation on June 25 at the Hendricks Motorsports Racing complex in Harrisburg, North Carolina. The purchase price of $47,250 included travel and lodging for new owners to attend the function.

There, they were greeted by Rick Hendrick; Jim Perkins, CEO of Hendrick Motorsports and former Chevrolet general manager; professional driver Terry Labonte; and Jeff Gordon's crew chief, Ray Evernham. Chuck Mac, a designer for HMS,

2010–2011 Hendrick Motorsports Performance Edition Camaro

In 2010, Hendricks Motorsports offered a three-tiered Performance Edition Camaro package that brought performance upgrades and custom bodywork to the fifth-generation Camaro.

It was available on both V-6 and V-8 Camaros that were equipped with either the manual or automatic transmission.

The 2010 Performance Edition was marked with a sharp angular front "Snake-Splitter" chin spoiler.

Top-tier LS3H versions featured a supercharger along with a carbon-fiber engine cover and air-intake tube.

Upgrades were done at the Hendrick Performance Center in Charlotte, North Carolina.

All three tiers were available with a carbon-fiber body-work package, bringing a body-colored "Snake Splitter" front lower spoiler and a rear diffuser. Graphic packages were available, including one that mimicked the RPO D90 striping seen on the 1968 Camaro and another with "fang" stripes that were mounted on the sides of the hood cowl.

Level 1: H.O. V-6 Performance Package

The first entry was the high-output V-6 package based on the Camaro 1LT. Under the hood, the engine received a Hendrick Performance air induction system, a performance exhaust, and a custom tune. After the upgrades, output was bumped to 325 hp. Other items included a Hurst short-throw shifter (on a manual transmission) and three-piece wheels with "H" center caps. For styling, the package included a carbon-fiber rear deck spoiler that was painted the body color.

To mark the cars, HP badges were applied to the front fenders, and a numbered plaque that was signed by Rick Hendrick was mounted on the dashboard.

Level 2: H.O. SS

Moving to the next level, the package could be applied to a Camaro SS. Improvements included underdrive pulleys and a badge on the engine cover that called out the new output of 465 hp.

Level 3: LS3H Supercharged SS

The highest offering was the supercharged SS Camaro package (identified as the LS3H), which brought a supercharger to the Camaro SS along with the rest of the included

equipment. The under-hood plaque was omitted. Output was rated at 588 hp and 555 ft-lbs of torque. Other items included a carbon-fiber air-intake tube and engine cover.

2010 Hendrick Motorsports 25th Anniversary Camaro SS

In 2010, Hendrick Motorsports celebrated its 25th anniversary and marked the occasion by commissioning Callaway Cars in Old Lyme, Connecticut, to build a limited run of special-edition Camaros.

Called the Hendrick Motorsports 25th Anniversary, a prototype (ID #00) was created and was followed by 25 more that were built on Camaro 2SS coupes (ID #01–25). All 26 vehicles came painted in Silver Ice Metallic. They were fitted with black leather upholstery and equipped with a 6-speed manual transmission.

The added Callaway hood featured a "PowerWindow," showing off the package's chrome supercharger.

Upgrades and Alterations

The 6.2L V-8 engines received upgrades such as a Callaway Eaton TVS2300 supercharger system along with a high-flow air intake and low-restriction exhaust system. After tuning, total output was rated at 582 hp and 546 ft-lbs of torque. The engine bay was dressed up with carbon-fiber injector covers that had Hendrick Motorsports and Callaway logos. The transmission was upgraded with a short-throw shifter fitted with a Corvette leather shift knob and boot. The knob's circle insert was replaced with one made of carbon fiber, painted the body color, and topped with the Hendrick logo.

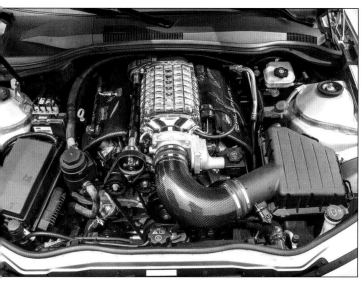

Other additions under the hood included carbon-fiber injector covers and a carbon-fiber air intake. This example (#8), like the rest, features signatures by Rick Hendrick and Reeves Callaway. It also features Dale Earnhardt Jr.'s signature.

Cabin additions included embroidered floor mats and a short-throw shifter topped with a Corvette shift knob.

Suspension upgrades included Callaway coil springs, shock absorbers, and anti-roll bars. Callaway also installed 20-inch 9-spoke alloy wheels, utilizing the stock Pirelli P Zero performance tires.

Exterior alterations included a new hood with "Power-Window" (inspired by the Corvette ZR1) with a carbon-fiber surround that showed off the supercharger. Other new body components included a carbon-fiber front splitter, rear spoiler, rear diffuser, and rocker panels.

Special anniversary badging was installed on the front fenders and rear decklid while Callaway lettering was applied down low on both rear quarter panels.

Inside, special anodized sill panels were installed, and the front headrests and floor mats were embroidered with anniversary logos.

The vehicles were marked by a serialized numbered plaque—one on the dashboard and another on the radiator shroud panel.

2010 Hendrick Motorsports 25th Anniversary Camaro 2SS: Equipment and Modifications			
Engine (582 hp/ 546 ft-lbs)	• Eaton TVS2300 supercharger • Honker air intake • Carbon fiber injector covers • Data plate with production number • Transmission: 6-speed manual		
Exhaust	Callaway stainless-steel cat-back system		
Wheels	Callaway 20-inch 9-spoke alloy		
Tires	F	Pirelli 245/45ZR20	
	R	Pirelli 375/40ZR20	
Suspension	Eibach/Callaway coilover system		
Exterior	Carbon Fiber	Front splitter	Rear diffuser
		Rear spoiler	Rocker panels
	• ZR1-style "power window" hood • Fender badges • Rear decklid badge		
Interior	• Callaway short-throw shifter • HMS-logo leather shift knob and boot • Embroidered front seat headrests • Embroidered floor mats • Anodized sill panels • Sequential dash plaque		
Vehicle Price	$76,181		

A carbon-fiber diffuser and spoiler were mounted at the rear along with a decklid badge.

Distribution

The first vehicle was shown at the 2009 SEMA Show in Las Vegas, Nevada, before the rest went on sale later that month. Each cost $76,181 and was only available at four dealerships: Hendrick Chevrolet in Cary, North Carolina; Kearny Mesa Chevrolet in San Diego, California (owned by NASCAR driver Jimmie Johnson); Rick Hendrick Chevrolet in Duluth, Georgia; and Superior Chevrolet in Merriam, Kansas.

2020 Hertz/Hendrick Motorsports Edition Camaro SS and ZL1

		Trim	Role	Total	HP/TQ	
Total	226	SS	Prototype	1	480	455
			Sweepstakes	1		
			Fleet use	199		
		ZL1	Prototype	1	750	730
			Fleet use	24		

In the fall of 2019, Hendrick Motorsports partnered with Hertz rental cars to offer a limited-edition run of performance 2020 Camaro SS and ZL1 models that customers could rent at

select airports across the United States. Hertz sponsored Hendrick Motorsports and NASCAR driver William Byron, who competed in a Chevrolet Camaro ZL1 1LE race car with #24 livery.

After a pair of prototypes, 224 (200 SS versions and 24 ZL1s) fleet vehicles were created under a unique RPO code of PEH. They featured the reverse of the race car's colors, coming in black paint with yellow center stripes and lower vinyl graphics.

A front license-plate bracket was supplied but never installed, as the vehicles were all titled in Florida, which doesn't require front plates for motor vehicles.

BONUS CONTENT

Scan to view the lists of airport rental locations.

www.cartechbooks.com/ct658-qr43

2020 Hertz/Hendrick Camaro SS

The Camaro SS received an assortment of factory options and Chevrolet accessories, including a strut-tower brace, sport alloy pedals, ground effects, a cat-back dual-exhaust upgrade, and a cold-air intake system.

Custom exterior touches included satin black 10-spoke aluminum wheels with custom center caps, Hertz fender badges, and yellow painted brake calipers. In the engine bay, new additions included reservoir caps bearing the number 24 and a serialized data plate. The cabin received upgrades including new door sills, yellow painted door trim, and embroidered mats and front seat headrests. A serialized dash plaque was also included.

As part of vehicle promotion, Hertz launched the Hertz

Continuing its storied Rent-a-Racer program, Hertz offered radical Camaro SSs and ZL1s to customers in 2020 at select airports around the United States.

The ZL1s were equipped with a Callaway SC750 supercharger that was powder coated yellow.

Ultimate Ride Sweepstakes and in March 2020 gave one (car #5) of the SS versions to winner Phillip Abma. In addition to the car, the prize also included a track day at the Charlotte Motor Speedway with the Hendrick Motorsports team.

2020 Hertz/Hendrick ZL1 Camaro

2020 Hertz/Hendrick Motorsports Camaro SS: Equipment and Modifications: RPO PEH				
Engine	• Yellow painted strut tower brace • Chevrolet cold-air intake • Brake fluid reservoir engraved cap (#24) • Engine oil fill engraved cap (#24) • Coolant reservoir engraved cap (#24) • Numbered data plate			
Exhaust	Chevrolet cat-back dual exhaust upgrade			
Wheels	with "24" center caps		Tires	
F	20x9-inch black aluminum		F	265/35ZR
R	20x10.5-inch black aluminum		R	305/30ZR
Brakes	Yellow painted calipers with HMS logo			
Exterior (Black)	• Second-generation carbon flash metallic • Ground effects* • Yellow rally stripes and graphics package • Hertz fender badges			
Interior (Jet Black)	Front Seats	• Recaro performance buckets** • Embroidered headrests		
	• Embroidered floor and trunk mats • Yellow painted door trim • Illuminated door sills with Hertz logo • Numbered dash plaque • Sport alloy pedals			
Package Total	$6,400			

2020 Hertz/Hendrick Motorsports Edition Camaro ZL1: Equipment and Modifications (RPO PEH)				
Engine Bay	• Callaway GenThree supercharger • Callaway TripleCooled intercooler system • Brake fluid reservoir engraved cap (#24) • Engine oil fill engraved cap (#24) • Coolant reservoir engraved cap (#24) • Numbered data plate			
Wheels	Forgeline gloss black aluminum			
Front	20x10 inch	#24 center caps		
Rear	20x11 inch	Hertz logo engraving		
Tires	F	285/30ZR	R	305/30ZR
Brakes	Yellow painted calipers with HMS logo			
Exterior (Black)	Carbon-fiber hood insert Yellow stripes and graphics Hertz fender badges			
Interior (J. Black)	Front seats	• Recaro performance buckets • Embroidered headrests		
	• Embroidered floor and trunk mats • Yellow painted door trim • Illuminated door sills with Hertz Logo • Carbon fiber dash panel insert • Numbered dash plaque			
Package Total	$3,190			

The ZL1 version included additions such as a carbon-fiber hood insert and Forgeline gloss black aluminum wheels with a Hertz logo engraving. The cars also received custom center

The exterior theme carried over to the interior, which featured yellow painted door trim.

caps. Other additions included painted yellow brake calipers and Hertz fender badges.

Under the hood, the stock supercharger was exchanged for a Callaway SC750 supercharger (powder coated yellow) that boosted the engine's output to 750 hp. The prototype received a painted yellow supercharger, water manifold, and snout. Other touches included a unique oil fill cap, brake fluid reservoir caps, and a serialized data plaque.

Inside the cabin, the front-seat headrests and floor mats were embroidered, and the doors received painted yellow accents. Hertz door sill plates were also installed along with a serialized dash plaque.

The package cost $3,190. Unlike the SS versions, the ZL1s incurred a $2,100 gas guzzler tax.

Each wheel was engraved with the Hertz logo, and the brake calipers were painted yellow.

In addition to yellow rally stripes, the vehicle featured lower striping bearing "24" and "Hendrick Motorsports" logo callouts.

## CHAPTER 10

BERGER CHEVROLET

One of the long-standing dealerships that is still serving up bowtie performance is Berger Chevrolet. Located in Grand Rapids, Michigan, Bill Berger began selling Chevrolets in 1922, and three years later, he opened his own establishment.

Now, four generations later, the locale is alive and well and is still dealing in nothing but Chevrolets. During the 1960s, the dealership made a name for itself by ordering the second-largest quantity of L72 427-ci V-8-equipped COPO Camaros after Yenko Chevrolet. In addition, it also received 10 1969 COPO Chevelles and the #3 1969 COPO Camaro ZL1, which was painted Daytona Yellow.

Besides that kind of ultra-hot inventory, Berger Chevrolet maintained an active speed parts department, supporting racers both far and wide. Things haven't changed much, and today, it remains as the sole muscle car dealer from the 1960s that is still operating.

Berger Chevrolet has been offering modified Camaro programs since the first generation of the iconic model.

The Berger SS: The Legend Continues

In 2000, the dealership celebrated a major anniversary marking 75 years of business. That motoring milestone had staff members thinking about recapturing some of their muscle magic from former days.

One of those passionate individuals was Dennis Barker, who was revved up for a special-edition Camaro after taking delivery of his own 1999 Hugger Orange Camaro SS.

The Pyramid of Players

To get such a special project off the ground, additional individuals need to get on board—just as it was in the 1960s. The first person, naturally, was Matt Berger, who readily liked the idea. Both he and Barker knew that for it to be successful, the cars had to move beyond mere cosmetics and boast serious performance upgrades.

Barker would run point on getting the cars sold once they arrived onsite, and with Berger on-board, the pair approached Chevrolet insider, Scott Settlemire, Camaro's assistant brand manager. The veteran corporate brass was essential for green-lighting any kind of large allocation of Camaros into the dealer's possession.

If Dennis was sales (under Berger's dealership umbrella) and Scott was supply, a third player was critical to making the whole plan work. This addition was one who dealt strictly with speed: Matt Murphy and his GMMG performance shop.

The GMMG story began with this custom Bright Orange SS Camaro modified by SLP. Matt Murphy took delivery of it at Berger Chevrolet, laying the groundwork for multiple fourth-generation Camaro programs.

Murphy came onto Berger's radar in August 1998 after taking delivery of SLP's 1995 Bright Orange Camaro show car onsite at the historic dealership. The one-of-a-kind vehicle had been built for the 1996 SEMA Show. It had an LT4 engine with 350 hp and 375 ft-lbs of torque.

Seeing the opportunity, Murphy stayed in touch with Matt Berger about a possible venture together. Being the right fit, Murphy was brought onboard to the dealership's anniversary project, which was now called the Berger SS. Together, Berger and GMMG became one the most dynamic powerhouses of fourth-generation Camaro modification and distribution.

BONUS CONTENT

Scan to view the Berger/ GMMG program players.

www.cartechbooks.com/ ct658-qr44

BONUS CONTENT

Scan to view GMMG fast facts.

www.cartechbooks.com/ ct658-qr45

Partnering with GMMG Performance

GMMG was launched in 1998. The running gag around the shop was the acronym stood for "Go Matt Murphy Go," given the light-speed pace the hard-working enthusiast kept. However, Murphy himself admitted there was no exact meaning behind the name. It's also been hinted that it stood for "General Motors Motorsports Group," but that is unsubstantiated.

Murphy was raised around the bowtie brand. His father, Matt Sr., was a Chevrolet regional manager. Matt followed in his footsteps, veering into the performance side of the industry, landing a job at tuner SLP in Troy, Michigan. He took much of what he learned there as a district representative and went out on his own, opening GMMG in Marietta, Georgia.

Growing GMMG

GMMG parlayed off that initial collaboration and went on to create additional limited runs of Camaros for other dealer partners. Its key to success was in standard performance and cosmetic upgrade packages that could be readily retooled to fit a variety of requests. Approximately 400 fourth-generation Camaros were modified in GMMG's shop.

From the get-go on Berger's anniversary Camaro, it was intended for GMMG to remain in the shadows as a purely behind-the-scenes participant. This is readily evident in the complete lack of its branding on this and other early shop efforts.

After GMMG's quick rise to stardom due to the popularity of its programs, the company's own unique badging began

Over the years, GMMG's shop was buzzing with performance activity. Here, 2000 Berger SS Camaros are lined up to undergo transformation. (Photo Courtesy GMMG Registry)

The 2000 Berger SS Camaro program offered customers improved looks and performance. A total of 29 vehicles were built in that year's run.

2000–2002 Berger SS: Production Quantities								
	2000			2001			2002		Total
Prototype	1 (PR-1)			1 (PR-2)			1 (PR-3)		3
Production	30	T-Top	25	27	T-Top	26	44●	T-Top	26	100
		Convt.	5		Convt.	2		Convt.	15	
		Coupe	0		Coupe	0		Coupe	3	
Total	31			28			45		105*
●	Includes car "00"				*			Includes CO-99

to appear on its creations. Most notably was GMMG's red, white, and blue crest motif, which harkened back to those used by 1960s legends, such as Don Yenko and Dick Harrell.

In addition to GMMG's branding efforts, it also expanded its offerings. Building on the original Phase 1 package, after 2002, the shop rolled out a tiered structure of upgrades using the Camaro's stock LS1 as well as a C5R-based 427 and 454 LSX option.

2000–2002 Berger SS

With all the proper people and pieces in place, and with Berger's anniversary fast approaching, the crew set to work hammering out final details. In early November 1999, the first Camaro of this Berger SS run, a Bright Rally Red T-top example, was sent to Murphy's shop. This first vehicle (referred to as PR-1) served as the prototype for the rest of the run and was heavily showed, attending events including the Hot Rod Power Tour. Years later, Barker's 1999 concept vehicle was given the title of CO-99.

Starting in the spring of 2000, 30 Camaros were ordered by Berger Chevrolet and shipped to Bill Heard Chevrolet in Kennesaw, Georgia. Upon arrival, they were dealer prepped

and filled with gas before GMMG's staff picked them up and moved them to the facility for alteration.

All came in SS trim, equipped with the factory-installed 320-hp, LS1 5.7L V-8 paired to a 6-speed manual transmission with factory Hurst shifter.

2000 Berger SS

Under the hood, the engine received GMMG's Phase 1 performance upgrades, including a high-flow air box, dealer

A new airbox that is topped with the Berger "Prescribed Power" graphic was added to the engine bay.

A chambered exhaust system gave the 2000 Berger SS (and subsequent GMMG-created Camaros) a distinct and retro sound.

Harkening back to the 1960s big-block engine Camaros, the taillight panel was painted satin black. Another addition was a body-color painted B-pillar hoop that replaced the factory black.

decal, and cat-back chambered exhaust. The distinct GMMG chambered exhaust was a custom piece specially developed to rekindle the acoustics of late 1960s Camaro V-8 engines. After these upgrades and tuning, output improved to 375 hp and 390 ft-lbs of torque.

Front and rear Eibach lowering springs were added, which dropped the ride height 1½ inches, while dimpled brake rotors were installed at all four corners.

Exterior Cosmetic Modifications

On the exterior, the car's B-pillar top hoops were painted the same color as the body. Harkening back to the big-block-equipped 1960s Camaros, the rear taillight panels were painted satin black. PR-1 had chrome infill lettering in the rear Camaro embossing, but at the request of Matt Berger, it was left off the rest of the run. Vinyl heritage rally racing stripes were added as well, coming in a variety of colors, according to the vehicle's exterior paint color. Inset on the stripe on the hood cowl were horsepower rating callouts.

Up front, a black billet grille insert was added, highlighted with a retro 1960s-era "SS" center emblem. Further setting the cars apart, the stock 17-inch cast-aluminum 10-spoke wheels were chrome-plated, which was an option that was not offered by the factory that year. GMMG's finishing touch was SS center caps. The stock Goodyear Eagle F1 tires were retained.

2000 Berger SS: Stripe Assignments			
Paint Color	Stripe	Coupe	Convt.
Onyx Black	Red	10	3
B. Rally Red	Black	7	2
Navy Blue Met.	White	4	0
Arctic White	Black	3	1
S. Silver Met.	Black	1	0

Anniversary Berger badging was mounted on the front fenders and the driver's side of the rear panel, joined by a "by Berger" metal emblem. Sequential white number graphics were applied to exterior of the base of the windshield on the driver's side and on the front of the rearview mirror that indicated the car's number in the run.

Interior Cosmetic Modifications

Inside, an anniversary badge was mounted to the center stack, swapping out the stock Camaro badge. A numbered heritage cloisonné was affixed on the center console's ashtray lid. White gauge faces were part of the package, highlighted with Berger's "Prescribed Power" logo. As part of the cluster alterations, an internal bezel frame surround (sourced from the Pontiac Trans Am) was added, breaking out and isolating the individual gauges.

SLP provided the front floor mats (as part of its SS conversion), and each car came with a pair of numbered key fobs and a fitted car cover from California Car Cover that featured the anniversary logo. In the spirit of Yenko's COPO Corvair Stinger and 1968 COPO Camaros, the vehicles received a serialized GMMG brass tag riveted inside the driver-side doorjamb.

As part of the package, the Berger SS Camaros received several interior additions.

The center console received this numbered cloisonné.

Following Don Yenko's lead in the 1960s, GMMG added numbered brass tags to each of its Camaro projects.

2000 Berger 75th Anniversary SS Camaro Registry and Related Vehicles											
#	Paint	Body	T	Ph.	HP	#	Paint	Body	T	Ph.	HP
CO-99•	H. Orange	T-T	6	2	435	15	D. Yellow*	T-T	6	1	375
PR1	Rally Red	T-T	6	2X	475	16	Navy Blue	T-T	6	2X	475
1	Arctic White	Conv.	6	1	375	17	O. Black	T-T	6	5	650
2	Arctic White	T-T	6	3	600	18	O. Black	T-T	6	1	375
3	Rally Red	T-T	6	1	375	19	O. Black	T-T	6	1	375
4	Rally Red	T-T	6	1	375	20	Arctic White	T-T	6	1	375
5	S. Silver	T-T	6	2X	475	21	O. Black	T-T	6	1	375
6	Rally Red	T-T	6	1	375	22	Navy Blue	T-T	6	1	375
7	Rally Red	T-T	6	1	375	23	O. Black	T-T	6	1	375
8	Rally Red	T-T	6	1	375	24	O. Black	T-T	6	1	375
9	Rally Red	T-T	6	1	375	25	Rally Red	Conv.	6	1	375
10	Navy Blue	T-T	6	1	375	26	Navy Blue	Conv.	6	1	375
11	Navy Blue	T-T	6	1	375	27	O. Black	Conv.	6	1	375
12	O. Black	T-T	6	1	375	28	C.M. Yellow*	Conv.	6	2	435
13	O. Black	T-T	6	1	375	29	Rally Red	Conv.	6	1	375
14	Arctic White	T-T	6	1	375	30	O. Black	T-T	6	1	375
HP	Horsepower	*		Custom Paint	PR	Prototype	•	D. Barker's 1999 Camaro SS—Concept			

Sales and Special Requests

The completed vehicles cost $38,360. A pair were painted unique colors in the dealership's body shop. They, and most subsequent custom-painted cars, started in Onyx Black, which was left visible in the engine bays after the color change, which was another vintage nod to classic Camaros of the past. One customer wanted his coupe (#15) painted 1969 Daytona Yellow to match the 1969 COPO Camaro that he purchased new from Berger Chevrolet. The black roof hoop was retained to simulate the classic car's black vinyl roof. Dale Berger Jr. made the other custom request, wanting his convertible (#28) painted 2000 Corvette Millennium Yellow.

2001 Berger SS

Due to positive response, Berger Chevrolet offered the package again for the 2001 model year. A prototype was created for marketing but was also given the first number of the production run. A prototype (PR-2) was created and used for marketing.

It was followed by a second batch of production cars of 27 units. The sequencing picked up where the previous year left off, so cars were numbered 30 through 57.

Again, all came in SS-trim equipped with a 6-speed manual transmission, Hurst shifter, traction control, and the LS1 V-8, which received a factory 5-hp bump to make total output 325 hp. After GMMG's performance additions, output was now

For 2001, the Berger SS carried over the exterior cosmetic additions, including the stripes and heritage grille insert.

This new center stack cloisonné was added, bearing the vehicle's engine performance ratings. This example has an upgraded Phase 2 package.

rated at 380 hp and torque increased to 400 ft-lbs. The cosmetic changes from the prior year's run were retained and carried over.

Changes and Additions

New additions to the package included 17x9.5 split five-spoke Mallett 396 chrome-plated wheels with special SS center cap stickers, a power antenna, and red powder-coated brake calipers.

A rearview mirror with a compass and auto dimming functionality was another upgrade. The mirror was made by the Gentex Corporation, an automotive supplier based in Zeeland, Michigan. A company executive purchased a 2000 Berger SS Camaro, and wanting to get his team involved with the new venture, he coordinated a deal to include the option on some 2001 examples, as well as subsequent GMMG-built Camaros.

With the dealership's anniversary having passed, the celebratory badging was replaced with "Prescribed Power" heritage badges. That included the center stack badge, which was replaced with one bearing engine performance ratings.

For 2001, customers could add an optional houndstooth seat insert.

Paint Configuration and Sales

#	Paint	Body	T	Ph.	HP	#	Paint	Body	T	Ph.	HP
PR2	Navy Blue	T-T	6	1	380	44	Onyx Black	T-T	6	1	380
31	S. Orange	Conv.	6	1	380	45	Arctic White	T-T	A	2X	475
32	Rally Red	T-T	6	1	380	46	Navy Blue	T-T	6	2	435
33	Rally Red	T-T	6	3	600	47	Onyx Black	T-T	6	1	380
34	Navy Blue	T-T	6	3	600	48	Onyx Black	T-T	6	1	380
35	Rally Red	T-T	6	1	380	49	Navy Blue	T-T	6	1	380
36	Navy Blue	T-T	6	1	380	50	Rally Red	T-T	6	1	380
37	Navy Blue	T-T	6	1	380	51	Navy Blue	T-T	6	1	380
38	Arctic White	T-T	6	1	380	52	Navy Blue	T-T	6	2X6R	525
39	Navy Blue	T-T	6	1	380	53	Arctic White	T-T	6	1	380
40*	Hug. Orange	T-T	6	2	435	54	Arctic White	Conv.	6	1	380
41	Onyx Black	T-T	6	1	380	55	Navy Blue	T-T	6	1	380
42	Arctic White	T-T	6	1	380	56	Arctic White	T-T	6	2X6R	525
43	Arctic White	T-T	6	1	380	57	Rally Red	T-T	6	1	380
PR	Prototype	HP	Horsepower	*	Custom Paint						

The 2001 Berger SS came in five factory colors; Arctic White, Onyx Black, Navy Blue Metallic, Bright Rally Red, and Sunset Orange Metallic. The color stripe assignments were the same as the year before.

Car #40, ordered by Matt Berger, received custom 1969 Hugger Orange paint with painted white stripes. It also was the first to get GMMG's Phase 2 performance package upgrades that increased horsepower to 435 and 410 ft-lbs of torque. Pricing for the 2001 Berger SS increased to $39,990.

2002 Berger SS

A third and final run of special Berger-commissioned SS Camaros was offered in 2002. A final prototype (labeled as PR-3) was followed by 42 production cars.

Berger now allowed customers to add more SLP second sticker upgrades, including the rear decklid mat, as well as the 1LE handling package, which featured larger-diameter anti-sway bars and Koni adjustable shocks.

As before, the run's sequencing picked up where the 2001 cars left off, becoming cars 58 through 100. New for 2002 was the option for customers to select any factory paint color along with the addition of two-tone or multi-seat surfaces, such as color leather inserts or houndstooth.

All the previous year's performance and cosmetic upgrades were added but with a new wheel package. For 2002, 17x9.5-inch

Fikse Classic FM5 3-piece forged techni-polished aluminum wheels were used. They were equipped with machined aluminum SS center caps and wrapped in BFGoodrich g-Force tires. The Gentex rearview mirror was upgraded to now include an exterior temperature reading.

Nine Camaros in the production run were ordered with GMMG's Phase 2 performance options and six of those were custom painted, receiving painted stripes.

This 2002 Berger SS (#93) received custom paint, being painted in Corvette Electron Blue. It also received a Phase 2 engine upgrade.

2002 Berger SS Camaro Registry										
#	Paint	Body	T	Ph.	HP	#	Paint	Body	T	Ph.	HP
PR3	Arctic White	T-T	6	1	380	80	Rally Red	T-T			
58	Arctic White	T-T	6	1	380	81	Arctic White	Conv.	6	2	435
59	Le Mans Blue•	T-T	6	2X	435	82	Rally Red	Conv.	6	2X	435
60	Rally Green•	T-T	6	2	435	83	Sebring Silver	Conv.	6	1	380
61	Arctic White	T-T	6	1	380	84	Rally Red	T-T	6	1	380
62	Light Pewter	T-T	6	1	380	85	Rally Red	Conv.	6	1	380
63	Sebring Silver	Conv.	6	1	380	86	Onyx Black	T-T	6	1	380
64	Navy Blue	Conv.	6	1	380	87	Rally Red	T-T	6	1	380
65	Rally Red	Conv.	6	1	380	88	Sebring Silver	Coupe	6	2X	475
66	Sebring Silver	T-T	6	1	380	89	Rally Red	T-T	6	3	600
67	Onyx Black	T-T	1	1	380	90	Rally Red	T-T	6	1	380
68	Navy Blue	T-T				91	Navy Blue	T-T	6	3	600
69	Navy Blue	T-T	6	2X6	500	92	Rally Red	Coupe	6	2	435
70	Navy Blue	T-T				93	C. Elec. Blue•	T-T	6	2	435
71	Navy Blue	T-T				94	Arctic White	T-T	6	2	435
72	Chrm. Illusion•	T-T	6	2X	435	95	Rally Red	Conv.	6	2	435
73	L. Pewter	T-T	6	1	380	96	Navy Blue	Conv.	6	2	435
74	Sunset Orange	T-T	6	1	380	97	Light Pewter	Conv.	6	1	380
75	Rally Red	T-T	6	1	380	98	Navy Blue	Conv.	6	1	380
76	Navy Blue•	T-T	6	2	435	99	Sebring Silver	T-T	6	1	380
77	Sebring Silver	Coupe	6	2	435	100	Hug. Orange•	Conv.	6	2	435
78	Oynx Black	Conv.	6	2X	500	00	Day. Yellow•	T-T	6	2	435
79	Oynx Black	Conv.	6	1	380	PR	Prototype	HP	Horsepower		•	Custom Paint

The exterior upgrades continued for the run of 2002 Berger SS Camaros, including the added stripes and painted black rear panel.

To cap off the run of vehicles, this 2002 Berger SS (#00) was created for Matt Berger and painted in Daytona Yellow.

Pricing for the package climbed again, as completed vehicles with all the bells and whistles cost as much as $59,995, which was more than the price of a then-new Corvette.

To commemorate the entire three-year run, a final Camaro (known as car #00) was built for Matt Berger. It received a Phase 2 performance package, custom Daytona Yellow paint with black stripes, and a Daytona Yellow and houndstooth leather interior.

2002 Camaro ZL1 Supercars

		ID	Paint			Built For
Prototypes	3	PR-1	1969 Le Mans Blue			Chevrolet
		PR-2	Bright Rally Red			Berger Chevrolet
		PR-3	Medium Plum M.			Helen Gibb
Production	69	Man.	67	Auto.	2	

Dialing up the performance, in 2002, Berger Chevrolet and GMMG offered the ZL1 Supercar, harkening back to the legendary 1969 COPO Camaro ZL1. This modern version utilized several contemporary Corvette Z06 components, including the model's five-spoke wheels.

2002 Camaro ZL-1 Supercars: Package Content and Equipment					
Phase 1	400 hp/410 ft-lbs	Package Total	$34,845	ID	GMMG 9560 ••
Engine	• 2002 LS6 GM Performance Parts Corvette warranty block • CNC ported and cast gray painted exhaust manifolds • New high-flow M.A.F. housing • Underdrive pulleys and belts • Carbon-fiber-type air-box lid with 1999 GM filter and tube • Cat-back chambered exhaust system with stainless tips • 180-degree thermostat • Coolant and emission stickers, Mobil 1 oil fill cap and decal				

Suspen-sion	• Eibach (front and rear) lowering springs (1.5 inch) • Penske Racing 7500 Series D.A. shocks • Special sway bars (front and rear) • 1LE: front and rear control arms and Panhard bar	Brakes			
		Calipers	Z06 Corvette (front and rear)		
		Pads	Hawk		
		Rotors	Slotted Z06		

Wheels	17x9.5-inch Z06 5-spoke	Tires	Goodyear Eagle F-1 SC 265/40ZR17

Exterior	• GM "SS" Hood and "SS" spoiler • Hood, roof, deck lid stripe with 400-hp decals • 35th Anniversary Satin Black hood decal • Charcoal Metallic Grille with 1969-style blue bowtie • Painted black rear panel with polished "CAMARO" insert lettering • ZL1 Supercar Fender badges
Interior	• Silver Face gauge insert with ZL1 Supercar logo* • Internal gauge cluster bezel frame surround • Front seat headrests embroidery • Black Hurst shift ball with short-throw shifter • GM power antenna and rearview mirror (compass, temperature, automatic dimmer)
Num-bering/ID	• Numbered HP/TQ dash cloisonne • GMMG numbered doorjamb plate (driver's side) • ZL1 car numbers graphics on front window and rearview mirror
Other	ZL1 key fobs, car cover, and floor mats
••	A play off the 9560 COPO designation from the 1969 COPO Camaro ZL1
*	Original plans called for each to be signed by long-time GM employee Jon Moss

Inspiration for the 2002 ZL1 Supercar arose after Ford's 2000 summer debut of the special-edition 2000 Mustang Cobra R. Chevrolet teamed with GMMG to build a one-off suitable Camaro rival concept that used the Corvette Z06's powertrain. The trim was all new for 2001, and the new LS6 engine was used. Based on the 5.7 LS1, the powerplant, which was rated at 385 hp and 385 ft-lbs of torque, featured an aluminum block, high-compression cylinder heads with improved porting, and titanium exhaust.

Scott Settlemire provided Murphy with a Camaro test fleet vehicle, an LS6 engine, and a set of Z06 wheels, tires, and brake components for what would be called the ZL1 pilot car.

Murphy had the prototype together in February 2001. Moving forward with an ancillary project, Murphy and Berger Chevrolet, pleased with the Berger SS program, planned to offer a run of these performance machines, which were to be christened ZL1s. That name harkened back to the legendary 1969 COPO Camaro of the same name. Sixty-nine of those classic legends were surreptitiously processed through Chevrolet's central office, and the first 50 were ordered by Fred Gibb Chevrolet, in LaHarpe, Illinois. Power came from a wild, all-aluminum 427-ci V-8 engine.

Murphy wanted to replicate their race-ready nature, the quantity of 69, and the name. Chevrolet wasn't willing to authorize the use of the iconic moniker, but an agreement was reached to call the cars "ZL1 Supercars."

Other dealers signed on to distribute the cars, including Tom Henry Chevrolet in Bakerstown, Pennsylvania, and Hendrick Chevrolet in Cary, North Carolina.

Ordering the B4C Batch

All 69 vehicles were ordered as B4C coupes in late winter of 2002. The B4C designation was a special police-use Special Service Package that was never officially available to the public.

GMMG's back lot is full of Camaro B4Cs awaiting transformation to ZL1 Supercars. (Photo Courtesy GMMG Registry)

ZL1s that have modifications in progress are stored in GMMG's back lot. (Photo Courtesy GMMG Registry)

Ordered through a six-digit fleet order, it simply repackaged a Z/28 but omitted the black painted roof and emblems. The only new parts were the rear trailing arms from the 1LE package. Under the hood was the stock 310-hp LS1 5.7L V-8. All ZL1 vehicles had a 6-speed manual transmission except two that were converted to be automatic (#1 and #21).

Setting the Scene

The first prototype was displayed at that year's SEMA Show. Originally black, Matt Murphy painted it Garnet Red, a 1969 Camaro color that was used on two of the original 1969 ZL1 Camaros. Settlemire used the car extensively for public relations, and eventually the car was repainted Le Mans Blue, which harkened back to Bright Blue that was used in 1969.

This example, PR-3, was one of three prototypes and was built for Helen Gibb, the wife of Fred Gibb. Fred owned Gibb Chevrolet and initiated the run of 1969 Camaro ZL1s.

While Gibb Chevrolet was no longer in business, the engine bay plaque on PR-3 was modified to celebrate the ZL1's heritage. Each ZL1 Supercar received a data plaque mounted on the driver-side shock tower.

The car was kept by the brand through 2009 when it was disposed of at auction due to the General Motors bankruptcy proceedings.

A second prototype (PR-2) was delivered to Matt Berger. Murphy built a third prototype (PR-3), which was painted Medium Plum Metallic and harkened back to a 1967 Camaro Z/28 that was campaigned by Gibb's dealership. It originally went to Fred Gibb's widow, Helen.

Performance Upgrades

Upon arrival to GMMG in March 2002, the car's stock LS1 V-8 was removed and upgraded with a 2002 LS6 Corvette engine block. Further modifications included underdrive pulleys and belts, a 180-degree thermostat, and a high-flow mass airflow housing. The setup breathed easier thanks to a carbon-fiber-type air box, ported exhaust manifolds, and a cat-back chambered exhaust with stainless-steel tips. This powertrain foundation was branded as the LS6 Phase 1 and was rated at 400 hp and 410 ft-lbs of torque.

2002 ZL1 Supercar: Engine Upgrades			
	1	2	3
V-8	LS6 (346 ci)		C5R (427 ci)
HP	400	475	600
TQ	410	440	575
Comp.	10.5:1	11.4:1	12:1
Price	$34,845*	$6,995	$23,995
*	Package total (performance and cosmetic)		
Note: Car #69 received Phase 4			

Each of the ZL1 Supercars was upgraded with an LS6 Corvette engine block along with numerous other modifications.

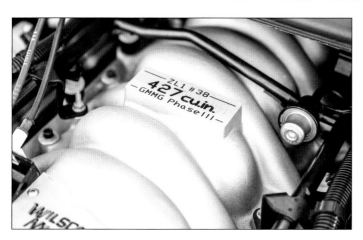

On cars that received the Phase 3 upgrade, the engine was topped with this Wilson intake manifold.

The cat-back chambered exhaust, combined with the LS6 engine, gives the ZL1 Supercars a distinct rumble.

The ZL1 Supercar engine block and cylinder heads were engraved with detailed data corresponding to each build. On this example, #23, you can see the car's VIN, that it received a Phase 3 upgrade, that it was built in the spring of 2008, and the initials of the GMMG employee who handled assembly.

Electric exhaust cutouts were part of the Phase 3 upgrade, allowing for even greater performance capabilities.

Phases 2 and 3

Customers who wanted more power could select a Phase 2 package (costing $6,995) with additional modifications (a lightweight flywheel and painted red valve covers), and output increased to 475 hp and 440 ft-lbs of torque.

GMMG pushed the ZL1 Supercar's performance one step further, offering a Phase 3 package. Costing $23,995, it equipped vehicles with the Corvette C5R's 427-ci V-8 race motor topped with a numbered Wilson Intake Manifold. After other modifications, output was rated at 600 hp and 575 ft-lbs of torque.

Besides the significant increase in performance, many customers opted for the Phase 3 to throw back to the displacement of the 1969 Camaro ZL1's 427-ci engine. Standard on Phase 3 cars were retro hockey-stick stripe decals that were interrupted by 427 numerals ahead of the front wheels. Car #23, which was built specifically for Matt Berger, had them left off.

Both option packages, including additional variants, were above the factory recommendations and not authorized by the Camaro brand team. Per the recommendation of the Camaro's chief engineer, output over 400 hp was pushing the vehicle's architecture to its limit. As such, neither were covered by the GM powertrain warranty, and they didn't comply with the emissions recertification.

In addition to engine packages, other performance options and upgrades were made available to customers, including items such as a roll cage and Hurst line lock.

An exclusive Phase 3 package cosmetic touch was used with the retro hockey stick–style side stripe. It was available in white, black, or red.

Suspension Upgrades

The suspension was equipped with Eibach lowering springs and Penske Racing shocks available in three different setups. Corvette Z06 front and rear brake calipers were installed along with Corvette pads and Z06 rotors.

Following the prototype, the ZL1 Supercar wheels also came from the Corvette Z06, using its painted dual-spoke, star pattern. At no charge, customers could select the chrome design as well as Cragar S/S or Fikse wheels.

Phase 3 Package Contents (Plus Phase 1 Upgrades)
• GM Motorsports aluminum C5R race block
• Forged 4340 steel crankshaft (Callies)
• Billet 4340 billet steel connecting rods (Callies)
• JE 4.125-inch lightweight pistons
• Hydraulic roller camshaft
• Phase III CNC ported LS6 cylinder heads
• High strength timing chain
• 4130 steel pushrods (Comp)
• Titanium valve springs and retainers
• Cometic composite head gaskets
• ATI crankshaft damper
• Wilson aluminum intake manifold with ZL1 engraving
• 1-7/8-inch diameter exhaust headers
• 3-inch Y-pipe with 4-inch collector
• Rear electric exhaust cutout with dash switch
Exclusive Cosmetic Content
• Hockey stick–style side stripe (white, black, or red)
• "427" graphics (on front fenders, interrupting stripe)

The standard Phase 1 Corvette Z06 wheel could be upgraded at no charge with either a chrome-plated Cragar S/S or a Fikse wheel.

Interior Upgrades

Inside the cabin, GMMG's usual upgrades were carried over, including the Gentex mirror, power antenna, and silver gauge insert that featured the ZL1 Supercar logo. A black or white Hurst shift ball with short-throw shifter was installed on manual transmission–equipped vehicles.

Other add-ons included special key fobs and the program's logo embroidered on the seat headrests and special floor mats, which was done by Marietta Auto Trim. As with other GMMG products, a horsepower and torque cloisonne was installed on the center console.

An engine performance data cloisonné was added to the center stack. This example is a Phase 3.

Cosmetic Modifications

The hood and rear spoiler were exchanged for SS components. Further visually setting the cars apart was the same exterior center stripe decal as found on the Earnhardt Intimidator SS Camaro. While those only came in Magnetallic Gray, the ZL1s were available in a variety of colors. It was further enhanced with the addition of the 2002 35th Anniversary Camaro's satin black hood decal applied ahead of the hood scoop.

The cars received the normal suite of GMMG's cosmetic touches with the painted black tail panel receiving stainless "CAMARO" infill lettering. Up front, the grille insert's SS logo was exchanged for a blue bowtie that mimicked the one

Embroidered floor mats and a Hurst shift-knob ball were some of the interior additions. An optional roll cage could also be installed.

As with other Berger/GMMG Camaro programs, the ZL1 Supercar received a trim bezel and special gauge face insert.

Included in the ZL1 Supercar's center stripe was a callout to Fred Gibb and Vince Piggins, two individuals who were instrumental to the 1969 COPO Camaro ZL1 program.

Each ZL1 Supercar received this brass door tag that features a new lower line of text calling out the ZL1 status.

found on the 1969 Camaro ZL1s. Custom badging was also affixed on the front fenders along with a GMMG badge on the rear panel.

GMMG's brass door tags were installed in the driver-side doorjamb along with the usual numbered graphics at the base of the windshield and on the rearview mirror. A new trapezoid-shaped badge showed up under the hood, mounted on the driver's side shock tower. It included the car's sequence number, the original owner's name, and the selling dealership.

Special Paint

Many cars received special paint, which was a $7,990 option. Because of the legendary status of the 1969 Camaro ZL1, many of the colors and schemes paid homage to the originals.

Standouts include the first production vehicle (car #1), which was built to commemorate Fred Gibb's original 1969 ZL1 Camaro Funny Car and was adorned with heritage-inspired livery.

Car #3 was painted Daytona Yellow to match the third 1969 Camaro ZL1, which was also painted Daytona Yellow and delivered to Berger Chevrolet. Car #23 was painted 1969 Hugger Orange for Matt Berger. The color was paired with a special orange leather upholstery with houndstooth seat inserts. Car #16 was purchased by Ken Barnhart and painted orange to match the 1969 ZL1 Camaro he purchased new.

Sales and Distribution

Completed ZL1 Supercars sold for approximately $57,000: $25,075 for the Camaro's base price, plus another nearly $30,000 to $34,000 for the GMMG package). When the other premium options, such as Phase 2 or 3, were added on, the price reached as high as $126,620, which was the cost of car #69. A variety of dealerships sold the 69 vehicles, and Berger Chevrolet sold the most, moving 28.

BONUS CONTENT

Scan to view the 2002 ZL1 dealership distribution.

www.cartechbooks.com/ct658-qr46

The first ZL1 Supercar of the run paid tribute to famed 1960s drag racer Dick Harrell. Harkening back to his 1969 Camaro race car, it featured $9,394 worth of custom paint and graphics, including door decals and a gold lace stripe package.

In addition to cosmetic upgrades, the ZL1 program brought serious performance upgrades.

2002 Berger Hot Rod Edition Camaro Z28: Registry

#	ID	Color	S	BS	T	P	HP	#	ID	Color	S	BS	T	P	HP
1	PR1	Rally Red	W	B4C	6	1	380	20	1984	Rally Red	B	B4C	6	1	380
2	PR2	Rally Red	W	B4C	6	1	380	21	1985	S. Silver	R	B4C	6	1	380
3	1967	O. Black	R	T-T	6	2	435	22	1986	N. Blue	W	B4C	6	4	680
4	1968	N. Blue	W	Con.	6	1	380	23	1987	O Black	R	B4C	6	1	380
5	1969	O. Black	R	B4C	6	1	380	24	1988	Rally Red	W	B4C	6	2	435
6	1970	O. Black	R	B4C	6	3	600	25	1989	Arctic White	B	B4C	6	1	380
7	1971	O. Black	R	B4C	6	1	380	26	1990	Rally Red	W	T-T	A	3	600
8	1972	O. Black	R	B4C	6	1	380	27	1991•	O. Black	R	Con	A	3	600
9	1973	L. Pewter	B	Con	6	1	380	28	1992	O. Black	R	Con	A	3	600
10	1974•	S. Silver	B	T-T	A	2X	475	29	1993	S. Silver	B	T-T	A	1	360
11	1975	Rally Red	B	T-T	6	1	380	30	1994	O. Black	R	Con	A	1	360
12	1976	L. Pewter	B	T-T	A	1	360	31	1995	S. Silver	B	T-T	6	1	380
13	1977•	L. Pewter	B	T-T	A	2X	475	32	1996	Rally Red	W	T-T	A	1	360
14	1978	Rally Red	W	T-T	A	1	360	33	1997	O. Black	W	Con	6	3	600
15	1979	L. Pewter	B	Con	A	1	360	34	1998	O. Black	R	Con	6	1	380
16	1980	O. Black	R	Con	6	1	380	35	1999	D. Yellow ••	B	T-T	A	2X	435
17	1981	Rally Red	W	Con	A	1	380	36	2000	N. Blue	BL	T-T	6	2	435
18	1982	N. Blue	W	T-T	6	1	380	37	2001	S. Silver	W	Con	6	1	360
19	1983	Rally Red	W	B4C	6	2	435	38	2002	L.M. Blue••	B	Con	A	3	600

PR	Prototype	P	Engine Phase	HP	Horsepower	BS	Body style	•	Equipped with SS upgrades
S	Exterior stripe colors: W: White, R: Red, B: Black, BL: Blue					••	Custom paint		

2002 Hot Rod Camaro Edition by Berger

Prototypes		2
T-Top	Auto.	8
	Man.	6
Convertible	Auto.	6
	Man.	5
B4C Coupe	Auto.	0
	Man.	11
Total Cars		38

In the fall of 2001, Ed Zinke, a *Hot Rod* magazine writer, discussed with Chevrolet building a commemorative Camaro to celebrate the close ties with the storied magazine. In 1966, the publication purchased a Bolero Red preproduction 1967 Camaro SS350 direct from General Motors. Over the subsequent years, it was modified and used for testing and documented in the magazine.

Zinke was rebuffed, mostly due to his desire for the car to be equipped with a red interior, matching the original example. He connected with Matt Murphy at the 2001 SEMA Show in

The 2002 Hot Rod Edition by Berger was created in conjunction with the long-running magazine. Each received a red bowtie grille emblem.

GMMG's parking lot in the back is full of completed Hot Rod Camaros awaiting transport and delivery. (Photo Courtesy GMMG Registry)

The front fenders received custom badges.

Las Vegas, Nevada, and shared his idea.

With Murphy's system of GMMG-modified dealer Camaros being a well-oiled machine, he suggested calling Dennis Barker at Berger Chevrolet. Zinke and Barker connected in April 2002, and the program was well-received by Matt Berger, who agreed to a run of 36 vehicles. Each marked the number of years that the Camaro was in production up to that point (1967–2002). Effectively, it mirrored the 2002 Berger SS Camaro program with changes limited primarily to branding.

Barker reached out to Scott Settlemire at General Motors for the allotment of inventory. The response was brief and to the point: no more Camaros could be had. Production on the iconic model was stopping in August, and here it was spring with the big request coming in.

A painted satin black taillight panel and custom badges were cosmetic additions to the rear of the vehicles.

Undeterred, Barker jumped to action, scouring the nation for needed vehicles. Wanting to fulfill the batch at any cost, the team forewent the traditional SS route and used more readily available Z28 Camaros as the starting platform coming in an assortment of convertible, B4C, and T-top bodystyles and with either the automatic or manual transmission. A month's time was needed, but 36 cars were secured, purchased, and shipped to GMMG.

Two prototypes were built, and both were equipped with a manual transmission.

Performance and Cosmetic Modifications

Each received GMMG's Phase 1 performance upgrades and its usual suite of cosmetic touches, such as the Gentex mirror, power coated brake calipers, power antenna, painted black tail panel, and roof hoop.

The ZL1 Supercar Phase 3 side hockey-stick stripes were added, interrupted with a horsepower callout ahead of the front wheels. Other exterior items included a grille insert with a red bowtie emblem. The package's wheels were chrome Cragar SS wheels that were wrapped in BFGoodrich g-Force KDW tires.

Special badging was applied to the fenders and tail panel along with unique door graphics that harkened back to the style found on the magazine's 1967 test car. Many owners opted to leave them off.

Inside, Zinke didn't get his full red interior, but the cars featured red seat inserts that were complete with headrest stitching. Other additions included silver-faced gauges, special key fobs, a fitted car cover, and embroidered floor mats. A numbered cloisonne was mounted to the center stack with the car's 4-digit year of celebration (1967–2002). That year was also mounted as a graphic on the windshield and rearview mirror.

Red seat inserts paid homage to the full red interior of the Camaro test vehicle that Hot Rod *magazine received in 1966.*

Noticeable changes under the hood included a new air box and Hot Rod Edition graphic.

Each vehicle received a center stack cloisonné with the year.

A new gauge face and trim bezel was installed.

Customers could return their vehicles to GMMG for additional engine Phase 2 through 5X upgrades and other performance options or custom paint.

Marketing and Distribution

The pair of prototypes participated in the Hot Rod Power Tour in June. While the overall concept was attractive to enthusiasts, sales were sluggish. Already having another run of GMMG-built 2002 Berger SS Camaros that essentially had the same performance capabilities available for sale, Berger Chevrolet effectively flooded its own market.

Eventually, buyers were found, and all Hot Rod Edition cars sold. The base price was $44,095.

2002 Berger Hot Rod Edition Camaro Z28: Registry

#	ID	Color	S	Body	T	Ph.	HP	#	ID	Color	S	Body	T	Ph.	HP
1	PR1*	B. Ral. Red	W	CPE	6	1	380	20	1984	B. Ral. Red	B	B4C	6	1	380
2	PR2*	B. Ral. Red	W	CPE	6	1	380	21	1985	S. Silver **	R	B4C	6	1	380
3	1967	O. Black	R	T-T	6	2	435	22	1986••	N. Blue **	W	B4C	6	4	680
4	1968	N. Blue **	W	Con.	6	1	380	23	1987	O. Black	R	B4C	6	1	380
5	1969	O. Black	R	B4C	6	1	380	24	1988	B. Ral. Red	W	B4C	6	2	435
6	1970	O. Black	R	B4C	6	3	600	25	1989	Arctic White	B	B4C	6	1	380
7	1971	O. Black	R	B4C	6	1	380	26	1990	B. Ral. Red	W	T-T	A	3X	630
8	1972	O. Black	R	B4C	6	1	380	27	1991•	O. Black	R	Con	A	3	600
9	1973	L. Pewter	B	Con	6	1	380	28	1992	O. Black	R	Con	A	3X	630
10	1974•	S. Silver **	B	T-T	A	2X	475	29	1993	S. Silver **	B	T-T	A	1	360
11	1975	B. Ral. Red	B	T-T	6	1	380	30	1994	O. Black	R	Con	A	1	360
12	1976	L. Pewter	B	T-T	A	1	360	31	1995	S. Silver **	B	T-T	6	1	380
13	1977•	L. Pewter	B	T-T	A	2X	475	32	1996	B. Ral. Red	W	T-T	A	1	360
14	1978	B. Ral. Red	W	T-T	A	1	360	33	1997	O. Black	W	Con	6	3	600
15	1979	L. Pewter	B	Con	A	1	360	34	1998	O. Black	R	Con	6	1	380
16	1980	O. Black	R	Con	6	1	380	35	1999	D. Yellow ***	B	T-T	A	2X	475
17	1981	B. Ral. Red	W	Con	A	1	380	36	2000	N. Blue **	R	T-T	6	2	435
18	1982	N. Blue **	W	T-T	6	1	380	37	2001	S. Silver **	B	Con	A	1	360
19	1983	B. Ral. Red	W	B4C	6	2	435	38	2002	L.M. Blue***	W	Con	6	3	600

*	Prototype	**Ph.**	Engine Phase	**HP**	Horsepower	**	Metallic	***	Onyx Black cars with custom paint

S Exterior stripe colors: W: White, R: Red, B: Black, BL: Blue • Equipped with SS upgrades

•• Equipped with a 454 C5R Phase IV upgrade (680 hp/650 ft-lbs) and other items, such as a carbon fiber GMMG Dick Harrell wide-body hood, a roll cage, Corvette brakes, and Nitto drag tires. Final vehicle price: $100,060.

2002 GMMG 35th Anniversary Performance Edition

2002 GMMG 35th Anniversary Performance Edition			
Prototype	2	PR1	Man.
		PR2	Auto.
T-Top	24	Auto.	11
		Man.	13
Convertible	23	Auto.	12
		Man.	11
B4C Coupe	3	Auto.	0
		Man.	3
Total Cars		52	

Building on Chevrolet's 35th Anniversary Edition Camaro, GMMG offered a Performance Edition, which added on to the cosmetic-oriented trim. Matt Murphy initially sought to build 100 vehicles. Two prototypes (PR-1 and PR-2) were assembled, both convertibles, followed by a proposed run of 50 production vehicles. Eight vehicles were part of the 50 Camaros that Chevrolet provided for use at the 2001 Brickyard 400 race. As such, they retained their unique door graphics. GMMG later converted two other festival Camaros (Z7D) that were part of the 2002 Brickyard 400 race.

While the original concept was to build the run strictly on 35th Anniversary Edition Camaros, that intention soon expanded to include non-Anniversary Edition Camaro SS cars. As such, these are lacking the red paint, unique seat inserts and embroidery, and special blacked-out wheels. Being created toward the tail end of GMMG's operations, this run's package uniformity was rapidly eroding.

BONUS CONTENT

Scan to view the 2002 Performance Edition package contents.

www.cartechbooks.com/ct658-qr47

The Performance Edition brought performance upgrades to the 2002 35th Anniversary Edition Camaros, which were all painted Bright Rally Red.

The taillight panel was painted satin black before receiving unique badging. This example, #14, received upgrades, including a Phase 3 engine package.

A bespoke gauge insert was added to the instrument cluster along with a new bezel insert.

Performance Edition cars built on 35th Anniversary Edition Camaros were identified by the package's (RPO Z4C) exclusive pewter seat inserts.

Package Contents

Murphy delved into his usual bag of performance and cosmetic tricks to craft the run, essentially giving them the same treatment as what was found on the Berger SS Camaro. As such, they received the Phase 1 engine upgrade with 380 hp and 400 ft-lbs of torque along with suspension upgrades and cosmetic touches, such as the grille insert and painted satin black rear panel.

Murphy marked the cars with red oval anniversary badging that nearly matched the version Chevrolet created for the 35th Anniversary Edition. GMMG tweaked it by exchanging the lower "Chevrolet Camaro" wording for "Performance Edition" text. The badge was on the front fenders, rear panel, special floor mats, and on a new silver gauge insert.

Each Performance Edition received this engine rating center stack cloisonné.

The Performance Edition logo closely mirrored Chevrolet's anniversary logo, merely changing the lower line of text.

Many Performance Edition owners upgraded from the base Phase 1 specifications. This example is equipped with the Phase 2X package.

As was customary, the vehicle's sequencing was marked with number graphics on the rearview mirror and the base of the windshield. The Performance Edition cars also received the center stack performance badge and the GMMG tag riveted in the driver-side doorjamb. Also included was a unique key fob and fitted car cover.

Pricing and Distribution

GMMG's Performance Edition package cost $9,895 with an extra $100 emissions recertification fee. All told, the vehicles cost $43,630.

As was the norm for its projects, GMMG's additional performance stages were available, and many customers took advantage of the extra options. Customers who opted for 427 powerplants received unique "SS 427" grille emblems.

For this run of vehicles, GMMG opened availability beyond its close working partners of Berger Chevrolet and Tom Henry Chevrolet, although many vehicles weren't finished until 2010.

2002 Berger Supercar: Dick Harrell Edition

2002 Berger Supercar: Dick Harrell Edition Camaro					
Prototypes	3	Coupe	3	Man.	
Other	2	Convertible	1	Auto.	
		T-Top	1	Auto.	
Production			30		
Coupe	7	Auto.	2		
		Man.	5		
T-Top	23	Auto.	6		
		Man.	17		

Example #24 was repainted black by City Chevrolet, the dealership that sold the car. The anniversary edition's checkered-flag stripes were retained.

2002 Berger Supercar: Dick Harrell Edition

Phase 1	Identified as GMMG 9427*	400 hp/410 ft-lbs		Package Price	$57,444–$59,221

Powertrain	• 2002 LS6 GM Performance Parts Corvette block • Ported and cast gray-painted exhaust manifolds • New high-flow M.A.F. housing • Ported throttle body with 180-degree thermostat • Underdrive pulleys and belts • GM Red Performance plug wires • Carbon-fiber-type air box lid with GM air filter and tube • Cat-back chambered exhaust with stainless tips • Lightweight SPEC flywheel • Coolant and emission stickers • Mobil 1 oil fill cap and decal				

Suspension	• Front and rear Eibach L. Springs (1.5 inch) • KONI C.D. adjustable shocks • Lower control arm brackets • Subframe connectors • Sway bars (front and rear, 1LE content)		

Brakes — Z06 Corvette Calipers
Pads — Hawk | Rotors | Slotted Z06
Wheel — FIKSE 18x11(F)18x12 (R)
Tires — Michelin (F:295/35ZR18, R:335/30ZR18)

Exterior Cosmetics	• Widebody kit (fenders, cowl-induction hood, and rear spoiler) • Charcoal Metallic Grille with gold bowtie emblem • Painted roof tops (body color) • Carbon fiber–style stripe package with 400-hp hood callouts • Painted rear panel (black) with polished insert lettering • Dick Harrell fender badges and GMMG badge (rear panel)

Interior Additions	• Silver-face gauges with DHS logo • Internal gauge cluster bezel frame surround (Pontiac Trans Am) • Front seat headrests embroidery • Black Hurst shift ball with short-throw shifter • GM power antenna and rearview mirror (compass, temperature, automatic dimmer)

Numbering/ID	• Numbered HP/TQ dash cloisonne • GMMG numbered doorjamb plate • Car number graphics on windshield and rearview mirror

Other	Key fobs, car cover, and floor mats

*	A play off the 9560 COPO number from the 1969 COPO Camaro ZL1

The pinnacle of GMMG's efforts, know-how, and vehicle craftsmanship was fully manifest in the 2002 Berger Dick Harrell Supercar. Facing daunting odds, the vehicle marked the team's final product before closing its doors for good. Due to its extreme nature both in performance and appearance, the Dick Harrell Edition Camaro went down in history as the ultimate fourth-generation Camaro available from a dealership showroom.

The Dick Harrell Edition was built to celebrate the life and legacy of 1960s drag racer Dick Harrell.

The project's origins are traced back to a radical Camaro show car that was built by the GM Performance Division and the brand's SEMA vehicle team. It paid tribute to the famed Camaro Z28 campaigned in SCCA Trans Am racing by Roger Penske and driven by Mark Donohue. It was on display at major automotive events, including the 2002 Woodward Dream Cruise, in Detroit, Michigan.

This contemporary interpretation sported a similar blue and yellow livery color scheme. More striking was its ultra-wide body that was comprised of larger front and rear fenders, which allowed for ultra-wide wheels and tires. At the rear was a high back blade spoiler, and up front was a massive cowl-induction hood. Power came from a 600-hp Corvette C5-R 427-ci aluminum race engine.

After seeing the vehicle, Matt Murphy was drawn to the unique one-off front fascia and wanted to incorporate it into one of his own GMMG projects. After connecting with John Heinricy, the director of General Motors Performance Division, it was clear: Chevrolet would only allow the entire car to be replicated—not individual pieces.

Undeterred, Murphy agreed. He recruited Matt Berger who set up Berger Chevrolet as the key distributor for this yet-to-be-named widebody Camaro project.

The next step was templating the vehicle and preparing mass production of the special panels. A donor vehicle was procured and sent to the design center at the GM Tech Center in Warren, Michigan. Murphy contracted a local supplier, and when the deal fell apart, he used a second manufacturer. The lost time was costly and was only one of many setbacks to come.

Procuring A Heritage Partner

With a working model in place and production methods established, the next step was finding branding inspiration for such an advantageous project. Since the ZL1 had already been taken on a prior project (Berger's ZL1 Supercar), Murphy struck up talks with Joel Rosen of Motion Performance fame. A contract was signed to incorporate the Motion name and appearance, but at the last moment it was called off due to design discrepancies.

Seeking another heritage partner, Murphy connected with Valerie Harrell, daughter of legendary 1960s drag racer and performance expert Dick Harrell. With Valerie on board, branding shifted slightly with the cars being labeled as Berger Supercars and this one becoming the Dick Harrell Edition.

With national supply dwindling fast, production was limited to 30 vehicles that were all sold through Berger Chevrolet. In March, past project sales champion Dennis Barker abruptly left the dealership, leaving the sale of these Supercars to colleague Dick Jacques.

Building the Beasts

Acquiring donor vehicles was nothing short of an impossible task because Chevrolet had stopped production of the fourth-generation Camaro. Being over a year and half later, new inventory was not available from the factory.

Tireless effort went into locating suitable Z28 and SS models from around the country that were either purchased or traded from other dealerships. Once acquired, they were shipped directly to Marietta, Georgia, for GMMG's modification.

A Pair of Prototypes

A pair of prototype vehicles were created. One identified as PR-1 was purchased by Valerie Harrell and was painted a radical Tangerine Orange. It was inspired by the appearance of the 1969 Camaro ZL1 that Dick had custom painted for his teammate driver, Shay Nichols.

The other, labeled as PR-2, was built in April 2004. It was the only vehicle in the run to have the added widebody panels made of carbon fiber. All other builds received carbon-fiber gas doors and hoods but fenders of fiberglass. The car was shown to an ecstatic public for the first time the last weekend of May in Atlanta, Georgia. From there, it attended national events and garnered media attention. A third prototype referred to as PR-3 was later built for Dale Earnhardt Jr.

Two other Camaros were given the widebody treatment, including a red convertible. The other was the pilot vehicle (referred to as the "clay car"), which was used to mock up the body panels.

It was a massive undertaking for Berger Chevrolet to sell all 30 of the Dick Harrell production run, but it was a fitting way to send off the fourth-generation Camaro.

Performance Modifications

As with the 2002 Berger ZL1 Supercar, the Dick Harrell's stock 310-hp, LS1 5.7L V-8 was removed and upgraded with a 2002 LS6 GM Performance Parts V-8 long-block. The Camaro's stock transmission options were retained, and the majority of the 33 were paired to the manual offering, which was upgraded with a lightweight flywheel.

The engine received other additions, such as a carbon-fiber air box, red GM Performance spark plug wires, underdrive pulleys and belts, a ported throttle body, and a cat-back chambered exhaust with stainless-steel tips. Total Phase 1 output was rated at 400 hp and 410 ft-lbs of torque.

Above this base configuration, further stages of power brought a reworked camshaft, heads, and tuning, which boosted output to upward of the 5XR's 750 hp—the highest rating for any of the GMMG-modified Camaros. Phase 5 packages came with a 454-ci LSX V-8 engine equipped with items such as a 92-mm throttle body.

The additional options found on the 2002 Berger GMMG ZL1 Supercar were made available, including a six-point roll cage, stronger 12-bolt rear end, and chrome-moly driveshaft.

2002 Dick Harrell Supercar: Engine Phase Upgrades						
Phase	1	3	3x	5	5x	5xR
V-8	LS6 (346 ci)	C5R LS6 (427 ci)		454 ci C5R LSX		
HP	400	600	630	650	680	750
TQ	410	575	600	630	650	675
Comp.	10.5:1	12:1	12:1	12.5:1	12:1	12:1
Price	*	$24,995	$24,995	$27,995	$3,595**	$36,000
*	Included in DH package price of $57,435			**	Plus Phase 5 price	

The Phase 1 engine package bumped output to 400 hp and 410 ft-lbs of torque.

A telltale sign of higher-Phase engine packages is the upgraded Wilson intake manifold.

Paint and Body

Because of the massive quantity of paint and body work, GMMG relied on several area body shops and local technicians for prep and assembly. One such example was Chris Lee, a painter for Cherokee County Toyota, a nearby dealership in Canton, Georgia. He arranged with management to work on the special cars on weekends in the company's paint booth. Chris painted six of the special Dick Harrell vehicles, spending upward of 50 hours per vehicle.

Upon arrival of each vehicle at the various body shops, the entire front and rear clip was removed and exchanged for the special fiberglass and carbon-fiber body components.

The cars received a black basecoat and then either Sikkens or House of Kolors paint. Available colors included stock Bright Rally Red, Arctic White, Sunset Orange Metallic, Sebring Silver Metallic, Onyx Black, and an assortment of custom colors. Around back, the rear taillight panel was painted black, and stainless "CAMARO" badging was inserted in the infill lettering.

To set the cars apart, a gold bowtie was mounted in the center grille insert along with unique side and hood graphics and fender badges. Phase 1 cars had a "400 HP" callout in the hood stripe, while higher phase upgrades received a "427 c.i." callout.

Car #23 received a blue bowtie to match the original owner's 1969 COPO Camaro. The single convertible also received a blue bowtie.

Adding the widebody panels was a laborious and time-intensive project, requiring upwards of 50 hours to complete. (Photo Courtesy GMMG Registry)

Fiske Profil 13 wheels with Michelin Pilot Sport tires were included in the package.

In addition to the spoiler and painted black tail panel, many cars received artwork showcasing Dick Harrell's nickname "Mr. Chevrolet."

After the radical bodywork was complete, the performance upgrades were added. (Photo Courtesy GMMG Registry)

Suspension Modifications

The car was lowered 1-1/2 inches and given other suspension upgrades including lower control-arm brackets, subframe connectors, and pieces from Chevy's factory 1LE suspension kit, including the front and rear sway bar.

The brakes were improved with Corvette Z06 front calipers and rotors. The stock wheels were swapped for polished Fikse custom billet aluminum wheels (just like the GM Performance Sunoco Camaro inspiration), wrapped in Michelin Pilot Sport tires. Some cars received BFGoodrich 335x30ZRx18 drag radials.

Interior Upgrades

The front seat headrests were highlighted with stitched Dick Harrell signatures along with the racer's iconic "Mr. Chevrolet" nickname. Many cars were equipped with standard Ebony leather interiors, but a few were upgraded with white leather.

Cars #21 and #23 are unique in that they received houndstooth inserts. The upholstery and stitching work was performed by Marietta Auto Trim.

Other additions included silver-faced gauge inserts that were divided using a new Pontiac Trans Am internal bezel complete with Dick Harrell's red, white, and blue shield. Cars

Embroidered floor mats, a short-throw shifter, and a Hurst shift-knob ball (in either white or black) were added to the cabin. Many cars, such as this example, were equipped with an optional roll cage.

A numbered cloisonné was added to the center stack.

A silver gauge face insert and trim bezel were added.

As was customary for GMMG Camaros, each Dick Harrell Edition received a numbered brass door tag.

The front seats received custom embroidery with Harrell's simulated signature and his "Mr. Chevrolet" nickname.

equipped with the manual transmission received black or white Hurst shift balls with a short-throw shifter. A numbered cloisonné was installed on the center stack along with GMMG's brass tag inside the driver-side doorjamb.

Special floor mats, special key fobs, and a car cover completed the getup.

Content for the special package also included a GM power antenna with a rearview mirror that featured a compass, the temperature, and automatic dimming.

Distribution

The completed cars, while impressive, were extremely difficult to sell, as these fully modified Supercars boasted prices as high as $140,000. Despite the staggering figure, enthusiastic buyers were found over time.

Making the sell more impossible was the timing. While the project kicked off in 2004, securing foundation cars further delayed the project. As the years dragged on, GMMG became overwhelmed with rapidly mounting research and development and production costs among other internal troubles.

As it became clear GMMG had taken on more than they could handle, several of Berger's repair staff traveled to Marietta to complete the final three unassembled vehicles. They weren't sold until early 2009, and GMMG closed in 2011.

With their dazzling colors, extreme body modifications, and over-the-top performance, the Dick Harrell Supercars are some of the wildest fourth-generation Camaros.

\multicolumn{9}{l}{2002 Berger Supercar Dick Harrell Edition: Registry and Related Vehicles}								
#	Paint	STP	BS	T	P	#	Paint	STP	BS	T	P
PR1	T. Orange*	BLK	CPE	6	3X	16	S. Silver	BLK	T-T	A	1
PR2	T. Turquoise*	BLK	CPE	6	3	17	Viper Red*	GLD	T-T	6	3X
PR3	G. Orange*	•	CPE	6	3X	18	Org. Green*	BLK	T-T	A	1
1	Cad. Red*	SIL	CPE	6	3X	19	O. Black	SIL	T-T	A	3X
2	Cor. Blue*	BLK	CPE	6	3X	20	L. Pewter	BLK	T-T	A	1
3	SSR Yellow*	BLK	CPE	6	3X	21	O. Black	SIL	T-T	6	5X
4	S. Orange	BLK	T-T	6	5	22	S. Silver	BLK	T-T	6	3X
5	Rally Red	BLK	T-T	6	3X	23	S. Silver	BLK	T-T	6	3X
6	Elec. Blue*	SIL	T-T	6	3X	24	Penske Blue*	YEL	T-T	6	3X
7	S. Silver	BLK	T-T	6	3X	25	Rally Red	BLK	CPE	A	3X
8	Rally Red	BLK	T-T	6	3X	26	Hug. Orange*	BLK	CPE	A	3X
9	Rally Red	BLK	CPE	6	1	27	Edelbrock Red*	•	T-T	6	1
10	Arctic White	BLK	T-T	6	5X	28	Arctic White	BLK	T-T	6	3X
11	Rally Red	BLK	T-T	A	1	29	Navy Blue	SIL	T-T	6	3X
12	Rally Red	WT	T-T	A	3X	30	Hug. Orange*	BLK	CPE	6	3X
13	Garnet Red*	BLK	T-T	6	1	\multicolumn{5}{l}{Related Vehicles}				
14	Bright Teal*	BLK	T-T	6	3X	PC	Red Met.*	BLK	T-T	A	2X6SR
15	S. Orange	BLK	T-T	6	3X	CV	Rally Red	•	CON	A	5XR
STP	\multicolumn{5}{l}{Stripe - BLK: Black; SIL: Silver, GLD: Gold, WT: White, YEL: Yellow}					P	\multicolumn{3}{l}{Phase}		
BS	\multicolumn{5}{l}{Bodystyle – CPE: Coupe, T-T: T-Top, CON: Convertible}					BS	\multicolumn{3}{l}{Bodystyle}		
T	\multicolumn{4}{l}{Transmission: 6-spd manual or auto}				•	\multicolumn{2}{l}{Graphics not applied}		*	\multicolumn{2}{l}{Custom Paint}	
PC	\multicolumn{2}{l}{Pilot car ('00 Z28)}		CV	\multicolumn{3}{l}{Convertible}						

Original Owners	PR1	Valerie Harrell	PR3	Dale Earnhardt Jr.	18	Matt Berger
25	\multicolumn{3}{l}{Bill Kummer, "Chevy Boys" 1960s racing team, Harrell friend}			27	Vic Edelbrock

Despite the rocky landing, the Dick Harrell Supercar was a fitting swan song and send off to the legacy of GMMG. It was ambitious and truly spoke to Murphy's big-picture thinking, his love of the Camaro's past, and his deep proclivity to push the pedal to the metal in all that he did and built.

2010–2011 Berger SS Camaro

	2010			2011		
Prototype	1			1		
Production	20	CPE	20	30	CPE	20
		CNV	0		CNV	5
ID	10BC01—10BC20			11BC11—11BC31		

Upon the Camaro's relaunch in 2010, Berger Chevrolet offered a limited run of Berger SS Camaros. A prototype was built by the dealership followed by a run of 20, all of which were on 2SS RS models.

As part of the Stage 1 engine upgrades, the 6.2L V-8 was given a Magnuson supercharger and chambered stainless-steel cat-back exhaust with output rated at 550 hp and 475 ft-lbs of torque. Two additional mechanical stages of upgrades were available. The top tier, Stage III, was performed by Custom Horsepower in Grand Rapids, Michigan. Four customers opted for it with output rated at 650 hp and 515 ft-lbs of torque. The suspension was upgraded along the wheels and tires. Customers could also opt for two additional stages of suspension upgrades.

Cosmetic changes included custom-painted rally stripes and the grille surround and rear taillight panel were painted black. A chrome "by Berger" text badge was mounted on the

The Stage 1 package added upgrades including a Magnuson supercharger.

Changes inside included a short-throw shifter and embroidered floor mats.

Shortly after the launch of the fifth-generation Camaro in 2010, Berger Chevrolet launched a performance Berger SS program.

Each vehicle received a data plaque on the ignition panel. It shows that this example is a 2010 (10) Berger Camaro (BC) and is car number 20 of the run.

2010 Berger SS Camaro: Registry							
#	Car ID	Paint	Stripe	Interior	Wheel	T	VIN
1	10CM2*	R. Yellow	Black	Black	Silver	M	W7A9100262
2	10BC1	A. Blue	Black	Black	Black	M	W0A9147312
3	10BC2	A. Blue	White	Black	Silver	M	W6A9148495
4	10BC3	V. Red	Black	White	Silver	M	W1A9149361
5	10BC4	I. Blue	Silver	Gray	Silver	A	J4A9150060
6	10BC5	Black	Silver	Black	Silver	M	W4A9150052
7	10BC6	Black	Red	Black	Silver	M	WXA9151237
8	10BC7	R. Yellow	Black	Black	Silver	M	W2A9149496
9	10BC8**	I. Orange	Gray	Orange	Silver	M	W2A9149496
10	10BC9	Silver I.	Black	Black	Black	M	W2A9153175
11	10BC10	S. White	Black	Black	Silver	M	WXA9155336
12	10BC11	V. Red	White	Black	Silver	M	W2A9154052
13	10BC12	R. Yellow	Black	Black	Silver	M	W0A9160299
14	10BC13	A. Blue	White	Black	Silver	M	W2A9156609
15	10BC14	I. Blue	White	Black	Silver	M	WXA9154977
16	10BC15	J. Blue	Black	Black	Silver	M	WXA9157314
17	10BC16	Red J.	Silver	Gray	Silver	A	J7A9159741
18	10BC17	I. Orange	White	Black	Black	M	W8A9156551
19	10BC18	S. White	Black	Black	Silver	M	W1A9154611
20	10BC19	A. Blue	White	White	Silver	M	W0A9142840
21	10BC20	S. White	Black	Black	Silver	M	W0A9156804
*	Prototype; CM standing for "Camaro"			**	Built for Matt Berger		

rear panel while the front fenders received SS and Berger's heritage badging.

The central gold bowtie on both the front and the rear was swapped for a retro-oriented prism blue emblem. Inside, the run of vehicles received items including a Hurst billet short-throw shifter, Berger SS floor mats, and a serialized dash plaque. A fitted car cover was included in the package along with a powertrain warranty.

Numbered decals were mounted at the base of the windshield and the front of the rearview mirror. The nomenclature was a five- and six-digit figure that stood for 2010 (10) Berger Camaro (BC) and the car's placement (1 through 20).

2011–2012 Berger SS Camaro

The package was offered again in 2011 with 26 cars being created in both the coupe and convertible bodystyles. Most of the equipment from the 2010 version was carried over with a few new additions. The package price increased to $21,730.

From a performance standpoint, the sole upgrade was a new rear sway bar. Forgeline split-spoke forged wheels with 11-inch width in the rear were now mounted on the cars. Output was slightly higher with Phase 1 manual-equipped cars delivering 550 hp and 530 ft-lbs of torque and automatic-equipped vehicles delivering 525 hp and 505 ft-lbs of torque.

New cosmetic changes included the roof shark-fin antenna being painted the body color. Houndstooth fabric seat inserts were optional for $1,595 along with an appearance package. It included a heritage grille, billet aluminum front and rear SS emblems, a "550 hp" hood emblem, and a GM blade-type three-piece spoiler with wraparound stripes.

The vehicles continued to be numbered and picked up where the 2010 left off. As such, they received numbers 11BC21 through 11BC47. Instead of receiving a numbered ignition plate, they were marked with a cloisonné mounted on the passenger's side of the dash.

The program continued into 2012 with two convertibles being produced.

#	ID	Paint	BS	ST	INT	WHL	T	VIN (2G1F)
1	11CM15	S. Green	CPE	BLK	BLK	BLK	6	T1EW3B9123281
2	11BC21	S. Ice	CPE	BLK	BLK	BLK	6	T1EW3B9101166
3	11BC22	Black	CPE	SIL	BLK	SIL	6	T1EW0B9128034
4	11BC23	I. Orange	CPE	BLK	BLK	SIL	6	T1EW4B9101483
5	11BC24	V. Red	CPE	BLK	BLK	BLK	6	T1EW4B9131261
6	11BC25	S. Green	CPE	BLK	BLK	SIL	6	T1EW9B9122667
7	11BC26	I. Blue	CPE	SIL	GRY	SIL	A	K1EJ1B9127790
8	11BC27	Red J.	CPE	SIL	GRY	SIL	A	K1EJ1B9128843
9	11BC28	S. Green	CPE	WHT	BLK	SIL	6	K1EJ1B9128843
10	11BC29	S. White	CPE	ORG	ORG	CHR	6	T1EW8B9132249
11	11BC30	I. Orange	CPE	WHT	BLK	SIL	6	T1EW1B9133906
12	11BC31	R. Yellow	CPE	BLK	BLK	BLK	6	T1EW1B9102087
13	11BC32	I. Blue	CPE	WHT	BLK	BLK	6	T1EW1B9102087
14	11BC33	Black	CPE	Red	BLK	SIL	6	T1EW3B9159293
15	11BC34	S Green	CPE	BLK	BLK	BLK	6	T1EWXB9130325
16	11BC35	I. Orange	CPE	BLK	ORG	BLK	6	T1EW4B9159285
17	11BC36	S. White	CPE	BLK	BLK	SIL	6	T1EW1B9161639
18	11BC37	V. Red	CPE	WHT	BLK	SIL	6	T1EW3B9100308
19	11BC38	I. Blue	CPE	SIL	BLK	SIL	6	T1EW7B9165131
20	11BC39	R. Yellow	CPE	BLK	BLK	SLV	6	T1EW8B9166398
21	11BC40	S. White	CPE	BLK	BLK	BLK	6	T1EW4B9100902
22	11BC41	S. Green	CON	BLK	BLK	BLK	6	T3DW1B9155935
23	11BC42	Black	CON	Red	BLK	SIL	6	T3DW2B9163686
24	11BC43	I. Orange	CON	BLK	BLK	BLK	A	T3DW0B9163279
25	11BC44	Red J.	CON	WHT	WHT	SIL	A	K3DJ0B9170238
26	11BC45	Red J.	CON	Tan	Tan	SIL	6	T3DW3B9175328
2012 Berger SS Camaro: Registry								
27	12BC46	R. Yellow	CON	BLK	BLK	CHR	6	T3DW9C9149172
28	12BC477	V. Red	CON	BLK	BLK	CHR	A	13DJ1C9109885

BS	Bodystyle—CPE: Coupe, CON: Convertible		ST	Stripe	INT	Interior
BLK: Black; GRY: Gray; ORG: Orange; WHT: White; CHR: Chrome					WHL	Wheel

## CHAPTER 11

OTHER DEALER PROGRAMS

The Camaro's appeal as a platform for performance and personalization has been far reaching. Throughout the model's six generations, numerous dealerships, performance shops, and additional players around the country have crafted and created their own special editions.

Some special editions feature power improvements, others feature head-snapping looks, and others harken back to the storied heritage and history. While each program is distinct, they all share the common goal of seeking to provide customers with a Camaro that readily stands out and delivers a truly unique driving experience.

1993–1996 Camaro ZR28 by G2 Performance Parts

During the late 1980s, Lou Gigliotti dominated the SCCA'S Class B series, competing in a third-generation Camaro race car. To house his race efforts, he opened L.G. Motorsports in Garland, Texas. In 1993, his sponsor, Young Chevrolet, in Dallas, Texas, provided him with a new 1993 Camaro Z28 (equipped with RPO 1LE), and Lou set to work crafting it into a serious competitor. Until then, Lou had varied the numbers used to identify his race cars. With this new Camaro, he chose

The ZR28 featured exterior modifications such as Enkei wheels and ground effects.

Some of the available powertrain upgrades included items such as a new K&N air filter and cold-air induction kit.

Modifications were light inside the cabin.

Many of the added components to the ZR28 came from Lou Gigliotti's race efforts and were included on the Camaro that he used in competition.

#28 and stuck with it for the rest of his competition career.

Part of the vehicle's build involved improving the aerodynamics and downforce. Having a close working relationship with Chevrolet, Lou collaborated with Clay Dean, who was one of the company's designers, to design a new five-piece body kit that consisted of a lower front air dam with a large central air inlet, rocker panels, a rear valance, and a rear spoiler. The pieces were fabricated by a composites manufacturer in Wausaukee, Wisconsin, and were painted the body color. The kit was included by Dale Earnhardt on his run of 1994 and 1995 Championship Series Special Edition Camaros.

Other ZR28 modifications included exclusive Enkei wheels and upgraded suspension components and graphics. Each piece was designed for competition. Having done the real-world research and development on the track and seeing the potential, Lou offered the components in a street-going package. He called it the ZR28, and the conversion happened at LG Motorsports. Young Chevrolet signed on to help with the sales and distribution along with a few other Midwest dealerships. Somewhere around 24 vehicles received the full package, and additional customers bought pieces individually and installed them on their own.

When the fifth-generation Camaro debuted in 2010, LG Motorsports crafted various components, including wheels and a hood, again under the ZR28 moniker.

2001–2002 Tom Henry Camaro SS

2001-2002 Tom Henry Camaro SS: Production Data							
	2001			2002			Total
Total	4	Coupe	1	28	Coupe	3	32
		Convt.	0		Coupe	6	
		T-Top	3		T-Top	13	
		B4C	0		B4C	6	
Paint Colors							
S. Silver	8	Navy Blue		2			
B. Rally Red	8	M. Maroon		1			
S. Orange	5	Arctic White		1			
Onyx Black	3	Mystic Teal		1			
Light Pewter	2	Hugger Orange		1			

Berger Chevrolet's success with its fourth-generation Camaro program was contagious, and once Tom Henry Chevrolet in Bakerstown, Pennsylvania, caught wind of the program, the dealership wanted its own piece of the action.

2001–2002 Tom Henry Camaro SS Registry									
#	Paint	Body	T	Ph.	#	Paint	Body	T	Ph.
1*	Onyx Black	T-T	6	1	17	S. Orange M.	T-T	6	1
2*	S. Orange M.	T-T	6	2••	18	B. Rally Red	T-T	6	1
3*	Mystic Teal M.	T-T	6	1	19	Sebring Silver M.	T-T	6	2X••
4*	Light Pewter M.	Cpe.	6	1	20	Onyx Black	T-T	6	1
5	B. Rally Red	T-T	6	1	21	B. Rally Red	T-T	6	1
6	Sebring Silver M.	Cpe	6	1	22**	M. Maroon M.	T-T	6	1
7	S. Orange M.	Cpe	6	1	23	Sebring Silver M.	B4C	6	1
8	Sebring Silver M.	B4C	6	1	24	Onyx Black	B4C	6	1
9	B. Rally Red	T-T	6	1	25	Arctic White	Conv	A	1
10	S. Orange M.	Conv.	6	1	26	Navy Blue M.	B4C	6	1
11•	B. Rally Red	Conv	6	2	27	Sebring Silver M.	B4C	6	1
12	B. Rally Red	Conv	6	2	28	Hugger Orange***	B4C	6	2X6••
13	S. Orange M.	T-T	A	1	29	Navy Blue M.	T-T	6	1
14	B. Rally Red	T-T	A	1	30	B. Rally Red	Conv	6	1
15	L. Pewter Met.	Conv	6	1	31	Sebring Silver M.	T-T	6	1
16	Sebring Silver M.	T-T	6	2X••	32	Sebring Silver M.	Cpe	6	2XM•••
#	Car number	T		Transmission—6: 6-speed manual; A: automatic			Ph.		Engine Phase
*	2001 model year		**	Z28 converted to SS trim		***		Onyx Black car with custom paint	
•	Ordered by Tom Henry; equipped with Baer Aluma Sport brake calipers, EradiSpeed rotors, McLeod clutch, and Red Line synthetic lubricants								
••	Customer returned car to GMMG for additional upgrades								
•••	Equipped with 2xM package with heads ported and polished by Mauex Racing; Output: 500 hp/475 ft-lbs								

Tom Henry Chevrolet partnered with GMMG to produce a limited run of fourth-generation Camaros.

Engine modifications were GMMG's Phase 1 package, which bumped output to 380 hp.

Second-generation dealership owner (and cousin of Camaro brand manager Scott Settlemire) Tom Henry encountered a Berger SS and Matt Murphy at an Indianapolis, Indiana, show in the summer of 2000. Seeing the potential, he connected with Murphy about crafting his own low-volume run.

A Tom Henry Racing (THR) division was quickly launched to market and sell the cars. Hardtop, T-top, and convertible bodystyles were all offered. They were all in SS trim and equipped with either an automatic or manual transmission and with the factory's optional short-throw shifter.

Four cars were created at the end of 2001 with 28 more being built and sold through the summer of 2002. Faced with the problem of Camaro allocation as it neared the end of its run, Henry purchased vehicles from other dealers to use in his performance program.

Modifications and Additions

The run essentially replicated the treatment as found on the 2001 Berger SS Camaro with a few alterations. All received GMMG's Phase 1 upgrades to the stock LS1 V-8, which raised output to 380 hp and 400 ft-lbs of torque (360 hp and 380 ft-lbs of torque for automatic transmission–equipped cars).

Some of the Berger cosmetic upgrades were carried over, too, in the form of the painted top hoop and satin black taillight panel. Henry's cars received chrome "CAMARO" infill letters, and no additional exterior badging was applied except for horsepower callout stickers on the hood cowl and rear panel. The dual rally stripes were left off, but some cars received hash mark graphics on the front fenders, inspired by the treatment seen on the 1963 Grand Sport Corvette.

The biggest variation was the wheels, which were 17-inch Torq Thrust II ARE wheels with a charcoal gloss center. Inside the cabin, a silver-faced gauge insert was installed. It was marked with a THR logo, while a black Hurst shift ball was mounted on the shifter. Just as with Berger's program, a custom car cover was part of the package—this one bearing the THR logo.

The run was numbered, and the same numeral graphics were on the rearview mirror, windshield, and GMMG brass door tag that was mounted to the driver-side doorjamb.

Liking the results of the GMMG Camaros, Tom Henry Chevrolet later sold six 2002 ZL1 Supercars (cars #39, 40, 41, 42, 50, and 51) along with a few of its 35th Anniversary Performance Edition vehicles.

Inside, changes were minimal.

Tom Henry Camaro SS by GMMG (2001–2002): Package Equipment		
Engine	• Cat-back chambered exhaust • Underdrive crank pulley	
Underhood	• Carbon-fiber air-box lid with THR and output decal • Mobile 1 oil fill cap and badge (passenger-side strut tower)	
Exterior	• Billet grille insert with "SS" emblem • Hood and rear panel horsepower callout stickers • Painted body-color roof hoop • Satin black painted taillight panel • Chrome "CAMARO" infill letters (rear panel) • Power antenna	
Wheels	• Torq-Thrust II 17-inch ARE with charcoal gloss spokes	
Brakes	• Red powder-coated brake calipers • Dimpled rotors (front and rear)	
Suspension	• Eibach 1.5-inch lowering springs	
Interior	• Silver-faced gauge insert with THR logo • SLP Camaro SS floor mats (front) • Gentex rearview mirror with compass and auto dimmer	
ID	Windshield base and rearview mirror	Numbered Decals
	Driver's doorjamb	GMMG brass door tag
Accessories	• Numbered key fobs (x2) • Fitted car cover (with TH logo)	
Package Price	$9,465	Vehicle Total	$38,955

The taillight panel was painted satin black, and horsepower callout graphics were added to the driver's side.

2010 Tom Henry Racing Camaro SS

Total	34	Auto.	9
		Man.	25
Naturally Aspirated			26
Supercharged			8
Paint Color Distribution			
Inferno Orange			5
Cyber Gray			6
Victory Red			1
Black			4
Silver Ice			2
Imperial Blue			2
Aqua Blue			5
Rally Yellow			2
Summit White			4
Red Jewel			3

As with the fourth-generation Camaro program, Tom Henry Chevrolet marked the 2010 version with numbered graphics on the rearview mirror and base of the windshield.

With the return of the fifth-generation Camaro in 2010, Tom Henry Chevrolet offered a special run of Camaros assembled in-house at the dealership.

Thirty-four coupes were created in V-8 trim. They were equipped with varying degrees of cosmetic and performance upgrades. Added items included cat-back chambered exhaust (featuring a THR embossing), cold-air intakes, long-tube headers, and a supercharger. Cosmetic additions included painted stripes with a ghosted Tom Henry Racing logo on the cowl sides, THR floor mats, chrome wheels, and a rear spoiler.

Like Tom Henry's run of GMMG-created vehicles, this batch was also identified with numbered stickers on the rearview mirror, at the base of the windshield, and on numbered door tags inside the driver-side doorjamb. They also received windshield banners. An extra addition was special fender and taillight panel badges.

2010–2011 Hurst Performance Vehicles Performance Series Camaros

After developing a modified vehicle program in 2009 for the then-new Dodge Challenger, in 2010, Hurst Performance Vehicles in Irvine, California, added a Camaro program to its offering with the arrival of the fifth-generation version.

It was offered in several different series of upgrades and modifications, and the top-tier Series 5 was supercharged. Other enhancements included new suspension and exhaust components and a new black chrome wheel design. Made by HRE, it was modeled off the original Hurst wheel of the 1960s and 1970s. The vehicle exterior also received a custom rear spoiler and custom painted striping and fender markings.

Inside the cabin, a "Hard-Drive" pistol-grip shifter was installed on cars with a manual or automatic transmission. The seats were covered in Katzkin leather with gold top stitching.

The Hurst Performance series package was striking, featuring painted stripes and accents.

A Hurst logo was embroidered in the seatbacks and on the package's floor mats. A numbered metal plaque was added to the dash.

A dealer network wasn't in place, so vehicle packages (costing upward of $30,000) were sold with cars being sent to nearby Aria Designs in Irvine, California, for the conversion and upfitting. As part of the rollout, a Series 1 kit contained items that could be sold to a dealership for onsite installation. About a dozen vehicles were created.

2010–2011 Hurst Performance Vehicles Series 4 and 5: Package Contents			
Engine	Magnuson Supercharger		
Exhaust	Magnaflow stainless steel cat-back		
Wheels	HRE 20-inch black-chrome with custom center cap	F	20x9 inch
		R	20x11 inch
Tires	BFG KDW performance tires		
Suspension	Eibach coilover adjustable suspension		
Exterior	• "Air-Speed" rear spoiler • Hurst grille badge • Aria badge (lower rocker panel)		
Paint	• Gloss black painted stripes with contrast outline • Painted fender markings		
Interior	• Katzkin leather interior with gold stitching and Hurst embroidery • Gold-anodized "Hard-Drive" pistol-grip shifter • Embroidered floor mats • Hurst logo car cover • Vehicle signatures (trunk lid): Hurst executive team, "Miss Hurst Golden Shifter" Linda Vaughn, and Jack "Doc" Watson • Certificate of authenticity		

Embroidered floor mats and badges on the dash were additions to the interior along with black leather upholstery with gold perforations.

2014–2015 Hot Rod Limited Edition Camaro by Todd Wenzel Chevrolet

Total		13	
2014	7	Option I	1
		Option II	2
		Option III	4
2015	6	Option I	1
		Option II	4
		Option III	1

In celebration of *Hot Rod* magazine's 67th anniversary, the publication teamed in 2015 with Todd Wenzel Chevrolet, in Hudsonville, Michigan, and Nickey Chicago Inc. to create a limited run of special commentative-edition Camaros.

One of the program's driving forces was Dennis Barker, the Camaro specialist for the dealership. Dennis was instrumental for assembling the 2002 Hot Rod Edition Camaro by GMMG when he worked at nearby Berger Chevrolet.

Originally, the team's plan was to create 67 vehicles: one for each year the magazine had been in circulation. In the end, only 13 vehicles were built, and all were assembled by the Nickey Performance shop outside of Chicago.

The cars were built on 1LE, 1SS, and 2SS coupes and convertibles with different levels of performance and cosmetic upgrades available. Each received side reverse Motion graphics inspired by the wild cosmetic schemes found on Camaros built by the *Baldwin Motion* duo during the 1960s and 1970s.

From the Option 1 equipment, customers could add additional performance packages (Option II and III) and options such as a short-throw shifter, cross-drilled brake rotors, valve covers, and plug wires. Optional Forgeline wheels were available that were designed specifically for this project.

The Hot Rod Edition cars were identified by serialized tags in the driver-side doorjam and by a number graphic at the base of the windshield.

Todd Wenzel Chevrolet created a run of 2015 Camaros to celebrate Hot Rod *magazine's 67th anniversary.*

Embroidered floor mats and sill plates were included inside. This example, #HR14001, has been equipped with the optional leather interior package (costing $2,795) as well as a short-throw shifter and shift knob ($700).

Several stages of performance upgrades were offered. Car #HR14001, the first in the run, received a 575-hp Stage III upgrade that cost $21,640.

Special badging was mounted on the rear decklid and front fenders.

2014–2015 Hot Rod Edition Camaro by Todd Wenzel Chevrolet: Registry

#	ID	Style	Trim	Paint	Interior	T	Stage	HP	VIN
1	HRPR*	Cpe.	SS 1LE	Red	Black	M	II	550	T1EW3E9176048
2	HR14001	Cpe.	SS	Black	Red	M	III	575	S1EWXE9287246
3	HR14002	Cpe.	SS	Black	Red	M	III	575	S1EW8E9136647
4	HR14003	Cpe.	SS	Black	Red	A	II	575	K1EJ2E9176632
5	HR14004	Cpe.	SS	Black	Red	M	I	475	T1EW3E9176048
6	HR14007	Cpe.	ZL1	White	Blk. with Blue	A	III	825	G1EW6F9128517
7	HR14067***	Cpe.	Z/28	Black	Black	M	IIITT•	800	UK
8	HR15005	Cpe.	SS	Silver	Red	M	III	575	G1EW9F9116331
9	HR15006	Conv.	SS	Black	Blk. with Gray	M	II SE**	550	G1EW6F9128517
10	HR15008	Cpe.	SS 1LE	Silver	Black	M	I	475	G1EW0F9128416
11	HR15009	Cpe.	SS	Black	Blk. with Red	M	II SE	550	G3DW8F9168711
12	HR15010	Cpe.	SS	Blue	White	M	II SE	550	G1EW6F9224891
13	HR15011	Cpe.	SS	Yellow	Black	A	II SE	550	H1EJ0F9226704

*	Prototype, referred also as PR14001
**	Equipped with Magnuson supercharger
T	Transmission—M: Manual; A: Auto
•	Twin-turbo setup, classified as a Stage III given the factory Z/28 427-ci V-8 engine
***	Customer purchased the 1st vehicle (HR14001) and what was to be the last. When the run was cut short, the second vehicle was relabeled 14067 to reflect the "bookend" desire.

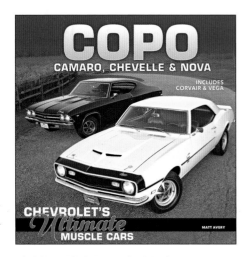
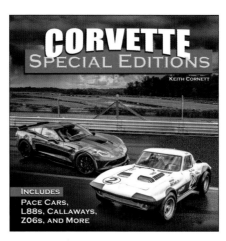
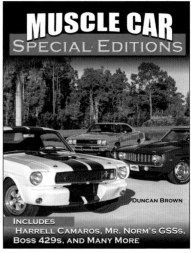

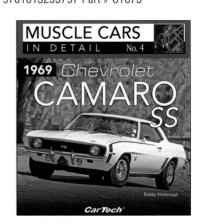